THE WORLD OF PETER SIMPLE

WAY OF THE WORLD: The Daily Telegraph

By the same author

BEST OF PETER SIMPLE
PETER SIMPLE IN OPPOSITION
MORE OF PETER SIMPLE
THE THOUGHTS OF PETER SIMPLE

THE
WORLD
OF
PETER SIMPLE

Extracts from 'Way of the World'
column in The Daily Telegraph
1971-1973

JOHNSON

LONDON

First Published 1973

I.S.B.N. 0 85307 126 8

SET IN 10pt. TIMES AND PRINTED BY
CLARKE, DOBLE AND BRENDON LTD., PLYMOUTH
FOR JOHNSON PUBLICATIONS LTD.,
11-14 STANHOPE MEWS WEST, LONDON, S.W.7

PREFACE

The last book of extracts from the "Way of the World" column appeared in 1971, with the title "The Thoughts of Peter Simple". For this new collection I have chosen what I hope are the best items from the column in the period from May 1971 to April 1973.

As in the previous books, the pieces—whether serious, satirical, fantastic, nostalgic or wholly nonsensical—appear in roughly chronological order without further arrangement.

PETER SIMPLE

1971

EXPLOSION————————————————————————————

DR LLEWELYN GOTH-JONES, the popular Medical Officer of Health for Stretchford, has welcomed the Government's report on population with an enthusiasm almost amounting to dementia praecox.

At an emergency meeting of the City Public Health Committee, called at his own urgent request, he demanded that Stretchford give an example to the country by immediately setting up 2,000 new family planning clinics throughout the city, that is, approximately one for every 300 people, as well as a 24-hour mobile corps of "contraceptive wardens" with what he called "statutory powers of persuasion" over the public.

He also suggested using the weapon of ridicule to deter couples from having children. People should get into the habit, he said, of laughing and pointing derisively at anyone they saw accompanied by more than one child (an occasional kick would not come amiss, either); teachers should encourage pupils who belonged to large families to feel shame at their own existence and anger at their parents for having brought them into the world: these and other methods would go far, in the long run, towards solving Britain's population problems.

As an expert, Dr Goth-Jones got a respectful hearing. As well as being Medical Officer, he is a director of Malebolge Chemicals, a subsidiary of Nadirco which manufactures hundreds of millions of contraceptive pills and other devices yearly.

He is also a director of the new Nadirco sex supermarket chain, with branches throughout the West Midlands; runs a popular network of abortion clinics (with supporting air and taxi services) in the Stretchford area; and has a controlling interest in an educational cinema at Nerdley which is now showing a film of women having intercourse with Alsatian dogs, horses and computers.

Yet one councillor at the meeting (evidently malevolent, half-witted or both) actually had the nerve to say he thought it odd that Dr Goth-Jones, while advocating non-stop sex, practical, cerebral or voyeuristic, for all, should so strongly condemn the natural result of that activity.

The Medical Officer of Health rose from his seat. "That is a typical example," he said, controlling himself with difficulty, "of the spite and envy of repressed middle age at the new, joyous and above all life-affirming and life-creating sexual freedom of youth today.

"Reactionary! Fascist! Racist!" he yelled, his eyes beginning to revolve like burning contraceptive pills. "I only wish I had you in my sterilisation clinic," he went on. "My assistant, Dr Jill Grese—one of a pioneering medical family—would know exactly what to do with you."

COMMON LABYRINTH————————————————

CONDITIONAL agreement reached on Commonwealth sugar! Virtual agreement (a more impressive form of agreement, as all must agree, than conditional) on Euratom, the nuclear research organisation! Agreement (conditional or virtual?) that Britain shall move towards Common Market price levels in six steps over a period of five years!

But persistent differences over apples and pears! And no mention at all of artichokes, soup, quince jelly, marmalade, string, four-inch nails, brass fenders, dog-collars and muzzles, cellular vests (men's) or other disputed items.

Meanwhile the people of England, Scotland, Wales and Northern Ireland are watching every smallest move of the negotiations in Brussels with bated breath. Or are they?

In fact, from my own observation, admittedly limited, they are not. These negotiations, infinitely protracted, pass over their heads like a battle in the clouds, a phantasmagoria, part abstract, part homely, which may or may not have meaning for those who are taking part in it, but for the great majority of people means as much or as little as the "currency crisis" which they hastily flicked over in their newspapers a few days ago.

They simply cannot understand how these mysterious comings and goings, these endless financial manipulations and convolutions, can concern them; or how, if they do concern them, they can any better control them than they can control the weather.

Is this invincible ignorance and apathy what the rulers of this country, or those who appear to be its rulers (the sense of mystery is infectious) are counting on as they prepare (or don't prepare) to "take us into Europe" (whatever that may mean)?

WARNING

"CREDITON could become a tourist centre if it exploited the name of St Boniface—the martyr who was born in the town—members of the urban council were told last night.

"Mr K. J. Stoneman said that perhaps the pulling power of St Boniface was not fully realised in the town. A developer could be persuaded to build a hotel with facilities to cope with a fairly large number of people and this could only be of benefit to the town" (*Exeter Express*).

Not necessarily. When Stretchford and Nerdley tried some years ago to exploit the names of the local saints St Oick and St Bogwena as tourist attractions, the result was not encouraging.

Admittedly neither of these two saints were martyrs. Indeed all that is known about them—both are briefly mentioned by Bede in his probably apocryphal life of St Chad, the apostle of Mercia—suggests that for Dark Age saints they led lives of tolerable comfort.

They were also deadly rivals, vying for the glory of converting the wicked pagan King Penda of Mercia by performing a series of fatuous and boring miracles, often to the discomfort of the ordinary Anglo-Saxon public. St Oick, for instance, caused a miraculous, inexhaustible spring of water to gush from the spot now occupied by the Tubal-Cain Carbon Brush Works in Hargreaves Road, flooding several popular mead-halls.

Nevertheless, a big public relations campaign was put in hand by the Stretchford and Nerdley councils. Rival luxury hotels, the Oick and the Bogwena, were run up in weeks on commanding sites, fully equipped with King Penda Grills, Olde Mercian Butteries and Hermits' Grotto Bars, and the two councils settled down to watch the money roll in.

But everything went wrong. The Bogwena's central heating would not work. An inexhaustible spring of liquid, later analysed by experts as mead, gushed from the floor of the Oick Hotel manager's office. And not a single tourist appeared.

Today the two hotels, in a state of partial collapse, stand as monuments of hope unrealised. "There must have been a jinx in operation, probably at administrative level," states Mr J. R. Shambles, chairman of the Stretchford Tourist Development committee.

But many local hagiologists put down the debacle to the continuing rivalry of the two saints and angrily demand their desanctification.

PHONEY WAR————————————————————————

"THE Battle for Washington." This headline is fairly typical of the treatment in the English Press and on television of the anti-Vietnam war demonstrators' unsuccessful attempt to bring the American capital to a standstill.

It suggests a clash between armed forces of equal strength and equal standing, a clash of which the outcome was long in doubt and which might have led to the occupation of Washington by the revolutionary forces and the setting up of a new American Government.

In fact, of course, there was no "battle"; simply the not very difficult suppression by a moderate force of police and troops of a mob of Leftist dupes, freaks and clowns, organised, in so far as such unsuitable material *can* be organised, by the conspiratorial enemies of the American State.

Is the dramatic, high-flown language used to describe this event merely journalistic licence, harmless exaggeration? Not entirely. It is one small example of the extreme distortion with which news of America is commonly presented over here.

English people are being led to believe—perhaps already do believe, as a thing beyond doubt—that the United States, disturbed admittedly, is now at the point of total, irredeemable collapse.

NIDGETT HITS BACK————————————

AT his Godalming home yesterday Gen. Sir Frederick ("Tiger") Nidgett strongly defended the industrial training boards. "In my view," he said, a smile playing about his Tailoring Corps tie, then spreading across his teak-like face to his piercing blue eyes, "these boards give your industrial chap—from manager and foreman right down to your run-of-the-mill sweeper, punkah-wallah or what have you—the discipline, guts, corps d'esprit, stamina, initiative, leadership, alertness, sense of values, smart turn-out and sheer physical fitness he can get no other way in Civvy Street.

"I see the Dismal Desmonds and Willie Wetlegs are bellyaching about people having to spend days assembling and reassembling bicycle bells, taking part in discussions about the drill involved, and so on and so forth. But this is precisely the sort of thing we had to do in the Army. It's the only way of giving a chap that sheer, unthinking instinct of split-second response to orders he'll need every bit as much in industry as in the fog of war if we're to win—as we must—the Battle of the Trade Gap.

"Theirs not to reason why. Theirs to jump to it—like greased lightning.

"My criticism of these training boards is not that they have too much bull, but that they don't have nearly enough. Daily kit inspections, polishing or blancoing of every thing in sight, even the ceiling, sudden turnouts in the middle of the night—that's the stuff to put real, down-to-earth moral fibre into your common-or-garden rookie industrial trainee and make him keen as the proverbial mustard.

"It's only a tip from an old soldier. But I shall expect the training boards to look to it, pronto.

"Good day to you all, whoever you may be, and cracking good hunting."

11

SUNT LACRIMAE————————

THE news of Herr Ulbricht's resignation as First Secretary of the East German Communist party, though not altogether unexpected, has brought sadness to Mrs Dutt-Pauker, the Hampstead thinker—sadness and long, long memories of youth.

The two first met in Barcelona in 1937, in the heady days of the Spanish Civil War. They were immediately drawn together by a mutual interest in the techniques of conspiracy and purges, secret police methods and the running of concentration camps.

Though 20 years parted them in age, passion bloomed swiftly under the velvet, star-throbbing night skies of Spain. Their parting, when it came at the behest of the Party, which assigned both to other, distant tasks, was as agonising as it must be to all lovers. But it was borne with Marxist fortitude.

There are those who have seen a resemblance to Ulbricht in Mrs Dutt-Pauker's daughter Deirdre; and an even more striking resemblance in Deirdre's four-year-old, bearded, baleful-eyed Maoist demonstrator son Bert Brecht Mao Che Odinga.

The Hampstead thinker has never admitted that there may have been fruit of the union. But every year, when Ulbricht's birthday postcard of the Berlin Wall arrives, a slight but unmistakable blush is seen to mantle the withered, dialectic-pale cheek of the chairman of House-wives for Peace.

Yesterday Mrs Dutt-Pauker, on behalf of the women of Britain, sent the retiring leader a telegram congratulating him on a lifetime of work for peace and higher living standards. But the sad occasion did not pass without further signs of the ideological split in the Dutt-Pauker family, Bert pointedly eating, with the encouragement of Gjoq, Deirdre's Albanian, pro-Chinese au pair girl, a record number of North Korean-made people's demo-cratic chocolate biscuits for nursery tea.

TRANSPLANTED——————————————

THE British Medical Association is urging doctors and surgeons to set an example to the public by volunteering as donors for organ transplants after death.

How will this affect surgeons like Dr Acula, the heart transplant specialist at St Bogwena's Hospital, Nerdley, or Dr Klingsor, of the new transplant clinic attached to the Mountwarlock Experimental Garden Centre?

Some medical experts doubt whether Dr Acula's heart would be in a suitable condition for transplant after his death, which can, of course, be brought about only by piercing his body with a stake through the heart itself.

Dr Klingsor, whose work on human-plant genetics and floral phantasmology has brought him world fame, is believed to suffer from the very rare condition medically known as acardia. This seems to rule him out as a donor altogether.

"IF only I could have my time over again, do you know what I would have been? I'll tell you—a merchant banker." How often have you heard a friend—a retired milkroundsman, perhaps, or an elderly tobacconist and newsagent—murmur these sad words? How often have you murmured them yourself?

The rising generation may well be free of these vain regrets, these bitter thoughts of what might have been. A new book, "Merchant Banking for All." by J. S. Goldvault (Viper and Bugloss, £3·50p; paper-back £1·25p) explodes some common misconceptions which have caused many a young would-be merchant banker to throw up his hands in despair and take to collecting matchbox labels instead.

Chief among these misconceptions is the idea that you need a large amount of capital, financial expertise and influential friends in the City to start a merchant bank. On the contrary. The author explains, in clear, concise language, how anyone of ordinary ability can start a merchant bank in his own home with no more equipment than a counting-house, a few confidential clerks, and a boardroom with a mahogany table.

He gives an example: a young deckchair attendant at Littlehampton, who, seeing no future in deckchairs, borrowed a few gold bars from a friend and set up as a merchant banker in the hut where his deckchairs were stored.

Soon he had expanded his business so enormously that he was able to open a merchant bank in the town itself. Within six months he had opened branches in several South Coast resorts and was doing a thriving trade with Antwerp, Zürich and other world-famous merchant banking centres.

The last time the author heard of the former deck-chairman he had a staff of 50 men continually moving bullion from one place to another and back again and was directing their work from his own personal deckchair of solid gold.

The secret? Keenness, hard work and above all, flair. It certainly makes one think. If only I could have my time over again. . . .

MORE! MORE!—————————————————

Last year more than 5 million tourists visited Westminster Abbey. This year 6 million are expected, and the London Tourist Board—how preposterous a body this would have seemed only a few years ago—how preposterous it will still seem if we only stop and think for a moment—the London Tourist Board is making plans to cope with them.

A "management consultant team" has worked out a scheme for a one-way flow round the Abbey which will come into effect from the beginning of June. But this is not enough.

It is not enough, in fact, to have only one Westminster Abbey. With modern building methods it would surely not be difficult to run up as many cheap replicas, suitably spaced out over London, as the tourists may require. Only experts and pedants could tell the difference, and who cares about them?

Some old-fashioned people may argue that Westminster Abbey was not built in the first place to attract tourists, or to help make money for London hotel-keepers. How strange! What very peculiar people its builders must have been!

DR HENBANE TALKING—————————————————

Good morning. And how are our allergies today? No, I'm not joking. The latest medical figures prove that of the 50 odd million people in this country, at least 49 million suffer from allergies of one kind or another.

Among the merry throng waiting in my surgery at Gorgon House most mornings I can count on a fair proportion who will turn out to be a prey to one of these medical puzzle-points. For let's face it, we medicos don't know a lot about allergies, their how, why and wherefore —yet.

The other day a patient, a middle-aged housewife, came to see me with a regular old tale of woe. It seemed that every time she drank a cup of tea red patches appeared on her forehead. If she drank tea out of the saucer, the patches turned green, if she left the spoon in the cup while drinking the patches turned blue.

She had tried drinking tea, she told me, out of a saucer with the spoon left in it—for good measure while standing on a table. But multi-coloured patches had appeared, the neighbours had begun talking; and her husband, a turntable setter at a local soapworks, was threatening to leave her for a younger woman, the proprietress of Chez Edna, a local hairdressing saloon.

Now here was a rare old dermatological carry-on! It was, of course, a case of what is called variable allergy, produced by a combination of factors—the tea itself, the comparative surface area of the liquid in cup or saucer, the angle of the spoon to the horizon, its metallic composition, the altitude at which the tea was drunk and so on and so forth.

That very morning, as it happened, a medical supplies traveller had left me, on approval, one of the new miniature medical computers which (we hope!) will help to smooth the thorny path of the much-tried GP. Why not give it a whirl?

No sooner said than done. I fed the patient's data into the machine, gave it a shake and Bob's your uncle! Out came the answer. "Cup, saucer and spoon allergy. Try drinking your tea through a rubber pipe direct from the teapot."

So the patient went on her way rejoicing. Good morning.

LET THEM BE LEFT——————————————————

ENVIRONMENTALISTS, conservationists, anti-pollutionists: the dull, pseudo-scientific words, endlessly repeated—imports, like so much else, from future-crazed America—can arouse in certain moods a perverse rage to build oil-refineries and cement-works all over Dartmoor.

The latest thing to come to their notice, I read, is the view from railway carriage windows, on the outskirts of cities. They say these squalid breakers' yards, heaps of scrap, derelict industrial sites, overgrown back gardens, half-scorched cuttings are eyesores. They must be cleaned up a soon as possible.

To the official mind, the mind which has invented national parks and conservation areas and areas of outstanding natural beauty, the mind which measures the colours of the Spring and assesses Wastwater and Ludlow by an index of aesthetic value, they are simply eyesores and that is all. To people who casually look out of railway carriage windows they may seem quite otherwise.

They are miniature wildernesses, places that men have made, certainly, but places which have the pathos of all things that have once been used but are now neglected and abandoned: tangled garden-plots, rusting springs, shattered bricks, shards, books sodden by the rain and, blistered by the sun, lumps of newspaper that no one will ever read again.

The train, held up by signals, slows down in the summer heat; the wondering eye looks through the glass into those suburban jungles and finds there, as in childhood, a mysterious poetry. Who knows what strange flowers—moly, nepenthes—may grow among that unloved, grimy undergrowth?

Perhaps it is as well this has not occurred to the official mind. Wouldn't it wish to institutionalise this sense of wonder, to incorporate it into its official system: tidy up almost all the eyesores in its own image but leave, for recreational and educational purposes, a few Protected Areas of Designated Suburban Railway Squalor?

BOOKDOOM

ONE of the events of this week in London will be the "Bedford Square Bookbang" (what stripe-shirted publicist, with what supreme intellectual effort, thought up *that* title, I wonder, then sat back purring and drooling with trendy self-satisfaction?).

This book trade jamboree is to be opened on Friday by Coco the Clown. "Across the road at the Architectural Association," reports the *Sunday Times*, "the most sensational event will probably be a free showing of"—wait for it—"Martin Cole's film 'Growing Up.' "

17

Milton, thou shouldst be living at this hour. The Muses thou used to know are keeping (or being forced to keep) peculiar company.

Meanwhile, in the disused Derbyshire lead mine which is his home, Julian Birdbath, last citizen of what used to be called, rather embarrassingly as some thought, the Republic of Letters, sits at his rusting typewriter among mouldering shelves of review copies, listening to the tune the dripping water plays as it falls through lodes of ore and crystal into gloomy subterranean pools.

No summons from the Bookbang has reached the ultimate heir of Gosse and Saintsbury. No smart, purple-jeaned, Sassoon-coiffured young publisher has climbed mincingly down the rickety, fungus-infested ladders from level to level to take him by the hand and lead him to the merrymaking in Bedford Square. Nor will any such miracle occur.

Perhaps it is just as well. What could the Last English Man of Letters do, as he blinked owlishly in the sunlight amid the gay booksellers' tents, bemused by the frenzied chatter of publishers, alarmed by the shrill cries of strange immodestly-dressed women novelists, appalled by the satanic howl and jungle boom of taped music, but give one last literary groan and die?

GERROUTOVIT!————————————————————
bellows JACK MORON

So the reactionary, Fascist, pro-Nazi Government of Spain (we old soldiers who fought in the Second World War won't easily forget the infamous Blue Film Division it sent to help the Germans on the Russian front) has had second thoughts about banning short-term holiday charter flights from Britain, has it?

It had better.

I say this, straight from the shoulder, with no holds barred, to the lisping, sherry-stained, paella-stuffed grandees of Spain, and to their haughty master, the aged Caudillissimo Francisco Franco. Who the blazes do you think you are?

A ban on inexpensive short-term holidays in Spain would be a deliberate slap in the face, not of the rich, but of the ordinary working people of Britain. And Mr and Mrs Average Britain do not take kindly to slaps in the face, particularly when they are delivered by the puny, palsied hands of superannuated Mediterranean dictators.

They will know what to do about it, too, if there are any further attempts to twist the lion's tail. All they have to do, to bring Franco's pathetically tottering economy, entirely supported hitherto by the long-suffering British holidaymaker, crashing down in shoddy, humiliating ruin, is this: stop taking holidays on Spain's much-vaunted, sun-and-dysentry-infected beaches and take them at Blackpool instead.

All right, señores?

ORDER YOUR COPY NOW!————————————

ARE you a married woman? Do you hate your children, your parents and relations, your husband's parents and relations? Do you hate all other people? Do you see them as a threat to your marriage?

If so, you are one among millions of women who'll want to read the new best-seller about sex, love, marriage and genocide, described by over three million British and American sex experts as the most shocking, frank and controversial book ever written.

It's called "Sex and People"; it's by attractive, brilliant writer and TV personality Doreen Gaggs, and long, shocking, frank, controversial extracts from it will appear in this column next week, starting on Monday.

Fearlessly, Doreen Gaggs gives her own recipe for married happiness. She tells, in language of searing, four-letter frankness, how to get rid of your children by locking them in the washing-machine when you and your husband want to make love in the kitchen; how to frighten away your husband's boss and office colleagues by new, scientific techniques of terror when you and your husband want to make love in his office; how to get rid of your parents by the new technique, approved by over four million marriage guidance experts, of strangling them and bunging them out of the window.

The message of this astonishingly frank book is clear. It is this: if the rest of the human race stand in the way of your right to the non-stop sex which is the secret of a happy marriage, then the rest of the human race has got to go.

You may agree with Doreen Gaggs or not. But if you are a woman (and let's face it, who isn't these days?) it is your duty to read her.

THE Royal International Dairy Show, which for 23 years has taken place at Olympia in London, has been looking for a new site, but without success. So there will be no Dairy Show this year.

The irony of it is that Seth Roentgen, England's greatest scientific farmer, has repeatedly offered to accommodate the Dairy Show on his own experimental showground at the Ohm Farm, only to be rebuffed. I talked to the veteran agrotechnologist in his lead-lined control-room overlooking the broad sweep of the showground, where experimental cattle, some over 20 feet long and with two or more heads, cropped the strangely-gleaming radioactive sward.

"Danged if I know what's amiss wi' they blamed old Dairy Show folk," mused Seth, offering me an earthen pipkin in which a new type of high-vitamin-yield, borborotoluene-reinforced buttermilk hissed and bubbled greenly. I declined it, on the ground that I had just had breakfast, drawing a shrewd look from piercing blue eyes.

"Here on the Ohm Farm they could have had all the facilities they needed—electronic stalls, nuclear-powered milking-machines, radioactive mechanical stockmen, everything a true dairyman's heart could desire. Seems as how they just don't want to know."

He shook his gnarled old head, absently moving the dials on the control panel which regulate the movements of the cattle outside. Suddenly a monstrous bovine face, with eyelashes a foot long, loomed up beyond the window, rasping the thick glass with a gigantic tongue, breathing fuliginously and lowing with a sound that shook the concrete shelter to its foundations.

"Come up, Daisy! Come up, Lightfoot!" crooned Old Seth. "Bless'ee, bor, the mommets know it be near milkin' toime," he went on, as he slowly put on his asbestos-lined protective clothing.

TERMS OF ENTRY——————————————————————

M. POMPIDOU'S speculations about the role of the French and English languages have caused a linguistic panic among suggestible English people. Many seem to believe that if this country joins the Common Market they will all have to speak French.

There is one obvious way to avoid any such injurious rivalry between the languages: make Latin, once the common tongue of Christendom, the official "working language" which all functionaries of a European Union would have to learn and use.

Let the Vatican simultaneously restore the Latin Mass; let the Six drop such dull, banausic titles as the Common Market and the European Economic Union and revive the name of the Holy Roman Empire; let them turn away, by that solemn token, from their present degrading aim of a union of supermarkets and embrace instead the ideal of a restored Euroepan civilisation (yes, from the Atlantic to the Urals), armed for whatever fate may come.

Let them do these things and I might even begin to favour the entry of Great Britain (and Ireland) myself.

NORMAN THE GOOD————————————

THE question of the Queen's financial position, affected by inflation like everyone else's, is under discussion. How different things will be in the Socialist Monarchy of the future, in Good King Norman's Golden Time! Yet even then there will be problems.

May 20, 2011

There were angry scenes in Parliament yesterday when Mr Stan Brootes, MP for Windermere New Town, asked why Queen Doreen had been given planning permission to open a postcard, souvenir and novelty stall near the entrance to the Council Palace at Bevindon.

The proposed stall, for which—as he had been told by an unimpeachable source (shouts of "Name it!" "Suez!" "Arms for North Vietnam!" "Yanks out!" "Fascist Pigs!" etc.)—for which large consignments of plastic souvenir Scotty dogs, crown, orb and sceptre sets and models of the Brigade of Socialist Guards had already been ordered, would take the plastic and cardboard out of the mouths of hundreds of ordinary souvenir retailers throughout the country.

It was privilege, privilege naked and unadorned,

privilege redolent of the gilded, marble-infested courts of Byzantium or Versailles, where tyrants lolled in slippered ease, with slaves, eunuchs and neophytes to fetch and carry. It made a mockery of the proper practices of a democratic, Socialist Monarchy.

The Chancellor of the Exchequer, Mr Ken Nobes, replying, said that the annual grant to the Monarchy had remained at the figure of £2,105·25 for the last three years. It was no longer adequate if the Monarchy was to remain a viable institution. That was why Queen Doreen had been compelled to seek ways of augmenting the Royal income.

The alternative was to reduce the Royal Family to public assistance level (shouts of "Means Test!" "Get Knotted!" etc.). King Norman himself had not had a new suit for five years and had caused comment recently when, as he was receiving the Dumbodian Ambassador's credentials, his threadbare trousers suddenly gaped open at the knees, giving a strange glimpse of long grey woollen underpants.

Former money-making ventures by other members of the Royal Family, such as Duke Len of Erdington's off-licence at Gidea Park Underpass and Princess Shirley's ladies' hairdressing boutique in Mitcham High Street, had not been an outstanding success. Rather than carp at Queen Doreen's enterprise, which as well as helping the Monarchy would bring in valuable currency from foreign tourists, they should hope fervently for its success (uproar).

ANTI-JUBILEE——————————————

THE National Union of Students reaches its jubilee next year. But it has not yet decided how to celebrate it.

Several ideas immediately come to mind. Some are unsuitable for printing in a column which is designed for family reading and may even come into the hands of respectable artisans.

But the most dignified way this so-called union could celebrate its jubilee would be by the resignation of all its officials together, and by a public announcement that it was dissolved.

So that there could be no misunderstanding it should

give the reason: that students, having no recognisable interests in common, cannot form a valid trade union any more than, say, men with ginger moustaches or people born under the sign of Aries; and that if they do so it can only be for the purpose of power-exercises and political mischief-making.

But what, you may ask, would happen to all the students who now spend their time so enjoyably in these activities? Wouldn't they become frustrated and neurotic, and eventually a charge on the State? That is a risk which would have to be taken for the greater good.

EVIL DREAMS————————————————————————

"SCIENTISTS are trying to find . . . a contraceptive that women will wear like perfume," reports the *Sun*. "They believe that women could eventually attract and repel men at will by dabbing an appropriate scent behind the ear. The idea is based on the way animals' mating habits are linked to the smell from gland substances called pheromones."

Have these "scientists" and their ideas been invented by the gifted satirists of the *Sun* in order to make its readers disgusted with this kind of "scientific" attitude? Unfortunately not. They are only too real.

And their ideas are perfectly consistent with the "scientific" view of human beings as animal-machines, with emotions and bahaviour basically the same as the emotions and behaviour of dogs on heat.

Nothing else can be expected from these false scientists. The only interesting question is: are people beginning to accept the things they say, to take their inhuman fantasies for true science, or do they still regard them (as they certainly would have done a short time ago) with the instinctive disgust, contempt and loathing they deserve?

NOTHING NEW————————————————————————

THE five-day congress of the Czechoslovak Communist party is over. Dr Husak, re-elected as leader for a further five years with the new title of Secretary-General, has done everything his Russian masters expected of him, even virtually eating his own words in public.

The man who, when the Russian and satellite forces invaded Czechoslovakia in 1968, spoke of a "tragic misunderstanding" now says he is grateful for the invasion. The only explanation he can give for the undeniable fact that the majority of his countrymen condemned the invasion is that they were victims of "mass psychosis." And the assembled Czechoslovak Communist party applauded him for saying so.

Husak is doing neither more nor less than a Communist leader must do in such circumstances. Truth is not bourgeois truth (or bourgeois attempts to approximate to the truth); it is what agrees with the current purpose of the party.

Make no mistake; we have our Husaks here, and our obedient party men; the whole apparatus of tyranny and lies in embryo. The British Communist party has been commended for refusing to send delegates to the Czechoslovak congress on the ground that the proceedings would be subject to censorship.

That is the line at present. But does anyone think that if circumstances required it the British Communist party would not find men to play the game of Husak here with dishonesty as abject and absolute?

WELL DONE!————————————————————

THE Briggs Memorial Cup for the dirtiest railway station in Britain, presented by the Friends of Litter, has been won by Lampton-on-Hoke (Staffs.) for the third year running.

Yesterday thousands of motorists, many with young children, jammed the approaches to the famous station, which was looking its very best in the grey, overcast weather. Scuffles broke out as disappointed people were unable to get a glimpse.

"We're doing our best here at Lampton to keep up a great tradition, and I think we can say we're succeeding," the stationmaster, Mr Donald Nobes, told a reporter.

He looked proudly round the single litter-crammed platform, with its filthy, malodorous benches, rusted old slot-machines and peeling posters pencilled with a rich pattern of obscene symbols. His eye lingered on the key-point of the whole composition—the splintered, hinge-hanging door painted in faded, almost indecipherable letters "ENTS."

"They tried to close this station down two years ago," said Mr Nobes. "But the local conservation people weren't having any of that. Now there's talk of preserving it as a National Monument, with a small admission fee, to be what you might call a Joy for Ever."

PROVINCIAL NEWS————————————

WHEN members of the Men of Stretchford society, a body concerned with local traditions, chained themselves to railings at the Victoria Road Carbon Brush Works, which is threatened with demolition, members of Destruction 71, a local demolitionist group, chained themselves to the Men.

Firemen who arrived with hacksaws and oxy-acetylene equipment to free the demonstrators accidentally welded themselves to the demolitionists. Later a Town Hall spokesman declined to comment.

SECRET HISTORY————————————

IN an article about the late Lord Chief Justice Goddard Bernard Levin, the journalist, reveals that when he wrote a previous uncomplimentary piece about Goddard in the late fifties more than 20 High Court judges were called together in secret to advise whether he should be prosecuted for criminal libel.

"In view of the fact that, quite apart from the principle involved there was an overwhelming likelihood that one of the judges at this clandestine gathering would have presided if I had had to stand trial," writes Mr Levin, "I could not help feeling that this episode was one of the most disgraceful legal improprieties that had ever taken place in this country."

In fact Levin is too modest about his own importance in the world, a common failing in us journalists. The full story, I can reveal, was even more extraordinary.

At the judges' secret midnight meeting, they were unable to agree. Lord Goddard himself, who had insisted on being present and whose hatred and envy of Levin bordered on dementia, suggested that an unrepealed statute of 1381 be brought into play. By this Goddard himself, acting both as judge and jury, could have tried Levin in secret and sentenced him to be hanged, drawn and quartered or even boiled alive.

From then on, events moved swiftly. At noon the Privy Council was summoned. It was decided, after heated argument, to defer the announcement of a State of Emergency for 24 hours. But at 5 o'clock the Chiefs of the Defence Forces met (I was present myself, of course, in an *ex officio* capacity) to discuss contingency plans.

All that day and most of the night the meeting went on in an atmosphere of mounting crisis, as ominous reports came in from home and abroad—protest meetings in the Home Counties, unknown submarines in the Channel, massive Russian troop movements. Just before dawn we broke up, tired out yet ready to face whatever might come.

Lights were still blazing in Whitehall as I strolled with a grim-faced group towards the columnar, Nelson-crowned hub of the Commonwealth. I remember how Harold Macmillan turned to me with his characteristically shrewd yet world-weary smile. "Roll up the map of Europe, Simple. . . ." All round us the people of London slept on, unconscious of their peril.

And even before they woke, as it happened, with President Eisenhower, Prime Minister Khrushchev and His Holiness the Pope all on their respective "hot lines" at my own urgent insistence, the crisis was over.

But that is another story.

BEING, NOT BEING, ETC.————————————

SOME civilians at Colchester, it is reported, were asked by Army officers to taunt a squad of soldiers on a riot exercise and were given clods of earth to throw at them, on the understanding that the soldiers, who were armed with batons, would not move. The soldiers, however, did move, and one of the civilians had to have four stitches in his head.

"I'm afraid some of the lads were excessively enthusiastic," an Army spokesman, evidently a particularly talented one, explained later. "It was very dark and they probably didn't realise there were real civilians involved."

This is one of those news items which cloud the mind with mystery and convey it subtly to the borders of existence and non-existence. What did the soldiers think the beings who were throwing clods at them out of the darkness actually were, if they were not real civilians? A special kind of civilian trained by the Army for this purpose and able to absorb blows on the head from batons without thinking twice about it?

Artificial civilians, manufactured in REME workshops? Or thought-forms produced by enchanters attached to the Army Training Directorate, able to taunt and throw clods of earth but without corporeal existence?

Perhaps it is best not to think of such things.

RAILWAY enthusiasts and litter enthusiasts alike will be interested in the railway authorities' plans for the famous station at Lampton-on-Hoke (Staffs) which, as I mentioned the other day, has won the Briggs Memorial Cup for the dirtiest station in Britain for the third year running.

In a far-reaching reorganisation programme Lampton is to lose its other station, Lampton (Bog Lane End), on the old Great Northern Line. This station, though not quite so dirty as Lampton-on-Hoke, is equally beloved in its way, and is said to be haunted by the ghost of a former refreshment-room manageress, Joan Squinge (1872–1908).

All facilities will now be concentrated at Lampton-on-Hoke, a notable victory for local litter conservationists, who have fought plans to demolish the station tooth and nail. They have volunteered to put in a few hours a week making the station even dirtier than it is now, if that is possible. They hope to get a grant from Nerdley Council, which is interested in Lampton's tourist potential as the Dirtiest Railway Station in the World.

Mr Jim Grudge, brother of the Labour MP for Stretchford North, now Sub-Area Manager at Nerdley, is to take charge of Lampton, and also of the unmanned halts at Hokewell and Newcastle-on-Stretch, which owing to subsidence are now almost entirely under water.

Mr Don Nobes, the present stationmaster at Lampton (Bog Lane End) is leaving the railway service and has been offered a post with the "Friends of Litter" organisation as Promotions Officer. Particularly fine items of squalor from the station (such as the famous Table of All the Fungi from the old waiting room) will probably be added to the Lampton-on-Hoke collection. The rest will be put up for public auction at Nerdley Town Hall in the near future.

AMERICAN military technologists, reports the *Observer*, are developing an Automated Battlefield. They are devising a complex system of sensing contrivances, laser beams, night-seeing automata and computers, to create an electro-magnetic environment of continual automatic surveillance in which no enemy can survive.

The human factor in war will thus be discounted. If such an electro-magnetic screen were spread from the North Sea to the Alps, it is claimed, many of the American troops, most perhaps, could be withdrawn. Eventually, by the same argument, most of the other Nato troops now guarding Western Europe could also be withdrawn, leaving this miraculous technological system to defend us on its own.

I have heard of something rather like this before, 40 years ago. It was called the Maginot Line, an impregnable system of fortifications which, we were told, would make it impossible for German armies to invade France ever again.

It did not happen quite like that in 1940. The Maginot Line was outflanked. But even if it hadn't been, would France have remained unconquered?

Would Western Europe remain unconquered, for all her lasers, sensers, automata and computers, should treachery, defeatism, failure of nerve or even simple error put them out of action at a touch, leaving no effectual defence behind them?

Moral: It is not technology which wins wars, but men (Mao Tse-tung).

PRODIGIES————————————————————

AMONG my favourite comic characters are the married "family planning" experts Dr Malcolm Potts and Dr Caroline Deys (she is the woman doctor, you may remember, who was once reported to have given her baby girl contraceptive pills to prove how harmless they are).

The precious pair's latest act is even more hilarious. "We are in the middle of a private family row at the moment," Dr Deys said the other day. "I want to be sterilised and he wants to be sterilised and we can't agree which one of us should have an operation."

She thought the dispute would be resolved by a compromise "I expect I shall stay on the pill. Of course this only highlights the feelings that every couple have," she

30

babbled on convinced as all true fanatics are that every-body else must share her particular kind of fanaticism.

Why don't *both* these comic-doctors have themselves sterilised? To keep up the joke and set an example, Dr Deys should go on taking the pill as well and if Dr Potts himself is not already taking it he should start now.

DON'T MISS THIS————————————————

A BOOK which nobody from the humblest raver to the scholarly specialist can afford to miss is "Ron Frabb's Illustrated Lyrics," due from Viper and Bugloss next week (£1·80; paperback £1·20; gift edition in half-calf, autographed with Ron's famous "X" mark and fitted with battery-operated auto-destructive attachment, £15·50).

It contains the full text of all the multi-millionaire pop singer's major lyrics, from the early "Love Crawled Under the Door" to this year's subtle "Blancmange in the Head" (banned by the BBC), with its veiled references to frontal leucotomy, pot, masturbation and other great issues of our time.

Ron's notes on the background and composition of each lyric are not only sensationally interesting in them-selves but shed new light on the nature of genius and the mysterious sources of human creativity.

"Like I mean, man, I was lying in bed looking at this fly on the ceiling," he writes of the inception of one lyric, "Fly on the Ceiling," "when the words 'Fly on the Ceiling,' or something, I think, sort of came into what you might call my mind. I forget what happened after that, but I must have mentioned it to Cliff Rampton, my manager, because the next thing I knew it had sold 145 million copies and been banned in South Africa.

"Like I mean, dad, it's all happening, innit? I mean peace, and communication, and the fight against war and colonialism, and opting out of our rotten, money-oriented society, and that."

A RAILWAY TRAGEDY————————

SIR—The Joan Squinge you mention in your column as being refreshment-room manageress at Lampton (Bog Lane End) Station at the beginning of this century and as haunting the station after her death in 1908 was a great-aunt of mine.

The story in our family is that after being seduced one night in the porter's room by the then stationmaster, Jude Nuisance, she took the only course open, in that far from permissive age, to a railway employee who had stooped to folly and flung herself in front of the first train to pass through the station next morning, the 6,14 workmen's special from Nerdley to Trent Junction (not stopping at Gnomesall Heath).

I have a photograph of Great-Aunt Joan taken in the refreshment-room about the time of the Russo-Japanese War, an event which caused great excitement in railway circles in the Midlands. She is standing behind the tea-urn holding up a large pork pie with an enigmatic smile.
RODNEY SQUINGE
Brownhills (Staffs.)

This correspondence must cease, or legal action may have to be taken to protect the public.—P.S.

MORE PERSECUTION————————

A MAN jailed at Essex Quarter Sessions after his eighteenth offence of driving while disqualified in 11 years was said to have been "banned for life and for 10 years after that."

He is such a compulsive driver that it is evidently thought he may return from the grave to haunt the car-parks and take the wheel of other people's cars.

His case may be taken up by the Free Motorists' Resistance Group, run by J. Bonington Jagworth, Britain's most eminent motorist. The Group's Honorary Chaplain, the Rev. John Goodwheel, known to millions as the "Apostle of the Motorways," said yesterday that the case was unique in his experience.

It seemed that the enemies of motoring, not content with persecuting motorists in this world, were now trying to harry them in the next world as well. Let them beware.

In that other world of motoring the proud were cast down and the humble exalted; and there might be more joy in heaven over one motorist who drove while disqualified than over ninety-and-nine who, with a clean driving licence, yet smugly kept their cars unused in the spiritual garage where moth and rust corrupt.

THE PEOPLE'S REVENGE————————————

SHREWD political observers in Britain believe that the infamous Tory Government, already shaken to its foundations by the scorn and hatred of the exploited workers, may be finally overthrown by its latest measure of class-discrimination, a proposal to charge for admission to museums and art galleries.

Yesterday a crowd estimated to be over a million strong demonstrated outside the British Museum, most of whose treasures, stolen from the people over the centuries, are kept locked away for the delectation of the Tory aristocrats and their flunkeys. A fiery speech by Andrew Faulds, the beloved poet of the people who is known as "the Lord Byron of the 20th century," was cheered to the echo.

A small group of journalists wearing the hated boys' death's head brigade uniform of the official Government organ, *The Daily Telegraph*, and including the notorious Government hack, spy and police informer Lord Peter Simple, were recognised as they arrogantly tried to shoulder their way through the crowd, and narrowly escaped a lynching.

Fortunately for these gentry, the attention of the workers was diverted by the appearance of a jewelled coach carrying priceless paintings looted from the Tate Gallery and bound for the gilded mansion of a notorious art-collecting grandee, the Duke of Eccles. The guards were swiftly overpowered and in a sudden reverent hush, punctuated by gasps of art-appreciation, the Jackson Pollocks, Mondrians, Kandinskis and other masterpieces were shared out among the rightful owners.

Serious disturbances are reported from other parts of the country. In the Windermere bauxite-mining area, thousands of tough miners, veterans of a score of cultural hunger-marches, wept as they called on Sir Anthony

Blunt, the much-loved Socialist art-historian and darling of the people, to take the lead in overthrowing the tyrants in Whitehall.

Troops, including élite formations of the dreaded mobile art gallery attendants' corps, have now been drafted to this and other areas, including the Ilfracombe Coalfield, and there is every sign that the climax, which will blow the lid off the seething volcano of revolution, cannot be long delayed.

(*Dutt-Pauker Azerbaijani News Agency.*)

OBVIOUS————————————————————

DR PIXIE DUTT-PAUKER, niece of the well-known Hampstead thinker and lecturer in Social Protestology at Stretchford University, is to demand an investigation into the case of three young soldiers who have been discharged from the Army after inquiries about drug-taking.

One expert who supports her is Dr Heinz Kiosk, chief psychiatric consultant to the Fudge and Caramel Advisory Council, who commented yesterday on the obscurantist attitude of the Army authorities.

"It seems almost unbelieveable," Dr Kiosk said, "that young soldiers in this day and age can still be denied the right to experiment with the mind-expanding agents which most forward-looking young civilians take for granted.

"Blimps and other reactionaries may argue that drugs impair military efficiency, and point to the experience of the Americans in Vietnam. But surely we do not want to place ourselves on a level with the Russians or Chinese,

34

in whose armed forces drug-taking is officially frowned on and military efficiency is a fetish?

"What is the purpose of our having armed forces at all? It is surely to bring about world peace. And everything points to the conclusion that the more militarily inefficient our forces are the sooner world peace will be achieved."

PRICE OF FREEDOM

In its quiet way the *Radio Times* must do as much to propagate Leftist myths and condition the minds of the public to accept Leftist assumptions as any openly Leftist publication. With its enormous circulation, indeed, it must do far more.

Here is an example from an article in the current issue on "The Price of Freedom—the Hollywood Ten," a radio programme in a new series on "major political trials."

"During the McCarthy witch-hunts a number of Hollywood directors, producers and writers went to prison rather than testify whether or not they were Communists . . . When senators and statesmen pointed an accusing finger, insecurity degenerated into hysteria and nobody—not even the richest and biggest names in the business—felt safe any more . . . It seems incredible to us now that the dangers of a Communist conspiracy could cause such mass hysteria . . ."

How many readers of this stuff suspect that one reason why some of these film people went to prison rather than testify whether or not they were Communists may have been that they *were* Communists, and as such were helping a conspiracy which if it was dangerous then is a thousand times more dangerous now?

If all this seems incredible to us now, so much the worse for us; and so much the worse for the *Radio Times*, which has done its smug little bit to reduce us to this state of foolish complacency.

"The Price of Freedom"—freedom to advance the cause of Communist tyranny—could there be a more monstrous travesty of a title? The price of real freedom—must I repeat it?—is eternal vigilance.

"NIGERIAN company wishes to import used clothing, cars, cleaning rags, refrigerators, etc. Can export gum arabic, cow bones, alligator pepper, fruits and onions" (advertisement in the *Holland Herald*).

*   *   *

"Well, Watson, what do you make of it?"

I stared at the scrap of paper Holmes had tossed over to me, a slight smile playing over his lean features.

"I confess I'm completely bewildered," I replied, after a pause. "This Nigerian company—why should it want used cleaning rags? And who in England wants cow bones or alligator pepper—whatever that may be?"

My friend slowly took up his violin, then laid it down again as a thought evidently struck him. His eye gleamed with inductive light.

"Let us assume," he said, meditatively filling his pipe, "that the list of imports is simply a blind, an attempt to get certain people interested. What sort of man would own a lot of used cleaning rags?"

"A man with a lot of cars and refrigerators?"

"Precisely. A man of considerable means. A man who has the means to indulge his whims, however fantastic."

"You mean—"

"I mean this, my dear Watson. Consider: what sort of pastime, hobby or interest would you connect with gum arabic, cow bones and alligator pepper?"

"What *is* alligator pepper?"

For answer Holmes opened a drawer of his bureau and took out a small, finely carved ebony box, evidently of African provenance. He opened it and I had hardly time to observe the fine yellowish grains inside when I fell back, overcome by a fit of sneezing which lasted for several minutes and left me limp and exhausted.

"First render your victims helpless with a powerful sneezing agent derived from the powdered claws of alligators," Holmes went on. "Then fix them to the ground or to a prepared base with gum arabic and glue made from boiled cow bones. It's one of the most powerful adhesives known. The ancient Egyptians used it to secure the foundations of the Great Pyramid."

"Amazing," I gasped. "But what does it all mean?"

"It means, my dear Watson, that the man we have to

deal with is a madman with a taste for living statuary, a madman, moreover, of vast wealth and curious knowledge. It means we have not a moment to lose. Come, Watson. To Paddington!"

As I stood irresolute, my friend seized a valise and threw a tartan travelling rug over my head . . .

CALLING ALL BORES————————————
by "NARCOLEPT"

ALL roads lead to Harringay, Mecca of the world's yawn fans, as the Intergalactic Boring Contests of 1971 unroll their age-old tapestry of stupefaction. But this year there is a cloud over the joyous festival of lethargy, a cloud no bigger than a man's hand as yet, but soon—who knows?

I refer, of course, to the problem of hooliganism, from which our own sport, unlike the sports of lesser breeds, has up to now been so blessedly free. Tell it not in Gath, lest the heathen rejoice, but there are ominous signs that our long immunity from this contemporary plague is over.

As I sat entranced in the Press box during yesterday's hard-fought match between Jean-Pierre Cafard, Canada's No. 2 seed, and Irgun ben Tedium of Israel, I noticed, as I nodded off, that several people in a near-by stand, including at least one elderly clergyman, were not merely wideawake but were actually standing up and shouting ill-mannered remarks such as "Get boring!" "You're interesting!" and so on, just as though they were at some petty village contest rather than at the sacred centre of the boring world.

Such conduct can only bring our beloved sport into disrepute, and I look to the top brass of the British Boring Board of Control to crack down on offenders hard wherever they may be found. As I always say, facilis descensus Averni, and I well remember, if I may quote an incident from my own personal experience which in my view at least well illustrates the nature of the problem, nevertheless, having regard to the facts of the case, not, but, inasmuch as, however (turn to p. 63).

37

FOR all my dislike of Hampstead thinkers and their thoughts, I have lived in Hampstead twice myself. I too have walked her winding streets and lanes and peered into her umbrageous gardens where rich progressive ladies sit under the trees and plan to overwhelm South Africa with blood and fire.

I too have tramped her noted heath in all weathers and listened darkling as groups of Indian economics students, among the most gifted bores in the world, passed nattering like clouds of flies with many a fine-wrought gesture of dissent.

I have hated Hampstead for her Left-wingery, but I have loved her for her strange, secret, leafy soul. Nowhere in London are green thoughts so green, especially in a rainy June, when the grass grows high in her innumerable gardens tamed or wild.

As "Wayfarer" says in his book "Afoot in London" (in the chapter called "Hampstead Heritage"), "a man may walk with stick and knapsack, map and compass a live-long summer's day from Archway to Finchley Road Underground Station, and so be he can read a map and have an eye for country, need scarce once put foot on tarmac."

I have often thought of trying this out, following the hidden, half-overgrown paths between garden fences, sometimes crossing the gardens themselves or even passing through houses when no other way seems open.

What adventures I might have in those damp and leafy solitudes! "Wayfarer," in the book I have mentioned, says there are parts of Hampstead which have never been fully explored; in one densely-wooded stretch, between the garden of Mrs Dutt-Pauker's Queen Anne house Marxmount and the Heath, there is a tribe of Left-wing pygmies of cannibal habits and strong views on racial integration.

That would be among the least of the perils I might have to face as I pushed on through the dense foliage or paused to eat my bread and cheese by some gay flowerbed, watched by indignant progressive eyes from a book-lined study or seized and dragged indoors to take part in a discussion on comprehensive education and the need for Socialist play-groups.

KATYN————————————————————

IT is beyond doubt that in the last war the Russian Communists murdered 10,000 Polish officers, the élite of the Polish Army, in the Forest of Katyn. When the bodies were discovered by the advancing Germans in 1941, the Russian Government blamed the massacre on the Germans themselves.

It is also beyond doubt that leaders on the allied side were aware of the truth but took an evasive and prevaricating attitude for fear of offending the Soviet Government. The British Government, as was shown in a recent debate in the House of Lords, is still sticking to that attitude, presumably for the same reason. After all, the same Soviet Government is still in power.

As Churchill said at the time to Sikorski, the Free Polish leader, who kept on embarrasingly protesting to the Russians, "If they are dead, nothing you can do will bring them back." Yet after 30 years it is surely desirable, for the sake of their memory and of historical justice, that the guilt for this crime should be placed unmistakably where it belongs.

There is another point. If this particular incident in Communist wartime history could be thus officially concealed and prevaricated about, with the connivance of the West, how many more atrocities are still lying undiscovered or unpublicised about the world?

TOURIST TRAP————————————————

ONE landowner who seems not to have been present at Lord Montagu's seminar at Beaulieu on "the management of country parks, historic houses and castles" is Lord Mountwarlock, whose historic house in Leicestershire is often called in the travel brochures "The Stately Home that is Different."

I should have thought the eight-foot-tall, Cyclops-eyed Earl would have had a lot to contribute to the discussions. Mountwarlock Park, with its fabulous monsters, Deadly Upas Tree, 18th century artificial volcano and bottomless pit believed to communicate directly with the Infernal

Regions, draws thousands of visitors during the season. Many find it literally impossible to get away.

An innovation this year is a Mediaeval Banquet, where for a mere £2 a head visitors can sit at the historic table in the Great Banqueting Hall under which Cardinal Umfravile was murdered by Fulke the Red in 1292. There

they can gorge themselves silly on peacock stuffed with red mullet, honey, tinfoil and minced wild boar's trotters while the estate harpies—a particularly disgusting breed—swoop down and try to snatch the food in their filthy talons amid delighted screams and cries of "Get away, you nasty thing!"

Phantomsby the major domo, one of the few practising werewolves still left in the Midlands, is in overall charge. He has fixed the next Mediaeval Banquet, by manipulating the calendar, for the night of the next full Moon. As he told me yesterday, with an infectious smile which revealed his large gleaming white incisors, he thinks it may be the most successful banquet yet.

GIFTED

IN a discussion about Equity, the actors' union, in the House of Lords, Baroness Lee, who used to provide such a lot of laughs by her pronouncements as "Minister for the Arts" in the last Labour Government, showed she had not lost her touch.

Unemployment among actors, those "gifted people," was so serious, she said, that "the cheapest labour in the market at the moment is gifted actors. You can hire them for 6s. 6d. [*sic*] an hour." She herself had employed a young actor in her garden.

I would not trust an actor in my garden. But a few months ago, when large numbers of unskilled workers in the "Way of the World" building—sweepers, assistant punka-wallahs, turntable underlookers, keyhole-checkers, water-carriers and so on—were laid off through sickness, I authorised Griffiths, the works manager, to take on a few dozen gifted actors as an experiment.

It was not a success. Not only were these gifted people unable to carry out the simplest task, such as turning a tap on or off, without supervision; worse, the only gift they seemed to have was the gift of talking incessantly, in the most boring, tiresome, modish-Leftist way, on subjects they knew absolutely nothing whatever about.

In the end they got on the nerves of the ordinary work-people—honest, ungifted English craftsmen with a proper pride in their work—so badly that a walk-out—it would have been the first since the ablative absolute turners downed tools in 1958—was actually threatened.

After that they simply had to go, taking their gifts with them.

CAN I HELP YOU?————————————
by "GENUFLEX"

"MY elder brother Eric, who is in holy orders and also holds medical and dental degrees, joined the police force some 10 years ago and has just been promoted detective-sergeant. Soon afterwards, through the death of a cousin, he succeeded to the baronetcy.

"When writing, how should I address him, as he is a stickler in such matters?" (Mostyn Sheep-Harris, Loughborough).

"GENUFLEX" replies: "The Rev. Det.-Sgt. Dr Sir Eric Sheep-Harris, Bt., DD, MD, LDS' is the correct form. Should your brother be appointed a Privy Councillor, join the Navy, Army or Air Force, or make a pilgrimage to Mecca, please write to me again."

MEMBERS of the Stretchford Municipal Symphony Orchestra are considering whether to come out in sympathy with the strike by the Bournemouth Symphony Orchestra, who are in dispute with the council over fees.

Yesterday, at a crowded meeting at the Sadcake Hall, in New Bridge Street, various suggestions were made. One of them was for a "selective" strike by which all members of the orchestra would refuse to play certain notes of the scale at their concerts. In the event of the dispute continuing, more and more notes would be withdrawn until at last only one note remained.

But the players could not agree on the order in which notes should be withdrawn, the militants favouring the immediate elimination of A and E flat, the moderates favouring a token withdrawal of G in all works of more than 20 minutes' duration.

Another suggestion, that all works should be played at a very slow tempo throughout and that certain sections of the orchestra should stage lightning walk-outs during performances, led to an exchange of blows between second violins and wood-wind, in which Prem Bakshi, the comatose Pakistani triangle-player, who had somehow got involved, had his triangle twisted out of shape.

No agreement was reached on strike action. But a new factor was introduced into the dispute yesterday when the Amalgamated Hole-borers' Union executive, on a show of hands, affirmed their union's solidarity with the musicians and offered to go and bore holes in their instruments and even pour cold tea inside them if required, all entirely free of charge.

GLITTERING AWAY————————————

"LORD SNOWDON is said to have thrown two glasses of wine—one white, one red—over Mr Cazalet's shirt-front at a glittering party attended by hundreds of guests" (*Sunday Express*).

A rather amateurish effort, I'm afraid. Any serious wine-thrower would have made a point of throwing a glass of rosé as well; an expert would have included glasses of sherry, champagne and port in the list, if possible in the correct order.

One of the most impressive feats of this kind I ever saw—and it was not even at a glittering party, but in an ordinary saloon bar—was performed by a woman.

Offended by a man, she threw a glass of gin over him, followed at short intervals by tonic water, ice, a slice of lemon and a dash of angostura.

FESTIVAL

A NATIONAL demonstration for "love and family life," to be called the "Festival of Light," will be held in September. Beacon fires will be lit all over the country to "alert Britain to the dangers of moral pollution." There will be a rally in Trafalgar Square and a "gospel music festival" in Hyde Park. The backers include such familiar names as Cliff Richard, Dora Bryan, Lord Longford, Malcolm Muggeridge and Mrs Mary Whitehouse.

To make fun of this kind of thing is the easiest thing in the world. Modish verbalisers have started the game already. In the event, the Festival of Light is likely to be accompanied in the Press, on television and elsewhere, by a Festival of Progressive Jeering bigger and more sustained than any yet known even in this country. The Mellies and Millers will have a field-day.

There is great danger here, If those who now want to stand up for love and family life against moral pollution—and they not only represent, even now, the majority of the population of this country, but include people a great deal more intelligent and sophisticated than the Cliff Richards and Lord Longfords of this world—if they cannot even get a hearing, or any answer to their arguments except automatic jeers, they may find themselves giving place, for lack of any alternative, to other, very different champions of morality and decency, who will light beacon fires of another sort and sing another kind of song.

To laugh *them* off will not be so easy.

WHAT'LL YOU HAVE, SQUIRE?————————

No need to ask! A dirty great pint of NADIRKEG BITTER, of course!

Watch as it comes all foaming, golden-green, chemical-rich and fully-pressurised from laboratory-cool cellars to hygienically-operated beer-pumps!

Savour the taste, cunningly blended by masters of the brewer's age-old craft to tickle your palate subtly and set your teeth pleasurably on edge—full, creamy, soapy, free from harmful alcohol—the Old English Ale that is different, the Ale for men that are Men.

It's the drink that makes men irresistible to women, too! See them gather round and rub themselves against you, purring as you sink your pint of this superb beer! But remember not to spill any on them as they try to kiss your feet—every drop is precious!

One more for the road, Squire? You bet!

NADIRKEG BITTER

THE BEER THAT PUTS HAIR

ON YOUR CHEST

[*advt*]

JAGWORTH SPEAKS

J. Bonington Jagworth, Britain's most eminent motorist, called an emergency council of his Free Motorists' Resistance Group at his Staines garage home yesterday to consider the new situation caused by the proposal to ban all parking within 20 yards of road junctions.

"The pretence that this is for the protection of motorists themselves," says a statement by group spokesman Royston Cylinder, "will deceive no one. It is simply one more move in a deliberate campaign to drive the already downtrodden British motorist out of his mind and finally suppress him altogether.

"If the object of the new rule were really to improve visibility at road junctions, it is surely obvious that this could be achieved much better by demolishing all buildings within 20 yards—or better still, 200 yards—of the junctions. This is a commonsense step which the FMRG has been urging for years without the authorities taking a blind bit of notice.

"The Ministry of Transport should be renamed the Ministry of Immobility. It stands revealed in all its naked horror as a whited sepulchre, a broken reed, a worn tyre, a leaking petrol-tank, a cracked engine-block, a windscreen-wiper which instead of cleaning the wind-screen of the mind with the clean sweep of reason befouls it with the opaque mud of anti-motoring prejudice."

CHANGE

Rejecting a referendum on the issue of the Common Market, Mr Heath said it would mean a major change in our system of representative parliamentary democracy. "I find it curious," he said, "that those who resist change in one respect should become ardent advocates of it in another."

This remark apparently got a big laugh from the Conservative's Central Council. I can't quite see why. It is perfectly reasonable for the same person to resist change where he thinks it harmful but advocate it where he thinks it good.

I myself, as you may have noticed, resist many kinds of change (not that it gets me anywhere). But at the same time there are some kinds of change I advocate strongly: the elimination of almost all technical advances made during the last 150 years, for instance, and an absolute ban on any more.

RESPECT

"A COMBINATION of the pill and abortions on demand for everybody may raise the question whether the status and respect for womanhood which we have known can in fact survive," says the Bishop of Leicester.

But the people in our country who are doing their best to bring about the social situation he describes do not want respect for womanhood to survive. They do not want respect for anyone to survive. They want to destroy the kind of respect we have known altogether.

The more foolish and thoughtless of them hope that when this respect has been destroyed they will enjoy instead a "sense of community," a perpetual "love-in," a lovely warm bath of physical and sexual contact for everybody in the whole world.

That is what they hope for. What they are more likely to get is conscription and forced labour for men and women alike; guns and pickaxes; the kind of society in which respect for authority, if not for womanhood, is not only enjoined but efficiently enforced.

MYSTERY INTRUDER

MRS BRENDA O'GOURKE, 46, housewife, of Termite Road, Nerdley, was accused at Nerdley magistrates' court yesterday of dishonestly handling 51 pork pies, the property of the Nadirco Fooderama in Effluent Road.

Chief Pork Pie Section Leader Mr Kevin Stentorian, 35, said that while watching his section on the closed circuit television screen he saw Mrs O'Gourke methodically levering off the upper casings, or "lids," as they were technically called, of a large number of pork pies with an outsize nailfile. She appeared to be checking the contents, occasionally writing in an outsize notebook.

When he questioned her Mrs O'Gourke said she was conducting an independent survey of the contents of Nadirco pork pies. There was no knowing what you might find in them nowadays. One friend of hers had recently found a hairnet, part of an alarm-clock and what seemed to be the incisor-tooth of a badger; another had found a long, rambling letter, possibly an appeal for help from someone who had been at one time imprisoned in the pie, for what reason she could not say.

Told her remarks were defamatory, accused became abusive and the police were sent for. Cautioned by Sgt E. J. Mackenzie, 32, of Nerdley Special Branch, Mrs O'Gourke tried to climb into one of the pies, damaging part of the main casing, or "side," and was arrested.

Giving evidence, Dr F. Gestaltvogel, 51, consultant psychiatrist at Nerdley General Hospital, said he had examined Mrs O'Gourke. Apart from disturbance in her sense of spatial relations, particularly where pastry was concerned, and a morbid horror of string, she was a perfectly normal member of society. He believed she would benefit from membership of a sensory contact group; failing this, euthanasia by a variety of methods was always available at his own clinic.

Binding Mrs O'Gourke over, the chairman, Dr Ellis Goth-Jones, 62, said that in view of her previous good conduct he would deal leniently with her. But he must emphasise the duty every member of our society owed to great national trading groups like the Nadirco Organisation.

He believed that many of the urgent problems of our society—such as pornography, subsidence on motorways, the generation gap, racial discrimination and a growing disillusionment with politics—stemmed from a basic failure of respect. But he did not think a referendum on the Common Market was necessarily the answer.

THINK IT OVER————————————————————

"CHRISTIAN Action is opening a bureau in Trafalgar Square, London, for tourists' complaints about overcharging, bad food and bad service in British hotels and restaurants" (*Observer*).

If only Christian Action had been operating in Bethlehem 1971 years ago! The paucity and bad quality of hotel accommodation for tourists in the Roman Province of Judaea, as contemporary reports show, was one of the major spiritual problems of the time.

Some theological economists think this was an important factor in the failure of the Roman Empire to maintain a dynamic rate of economic growth and its consequent collapse.

TRIUMPHS OF REASON————————————————

"ALL but a handful of fanatics, Irish earls or dowager ladies, with ample private means and time on their hands, now recognise that the great mass of people are not unduly concerned, one way or the other, over "charters for queers," four-letter words, nudes, profanity or dirty postcards so long as checks are kept on prices and unemployment."

This passage comes from the Annual Report of the National Secular Society, whose "Distinguished Members' Panel" (*sic*) includes Michael Foot, MP, Brigid Brophy, Baroness Wootton, Lord Willis and George Melly.

The Society was founded in 1866 by Charles Bradlaugh. He and his fellow-Victorian secularists, however basically silly they may have been, at least thought themselves serious and high-minded people. What would they have thought of the cheap, vulgar, frivolous stuff their heirs are dealing in today?

They may well have had an equally patronising and contemptuous attitude towards the working classes. But they would have hoped, in however misguided a way, to improve them.

If they had thought that after a century the working classes might come to be totally uninterested in anything except money (as the National Secular Society seems insultingly to think), they would have deplored the fact, not giggled over it. If they were honest, they might even have had doubts about helping to rob the working classes of their morality and religion for such an end.

LAST night's GPI Television Network analysis of the problems of Ulster, in the "Hear All Sides" series, was well up to the standards of this admirably balanced programme.

It took the form of a discussion between Mrs Dutt-Pauker, the well-known liberal housewife and authority on Irish affairs (she has a house in Kerry, Leninmore); liberal film-producer Max Burst, who is planning a documentary on cannibalism by British troops in Belfast; another liberal, Brigadier Seán MacGuffog of the IRA, who claims to have shot several policemen; British Left-wing Labour backbench MP, Reg Duttcliffe; and (to dispose in advance of any foolish clamour about "bias" from the lunatic backwoodsmen of the Right) a senior British Army representative, Lt C. R. Wafer, a 56-year-old officer who is due to be discharged from the Royal Army Tailoring Corps shortly as his fits of uncontrollable trembling are not yielding to medical treatment.

With such a team as this there could be little doubt of the outcome. The case for the present British policy in Ulster was soon exposed as a pitiful sham, and after Brig. MacGuffog had reduced the Fascist Lt Wafer to tears by spitting on him and threatening him with a rusty machine-gun, all agreed that the British Army should be withdrawn immediately, the Stormont Government abolished and a United Nations peace-keeping force, preferably with a strong component from the Eastern European democracies, sent in.

It seems incredible that the GPI Network, in spite of all its trouble, should have received several telephone calls suggesting that the programme was not perfectly bal-

anced. To remove all doubts, a spokesman pointed out that Lt Wafer was to be given thirty seconds to argue his case again that very night on "Late Night Hold-Up," provided he recovered consciousness in the meantime.

LOADS OF GUILT————————————

DR HEINZ KIOSK, the well-known psychopenologist and chief psychiatric consultant to the Plastic Gnome Advisory Council, was quick to comment yesterday on the Police Federation's call for tougher action by the Government and the courts against violent criminals.

"As reasonable people," he said, "we may feel inclined to ignore this hysterical outburst or dismiss it as coming from a vociferous minority of uniformed cranks and neurotics obsessed with the so-called 'war against crime' which is their own most cherished illusion.

"But there I think we should be wrong. The statement by the Police Federation is unmistakably a cry for help, the desperate cry of sick people who are unable to come to terms with reality and with the society in which they live. It demands not our disapproval, contempt or ridicule, natural as these may be, but our compassion. The plight of these policemen concerns each and every one of us. We are all guilty.

"The primary need, of course, is for education. These deluded policemen, with their insistent talk of 'criminals,' 'the law,' 'protecting society' and other outmoded concepts, must learn to accept a society based on those basic values of dissent and social awareness which the 'violent criminal' of their fevered imagination represents and embodies more compellingly than most of us can hope to do.

"It will be a long, hard road. For policemen—a 'maverick' social group inclined to accept unthinkingly the values of the past—it will be particularly hard. But unless they are prepared to take it, like the rest of us, how can policemen play their part in building the future society, let alone have any place in it themselves?"

PROVISIONAL results of the 1971 Census show that the total population of England and Wales is about one-third of a million fewer than was predicted. This, says a statistician, "is really the only big mystery produced by today's figures".

Where have these missing people got to? One possibility is that many if not all of them are people who out of disgust with modern England have taken refuge in this column.

Hundreds of such refugees, usually carrying a pathetic jumble of possessions they have saved from the wreck of all they hold dear, such as Fabergé Easter eggs, fragments of blackleaded old kitchen-ranges, shooting sticks, silver duck-presses or stones from the summit of Cross-fell, arrive at the columnar frontiers daily.

Most are admitted, since the agony they show even at the thought of being sent back to the technology-corroded land from which they came is more than the most hard-hearted immigration official can bear. A few questions about Bruckner or Byzantine art, designed to establish their bona fides, a simple language test in Cornish or Old Sorb and they are in.

The problem of resettlement is another matter. Most of these people are not physically robust enough for subsistence farming or manually expert enough for the main columnar industries of organ-building and illuminating manuscripts.

Many of them, when their small savings are exhausted, turn to wandering the dusty roads as pedlars, fortune-tellers, mountebanks or amateur dentists; become holy men, genuine or feigned; or seek minor employment in the households of the great nobles as professional domino-players, bed-warmers, flatterers or mirror-men.

AGREED————————————————————————

THIS is the last day when the penny and the threepenny piece are legal tender, and it is a sad day for England. It is good to know that the "Anti-Decimal Group" is still fighting bravely on for the restoration of the old coinage.

Oddly enough they have support from an unexpected

quarter, the mammoth Nadirco Consortium, which runs a chain of supermarkets throughout the Midlands. A spokesman said yesterday that the effect of the change-over to decimals on the company balance sheets had been most encouraging. There was every reason to think that a change-back in due course would be equally beneficial.

As far as Nadirco was concerned, he added, laughing so heartily that he almost fell into a yawning cash-register behind him, the Government was welcome to arrange a switch between decimal coinage and £ s d, and vice versa, as often as it pleased.

FESTIVAL OF YOUTH————————
by VIRGINIA FERRET

THE great Grampus Moor Pop Festival, which drew a crowd of teenagers estimated by some observers at over 3 million to this quiet Midland village, is over.

Today nothing marks the site except an estimated 40,000 tons of rubbish, a few piles of "offensive weapons" still not collected by the police, the shattered ruins of several cottages and, here and there, the recumbent bodies of fans still too weak to move, who have so far escaped the notice of the Nerdley Municipal Cleansing Department.

What has impressed most people in the neighbourhood is the extraordinary orderliness, friendliness and peace-fulness of this mass-gathering of Britain's youth, their consideration for others, their social kindness, their essential *goodness*.

Apart from a few cases of violence and looting (only about 10,000 people were arrested), apart from preventing anybody in the neighbourhood from sleeping or attending to ordinary business for three days and nights and producing an exodus of refugees estimated at 5,000, the pop festival caused no problems whatever.

So much for the forebodings of the fuddy-duddies, always ready to pick on the alleged shortcomings of Britain's youth and throw up mittened hands in horror at new fashions in dress, music and public sexual inter-course.

Most of the older folk who have decided to remain in

the area, mainly tradespeople, say they are keenly hoping for another Pop Festival soon.

"It was a real vindication of Britain's youth." Mrs Linda Hinge, 46, a typical local widow, told me, smilingly surveying her cottage, its chimney just emerging from an enormous mass of malodorous litter.

"After all, these young people could easily have murdered me and set my cottage on fire. But they didn't. Whatever the moaners and groaners may say, there's nothing much wrong with young people like that."

HAND-OUT

"IN late 1919 more than nine-tenths of the Soviet Union was occupied by the British, Americans, anti-Bolsheviks, White Russians and their allies. Lenin and Trotsky were fighting for their lives in the remnants of their country around Moscow. More than 13 million Russian men, women and children died from starvation, disease and armed force during the Allied Intervention and the Civil War it did so much to bolster."

This is an extract from the BBC's publicity hand-out for a television programme, "The Forgotten War," to be broadcast this week. I can say nothing of the actual programme, which may, for all I know, give a reasonably fair account. But for sheer bias and partisanship the hand-out could hardly go further. That it merely repeats the accepted myths about this period of Russian history is no excuse. Isn't it one of the supposed functions of the BBC to educate, to "make people think," as the Leftists say?

Who would imagine from this hand-out that the White Russians, anti-Bolsheviks and their allies were fighting in 1919 to defend the legitimate government of Russia against Lenin and Trotsky, who by conspiracy and terror had usurped power in "their" country?

Who could have imagined then that for their defence of that legitimate government against the Bolsheviks, the allies, including Britain, could be accused by a British Broadcasting Corporation 50 years later of having practically *caused* the suffering and death of 13 million Russians?

And who would guess from this hand-out that if the

53

allied intervention in Russia had succeeded (as, given determination and realisation of what was at stake, it would have done) the subsequent history of Russia, Europe and the world would have been immeasurably happier?

EVERYBODY SATISFIED?————————

To some the Concorde is "a superb technological wonder." To others she is "a crime against humanity," the most striking example so far of technological advance for its own sake, without thought for human welfare.

In my Utopia these two seemingly irreconcilable attitudes would be reconciled. We should go on building a few Concordes but not allow them to fly. People who love these undoubtedly impressive and even beautiful machines could go and look at them in museums, while people who do not love them would not have to be deafened or frightened out of their wits.

Once every five years, perhaps, there would be a Technological Saturnalia, in which the strange human passion for technology could be indulged without restraint *for one day only*.

Scientists would put on their best white coats and go about researching and measuring things to their hearts' content, building the most advanced kinds of nuclear accelerators and pulling them to pieces again, examining each others' brains and playing about gleefully with genes and amino-acids and memory-banks, while overhead the Concorde flew, shattering their delighted eardrums with its sonic boom.

As night fell their technological pleasures would mount to frenzy; for they would know that when midnight tolled from the great cathedral bells they must put away their toys and take up the burden of human sanity again.

DANGER————————————————————

AFTER a ranger in the Duke of Bedford's "monkey jungle" at Woburn had repeatedly told a visitor to close the windows of his car the man got out and knocked him unconscious with a wrench.

Incidents of this sort sometimes happen even at Mountwarlock Park, Lord Mountwarlock's "stately home" in Leicestershire where the unique collection of fabulous monsters—wyverns, gorgons, basilisks, chimeras, harpies and so forth—can be seen in their proper unnatural setting and attract thousands of visitors every summer.

Precautions are taken to protect visitors, particularly from the gorgons. This is not so much out of concern for

the visitors themselves as to prevent the whole park from being cluttered up with people who have been turned to stone.

At one time these were sold off as garden ornaments, stone middle-aged women with outsize handbags being an especially popular line, but after complaints of unfair competition from the Plastic Gnome Council a quota system was agreed on.

Gorgons, of course, cannot turn people to stone through the windows of cars, though tyres may be petrified in certain conditions. So the Head Ranger, 46-year-old ex-ghoul Jabez Doomwright and his assistants perpetually haunt the gloomy glades of the fabulous monsters' realm, enjoining the visitors in awful tones to keep their windows closed.

But accidents will happen. Only the other day one visitor, a dynamic young naphtha salesman with the typical truculence of his kind, leaped out of his Boggs Super-Oaf and made to attack one of the gorgons with his metal-edged document-case.

He was a statue before he had gone two paces; and a few minutes later, grey and lichened, half sunk in long grass, with a few raindrops running down his stone executive's suit, he looked as if he had been there for hundreds of years already.

THE "great problems of our time," we are continually told by modish publicists, are racialism, poverty, "the population explosion," "the threat to the environment," war. But there is another and greater threat than any of these: the process by which our inherited capacity for feeling, perceiving and responding to things in a human way in being destroyed by a spirit which is steadily reducing and dehumanising our lives.

That spirit takes innumerable forms; it is present alike in the attitudes of computer engineers and sex educationists; of humanist thinkers and authors of books about the Naked Ape; of the translators of the New English Bible and pornographic entertainers; of fashionable pseudo-scientists, pseudo-artists, pseudo-philosophers, pseudo-mystics of all kinds.

It is everywhere; it disguises itself as its opposite; it takes good causes—the defence of the "environment," charity and mercy, freedom from toil, sexual happiness—and turns them into bad; it breaks down human language and makes it meaningless; it is supported by a vast body of organised lies—the dogmas of orthodox liberal enlightenment—which are everywhere accepted as unquestionable truth.

So powerful is that reductive, inhuman spirit that it seems by this time like the air we breathe, irresistible. Yet it must be resisted. How? In the first place by teaching people how to recognise it, by exposing its deceits and disguises and analysing its pervasive and seductive jargon.

ETERNAL RECURRENCE————————————————

THE Department of the Environment has a plan to set up a network of special thief-proof lorry parks along the motorways. They will be surrounded by moats and barbed wire fences and patrolled by guards and dogs. They will include sleeping quarters and canteens for the lorry drivers.

Here is a fine chance to get back to the Middle Ages. Mobile criminals, who grow bolder every day, will not be put off simply by moats and guard dogs. The parks should also have drawbridges, guard-houses, elaborate systems of walls and strong-points, double or treble, and a central donjon or keep where the most valuable goods can be stored in the event of a prolonged siege.

What a chance too, for the architects who design these castles, whose crenellated walls and towers will loom grandly over the ignoble huddles of buildings now called "service areas". In time, as history takes its course, the biggest, strongest and cleverest lorry-drivers, or in some cases the biggest, strongest and cleverest thieves, will turn into castle-holding barons; and a new feudal order will arise.

And when that age is over, when ferns and bushes cover the motorways and the very word "environment" is forgotten, what splendid ruins these castles will make: the haunted Castle of Watford Gap; grey, lichened, melancholy Trowell; romantic Leicester Forest East, still guarding with its broken bulk the leafy solitudes of Charnwood.

GET UP AND GO!

Do you envy the man who not only runs several shopping centres in Devon and Cornwall but has laid out a whole airfield near Bodmin Moor, including two 600-yard runways, without planning permission?

Don't stand there dithering! Get up and go! You too can build as many airfields (and shopping centres) as you like with the aid of two new volumes in the "Way of the World" "Do It Yourself" Series: "Home Airport Construction" and "Build Your Own Shopping Centre."

"Home Airport Construction" gives clear, concise instructions on Selecting Your Site (preferably in an attractive and relatively peaceful part of the country); Levelling the Ground and Removing Hedges, Trees. Villages, Churches, Farmhouses, etc. (here a companion volume in the series, "How to Build Your Own Earth-moving Machinery," will be useful); Laying out Runways for Maximum Noise Value; Airport Building Design; and many other fascinating topics.

A useful chapter gives hints on how to deal with so-called "amenity" and "conservation" cranks, local residents, doctors, schoolteachers, people and others who may object to your project.

The specimen letters to the Press, explaining that your airport is in the national interest and will benefit the export drive, the balance of payments, employment, standards of living, etc., etc., and that it is only opposed by a vociferous minority of long-haired neurotics, reactionary killjoys and unpatriotic misfits, are written by experts in this field.

STRANGE———————————————————

"No Government," says a political commentator, "can make the people of Northern Ireland love each other. But a British Government can at least try to remove the most obvious causes of hate, and this it is ready to do. In effect it is ready to take political control, and to create the conditions in which the Catholic minority can live worthwhile lives."

What is most appalling about this statement is the implication that people cannot live "worthwhile lives" unless certain "conditions"—universal suffrage, equal rights in housing and employment and so on—are created.

What a strange view of human life is this! Logically it means that the Protestant majority in Northern Ireland live more worthwhile lives than the Catholic minority. Is that really what the writer meant to say?

RUN FOR YOUR LIVES———————————

An "Itinerant Theatre Company" is being formed, "to bring back to London streets the concept of the strolling player." It will "move from site to site presenting musicals, contemporary drama, classics, vaudeville, discotheques and children's matinées."

Outside Central London, says one of the organisers, "there is very little professional theatre available. We want to take professional theatre into the boroughs and give them something new." "We want to create a new environmental theatre," says another member of the gang.

So a new horror is to be added to the mounting horrors of common life. Up to now this kind of "theatre" (and incidentally it is largely dominated by people of Leftist and progressivist persuasion) has mostly been confined to indoor performances where at least it could not be a nuisance to the general public.

Now the theatrical gangs are to take to the streets, pursuing their victims with wholly unwanted posturing, dancing and uproar to the remotest boroughs and, if need be, to the uttermost ends of the earth. Nobody will be safe anywhere.

Most ecologists agree that there are already far too many actors in this country. With this new outlet for their tedious goings-on the number may soon swell from the present estimated two million to five or ten million, with disastrous effects on the environment.

Moreover, actors, pampered and flattered as they are by those who ought to know better, are already remarkable for their ignorance, conceit and insolence. With this new licence to persecute anybody anywhere at any time they are certain to get a hundred times worse.

What can people do to protect themselves against this nuisance in the streets? The phrase "strollihg players" gives a clue. To prevent people taking matters into their own hands (and there have already been a few cases of attacks on street theatricals) the Elizabethan laws relating to strolling players and other vagabonds, which were understandably severe, should be revived.

59

THINGS TO COME

In Japan policemen are killed and wounded as farmers and Left-wing students demonstrate violently against the building of a new international airport near Tokyo. Barricades are thrown up and fortified points built against bulldozers, earth-movers and water-cannon as the police try to take over the requisitioned land.

Today Japan, tomorrow (perhaps) the whole world. Conservatives, Neo-Luddites, Green Fascists, Conservationists, Lovers of the Countryside—when the barricades go up, on which side shall we stand?

COMING SHORTLY

The BBC has followed Dr Dale and Drs Cameron and Finlay with a Welsh-born physician, Dr Owen. Of the four nations of the British Isles only Ireland remains to be ransacked for lovable doctors.

This time the GPI Television Network has beaten the BBC to it, and with its usual progressive outlook has killed two birds with one stone. Its new medical series "Dr Mfumbiro's Diary," due to start shortly, has a coloured doctor as hero and is set in Northern Ireland.

"A graduate of Bungrafta University, Gombola," says a handout from Paralysis House, "Dr Nelson Mfumbiro, with his two attractive girl assistants, Dr Bernadette O'Grady and Dr Jean Cairns, and his fey, dour-spoken housekeeper Seanette O'Ritchie, runs a large, old-fashioned practice in the typical, quiet Ulster village of Glenfrenzy.

"The first episode, 'Should a Doctor Tell?,' shows Dr Mfumbiro already in the thick of local problems when he discovers a large arms cache in the new Gombolan-designed encephalograph-machine he has installed in his surgery, causing raised eyebrows among the superstitious villagers.

"The mutual suspicions of Drs O'Grady and Cairns, a booby-trapped high tea prepared by Seanette and the arrival of the mysterious Pat, a high-ranking officer in the IRA Dental Corps, are all ingredients in a fascinating epic of divided medical loyalties."

A NEWSPAPER reader who travels regularly between Warrington and Knutsford near the stretch of the M6 where last week's multiple pile-up took place in the fog, reports that many motorists had taken their cars for "family outings" and parked where they could get a good view of the scene. "I was surprised no one had started selling tickets," he says.

Among the first motorists on the scene were those dedicated motorway fans Harry and Janet Nodule of Brassgrove Park, who set off as soon as the news came through and were lucky enough to find a good vantage point.

They were indignant, though, that the police prevented them from collecting souvenirs from wrecked vehicles. "One policeman was really quite rude about it," Harry complained, fingering the top of his head where it comes to a marked point.

"You'd think they actually didn't *want* to attract visitors. Surely spectacular accidents like this could be a great asset to the tourist industry and sort of help the balance of payments. Then they could build more motorways all over the place."

"Never mind, dear," said Janet, a smile appearing on what was evidently the front of the lower part of her head, "we got some lovely colour snaps of skid-marks, didn't we? And there'll always be a next time."

THREAT OR PROMISE————————

THE old-fashioned Leftist playwright Arnold Wesker is in trouble with the more up-to-date militant Leftists of the anti-apartheid industry because he has agreed to allow his plays to be performed in South Africa.

"The production in the townships of major contemporary plays," he says, defending himself with typical jargon-ridden solemnity, "could make an extraordinary contribution to developing that political and human awareness which gives men the knowledge that they can change their social conditions."

The production of one of his own appalling major contemporary plays in any Black African township would be more likely to reduce the inhabitants first to bewilderment and then to anguished boredom. Unless sleep mercifully supervened, this might easily turn to anger and large-scale rioting which would invite further repression by the White authorities.

Is it fair, just for the sake of having "Chips with Everything" performed before an audience of Zulus (though admittedly it would be a unique curiosity), to set back the cause of Black African advancement for a hundred years?

BETTER SEE A DOCTOR————————————

EXPERTS believe that National Health Service records are so out of date that doctors are being paid for about 1,500,000 patients who have moved, died or emigrated.

Somewhere there must be a GP whose practice is entirely composed of these unreal patients. There he sits behind his desk in surgery hours, waiting for nobody. His bell never rings; his telephone never sounds; from his chilly waiting-room next door no rattling cough is ever heard.

Does he dream through the sunny days, remembering patients who now live in Yeovil or Edinburgh, or trying to reconstruct the faces of a whole family of hypochondriac masochists who long ago emigrated to Canada?

Does he dread those evening non-surgeries in the winter when bare branches tap against the windows and the ghostly echoes of complaints and groans penetrate the padded door dividing him from "them"? Does he start uneasily, hearing once more the voices of those who came too often, beating their phantom fists against the door and begging him to speak the official National Health Service word which will release them to whatever limbo they long for?

Perhaps I had better check up on my own National Health doctor. He might be getting, in a manner of speaking, out of practice.

COSY CORNER

"IF aggression has outlived its usefulness, what better substitute than exhilarating exploration of our sexuality in word, deed and fantasy?" (Richard Neville, philosopher of the "alternative society").

Copy to GHQ, Soviet Occupation Forces, c/o Alternative Society, Czechoslovakia.

INDUSTRIAL NOTE

"TOURIST promotion can bring obvious economic benefits without despoiling the area or ruining the very assets which make the Ribble Valley so attractive to tourists. We must sell solitude profitably to the multitude without ruining our countryside" (a spokesman for the proposed Ribble Valley Tourist Association, quoted in *Longridge News*).

Many businessmen (writes a City Correspondent) must have thought of selling solitude profitably (and obviously nobody would want to sell it at a loss) to the few. But to sell solitude to the multitude is real, get-up-and-go business enterprise.

Now that deposits of solitude are beginning to be worked out in obvious, solitude-rich areas like the Lake District, it is natural for the developers to turn their attention to less obvious places like the Ribble Valley, where the yield, though less spectacular, can still be rewarding.

Once the solitude bonanza really gets going in any particular area, of course, and up-to-date extraction-plant is brought into use, the market tends to expand automatically until solitude resources are exhausted.

But such "environmental" factors as "ruining the countryside," though worth a mention in a company prospectus, are irrelevant to a modern solitude industry whose function is to attract an ever increasing multitude.

THEY CHOSE FREEDOM
by VERNON GHOULES

THE Post Office announces an intensive drive against television licence evaders this winter, employing 29 detector vans and a barrage of propaganda on the television screen itself.

"Let them come. We shall be ready to meet them, wheresoever, whencesoever and whomsoever they may be," says Attila Craggs, chief of the "extremist" wing of the Television Licence Evaders' Liberation Army.

Speaking at a secret hide-out "somewhere in South London" last night, the legendary "Che Guevara of the Wandle," a ginger-moustached, middle-aged man of medium height whose deceptively mild exterior conceals an ice-cube brain and a sense of ruthless determination, told me in a low, tense voice of new methods which may be used against the Post Office forces this winter campaigning season.

They include dummy pillarboxes; ice-cream vans which can jam the enemy's detection apparatus; elephant-pits; and a decoy house, somewhere in the labyrinthine recesses of the Turgis Hill area, which contains more than a hundred unlicenced television sets all operating simultaneously.

"We shall also use the ordinary hit-and-run tactics and ambushes which have paid such handsome dividends in the past," added Craggs, his eyes glinting under his trilby hat as he indicated a row of shrunken heads, obviously those of Post Office engineers, grinning ruefully on the wall.

It was a striking testimony to the fanaticism and effectiveness of men who, with a hundredth part of the time, money and effort involved, might tamely pay their licence fees—but instead choose freedom.

DISCOVERY

A PSYCHIATRIST at a Belfast hospital who is doing research on "the effect of civil unrest on the mind," has made what he evidently regards as a surprising discovery. "Make no mistake," he says, "the children you see throwing bombs and stones in a riot are not suffering a serious mental disturbance . . . the fact is these children are thoroughly enjoying themselves."

What does he expect? If these children were not enjoying themselves, would they throw bombs and stones at all? They are not conscripts.

Most—in some circumstances almost all—human beings are capable of blind pugnacity. Most—probably all—human beings are capable of taking pleasure in violence and destruction. Doesn't the whole of human history prove it?

To admit a fact is not to approve of it. But unless we admit a fundamental part of human nature how can we even begin to understand what is happening now in Belfast and may soon be happening nearer home?

LOOK WHO'S TALKING————————————

"IT's you who choose your MP, and you not only choose him—if you want to, you can change him." Thus Mr Ian Mikardo MP, chairman of the Labour party, addressing an audience of constituency party and trade union delegates.

He is right, of course. It is the constituency party and trade union delegates and not (as some might innocently think) the ordinary Labour voters who in practice choose who their Labour MPs are going to be.

That is one reason why this tireless Old Red has been a Labour MP for most of the last 26 years. If most of those who have actually voted for him had understood what sort of Socialism he stood for, and what sort of country they would have to live in if its policies were put into effect, would they have sent him to Westminster?

Wouldn't those voters have insisted on wresting that right which Mikardo now extols—the right to choose and change their own MP—from those who have usurped it?

TEETHING TROUBLES————————————

A MARCH of protest in London against the Government's Immigration Bill, scheduled for last Sunday, had to be called off because only 400 people attended the initial rally, whereas several thousands had been expected.

A spokesman for Rentacrowd, the giant consortium which supplies demonstrators for all occasions, denied yesterday that his organisation was responsible for the mix-up. The organisers of the demonstration, he suggested, might have placed their order too late, or, through inexperience, have ordered supplies of the wrong sort of demonstrators for this occasion.

Rentacrowd have now installed giant computers to handle the bulk of the work in their wholesale order department, though small orders for special lines of "quality" and hand-made demonstrators are still dealt with by traditional methods.

As with all computer work, the possibility of error is always present. Only the other day an organiser in Lancashire who ordered two dozen "Winsome Leftist Toddler No. 1" models from Rentacrowd for a demonstration demanding free school milk was supplied with 25,000 semi-automated models of "Student Fuzzy-wuzzy No. 2" and 50,000 assorted ecologists.

DIRECT CRITICISM————————————

THE Yorkshire Art Association is said to have plans to turn the county "into an open-air gallery" by setting up pieces of abstract sculpture in places like Spurn Point and Ilkley Moor. But in most cases their proposals have been turned down flat by landowners and local authorities.

This is encouraging. It shows that Yorkshire people, at least, are still ready to stand firm against modish artistic aggression and daft London notions. The great tradition personified in Alderman Jabez Foodbotham, the 22-stone, crag-visaged, indigo-waistcoated, iron-watch-chained, grim-booted chairman of the Bradford City Tramways and Fine Arts Committee in the great days, is worthily maintained.

The great Alderman, who refused to take cognisance of any English art-works later than those of Sir Frank Dicksee RA, would not, of course, have been satisfied with merely turning down flat a proposal to place, say, a group of distorted aluminium drain pipes on the sacred slopes of Cleckheaton Moor.

He would personally have flattened the offending artefact with one blow of his gigantic fist, finishing off the work by jumping up and down on it slowly and impressively in a way which as eye-witnesses of such incidents still living can testify, seemed to—and indeed did—defy the laws of nature.

IS THIS YOUR PROBLEM?————————
by CLARE HOWITZER

DEAR CLARE HOWITZER—I live on a very "with-it" council estate where all the other wives seem to have husbands who make love to them all the time. Most of them, I gather, rush back from work every day in the lunch-time—or even several times a day in tea-breaks—for this purpose.

My own husband, Jim, who works in a local turntable factory, seems to be the "odd man out." Now the other wives are beginning to laugh at me, particularly my neighbour, a blonde of 50 who has taken to standing on the roof every lunch-time in seductive postures, wearing a bouffant hair-do and "see-through" nightie and shouting about sex, etc., in a sing-song voice.

When I told Jim about this the other day he stayed at the factory all night. He has now been sacked for assembling more than 4,000 unwanted turntables. Is there something wrong with us? (Mrs L. Tropes, Nerdley).

CLARE HOWITZER replies: This is a problem which is facing more and more husbands and wives who find they cannot cope with the Sexual Revolution in this permissive day and age, when it is becoming more and more difficult to reconcile the claims of booming productivity, full employment and the "leisure explosion" with meaningful relationships in the context of traditional marriage.

If all else fails, and your husband cannot understand your difficulties, I suggest you join your local group of Women's Liberation urban guerillas on a part-time basis.

MEDICAL NOTES————————————

A DOCTOR who prescribed rosewater for a patient was asked by the Health Executive Council to explain why. He did not reply and now the cost is to be deducted from his National Health Service remuneration.

The "Way of the World" medical expert, Dr John Henbane, comments: This raises an important issue of principle. If doctors are liable to be asked to explain themselves to the health authorities every time they prescribe anything, the whole basis of the National Health Service will be undermined.

"Impulse prescribing," as it is technically called, is a different matter. We doctors are all subject to this at times, particularly when overtired and liable to "free association." Only the other day, confronted with a patient who had an unusually pallid, shiny bald head (I'd been up most of the night with a tricky case of acute labyrinthitis) I found myself automatically scribbling a prescription for brown shoe-polish!

But at its most serious, "impulse prescribing" can be a pathological condition and a most intractable one at that. A former colleague of mine at Watford would prescribe, at the mere sight of certain patients, a variety of substances ranging from a gallon-jar of red ink to a dozen trilby-hats or a cwt of brass curtain-rings.

After a time, chemists began to query his prescriptions, the local Health Executive Council took a hand and he went in as a voluntary patient to the National Hospital for Iatropathic and Prescriptive Disorders at Boreham Wood, where he remains to this day.

HAS Nature's Ultimate Secret—regularly discovered in the science columns of Sunday newspapers every week—been unearthed again? A team of biologists working in Stretchford University's prestigious Nadir Institute under the redoubtable Prof. Ron Hardware believe they have stumbled on a genetic secret which could not merely revolutionise human life in a matter of seconds but even force many scientific journalists to look elsewhere for their subject-matter in future.

Briefly (and in non-technical language) it has been found that at sub-enzymic level the well-known "G" effect of metabolised cromagnonose on the genetic structure of the average unhealthy human body does not operate uniformly, as has hitherto been thought.

There is a "retardation factor"—Hardware calls it "lag"—which in certain conditions—at temperatures exceeding 4 million degrees centigrade, for instance—can slow down the ageing process and even reverse it—*but only for periods of less than 5 millionths of a second.*

The problem, as Hardware and his team see it, is to "universalise" this process, thus realising the age-old dream of human immortality. The snag, as always, is lack of money—and the obstructive attitude of our still backward-looking social system, conventionally-minded scientists included.

"All we need," says Hardware, "is a few thousand billion pounds, a laboratory in which temperatures equivalent to those in the interior of an exploding super-nova can be created and a few hundred million human experimental subjects—and Bob's your uncle!"

It doesn't seem a big price to pay. But once again it looks as though Government timidity and professional jealousy will combine to smother at birth one more boon which Science is only too anxious to place in Man's hands for good or ill.

SHOCKING UNFAIRNESS————————————

"IT is the natural reaction of the British Press, in colonial situations, to create an over simplified contrast between *our* good brave boys and *their* fanatical terrorists," says a writer in the *New Statesman*, complaining of the tendency of British newspapers, on the whole, to report the activities of the British Army in Ulster more favourably than the activities of the IRA.

People who write like this (apart, of course, from those who are secretly or openly on the side of the enemies of this country) live in a strange world. It never seems to occur to them that in the real world—as opposed to the world in which abstractions like "colonial situations" and so on take the place of reality—to have at least *some* prejudice, however slight, in favour of oneself is simply a condition of surviving at all.

When the Red Army parachutists, after Ireland has been occupied, are actually descending on this country, will the *New Statesman* still be complaining that the British Press is unfairly biased against them?

After all, we really should be in a colonial situation then.

BEWARE———————————————

A SPECIALISED agency of the race relations industry called the Working Group on Education for the Eradication of Colour Prejudice (no, I have not invented this) declares that schools should get rid of text-books "which reflect attitudes more suitable to a colonial generation."

This is not the half of it. Spokesmen of the industry are already beginning to hint that books in public libraries should be vetted in the same way and very large numbers of them thrown out.

Make no mistake about it. What these people are after (and they are often the very same people who in all other matters favour total licence) is censorship, the rewriting of history, thought control.

They justify their attitude by the absurd assumption that "colour prejudice" (which can mean anything from psychopathic hatred to the mild, instinctive preference most, if not all, people of all races, tribes, nations and comunities have for their own kind) is the worst evil in the world.

Do not believe them. It is not. A worse evil is thought control; and this proposal to censor schoolbooks in the name of "social justice" is a small, sly but unmistakable step towards it.

MUSEUM———————————————————————

THAT esteemed body the Trade Union, Labour, Co-operative-Democratic History Society is reported to have approved a proposal to set up a "unique trade union and labour movement museum" at Harlow, Essex.

It will hardly be unique. It is five years now since Mr Len Gollip, general secretary of the Amalgamated Hole-borers' Union, formally opened the AHU Museum at Soup Hales, in the Stretchford Conurbation.

It occupies a council house built on the very site of the tiny cottage where once lived the immortal "Soup Hales Martyrs," the 278 men and women holeborers trans-ported to Botany Bay in 1821 for forming an "illegal combination," after sentence of death, pronounced by the infamous Judge Cattermole, an expert in the mis-direction of juries, had been overruled on the direct orders of Lord Liverpool.

The Museum contains many relics of the Martyrs themselves, including several holes bored by the primitive brace-and-bit method in the sweated labour conditions of the time; as well as exhibits illustrating the steady, even remorseless growth of the Holeborers' Union in the context of the trade union and Labour movements.

There is an ingenious working model of a modern holeborers' branch meeting made by the Curator himself, Mr Stan Naggeridge, brother-in-law of Mr Gollip. Provided a coin is inserted every two minutes the model can be kept going realistically for as long as 24 hours at a stretch.

71

FRACAS

THE visit of the Soviet Russian Prime Minister to Mr Trudeau's Canada has not been quite the smooth affair the well-known Canadian fun-politician must have hoped for.

Bombs intended for the Russian Embassy in Ottawa were discovered only just before they were due to go off. And as Mr Kosygin was strolling along outside the Parliament building with his Canadian opposite number a young Hungarian jumped on his back, seized him round the neck and forced him almost to the ground.

"A very humiliating event for Canadians," says Mr Trudeau. But whatever Canadians in general may feel about the unseemingly fracas, at least the young Hungarian has had his hour.

Whatever may happen to him in the future, he will remember that once, for a brief moment, he got his hands, not metaphorically but in fact, on a principal representative of the system which took away, by force and fraud, the liberties of his country.

ONCE AGAIN

A STUDY group from a body called, for some reason, the Greater London Young Conservatives has issued a statement demanding that all local authorities be forced by law to provide "family planning facilities" from the rates.

Unless the size of families is limited voluntarily now, with the official encouragement (to put it mildly) of the State, they say, "It is our belief that in 10 years' time it will be necessary to introduce compulsory control. . . .

"If no policy is introduced at either stage . . . the world problem of over-population will be solvable only by way of virulent fatal disease or large scale war."

Stripped of fashionable but humanly meaningless verbiage about "problems" and "solutions," what does this mean? It means that for the sale of a hypothetical future which, though it can be statistically predicted a million times over, cannot possibly be *known*, the State should set about controlling, deforming and corrupting the personal lives of all its citizens *now*.

Plagues or wars may or may not arrive. If they do, it will not be solely or even mainly because there are too many people in the world. And what is more, even plagues and wars, however hard the saying seems, might be the lesser of two evils.

EXPELLED

AMID the wild cheering, shouting, screaming and desk-pounding of United Nations delegates, the Nationalist Chinese are expelled from that organisation and the Communist Chinese take their place.

So a country of more than 15 million people, prosperous, well-governed, peaceful and friendly to the West, is now unrepresented in the so-called "councils of the world" while the representatives of any African pseudo-State can raise ignorant and prejudiced voices on any subject they please.

After the disgusting farce had been played out, the Foreign Minister of Nationalist China said it was a relief that it was all over. He might have added (but was probably deterred by natural politeness) that to be expelled from such a body as the United Nations, a body essentially fraudulent and potentially evil, is an honour.

What a great day it would be for our own country if it were expelled and excluded from that gigantic lie—or better still resigned!

TOWERS OF FEAR

TOWER blocks, as more and more people now realise, are a form of housing which could not be more certain to produce a race of mentally disturbed and violent delinquents, the riot and revolution fodder of the future, if it had been deliberately designed to do so.

Unfortunately it is hardly possible now to pull the whole lot down and build on their sites a new, reasonable and human form of dwelling. And in spite of the example of Ronan Point, most of these blocks, left to themselves, will probably remain standing for some time to come.

What is to be done with them? A new book suggests

that in future the policy should be to move into them only the sort of people who by temperament and upbringing are suited to the kind of life that has to be lived there.

But as a start it would be just to move into these lunatic dwellings, by compulsion if necessary, all those who planned and raised them: planners, architects, builders, civil servants and all manner of social theorists and social engineers.

BUILT-IN BIAS————————————————

" 'WHY have we, the peoples of Western Europe, had such a great History?' asks 'The Earth—Man's Heritage,' a secondary school textbook, still in common use."

Taking this as his text a writer in the *New Statesman* preaches a sermon on the "built-in bias" in favour of the Western European peoples which is found in school textbooks and which, he believes, has a corrupting effect on the minds of children.

The answer to this "problem," he thinks, may be the disappearance of textbooks and their replacement by "packaged kits of documentary material" which are genuinely objective.

An even better answer might be to abolish the teaching of history altogether and replace it by hypnotism or techniques of brainwashing by which all knowledge of the fact that the peoples of Western Europe have indeed a great, even an uniquely great, history may be expunged from children's minds.

To take a certain pride in the achievements of one's own people and to have a certain bias in favour of them is as natural (and as necessary to survival) as to take a certain pride in oneself and to have a certain bias in one's own favour. To extirpate these basic human tendencies (in the case of the white races only, of course) will take great ingenuity and some little time. Nevertheless, we are told it must be done.

Together with all the other measures ceaselessly advocated by the *New Statesman*, this will help to ensure that the peoples of Western Europe, writers in that journal included, will have a small and pitiable history in the future—and perhaps no history or future at all.

MEMORIES, MEMORIES————————————

THE news that a Black Arrow rocket has been launched successfully into space from Woomera in Australia comes like a breath from the past, redolent of old-world rocket-fuel, skiffle-groups, Krishna Menon, Podola and World Mental Health Year.

Most people must have thought, like myself, that the scientists and technologists at Woomera had long ago given up their absurd attempts at rocket-launching and had settled down among their rusting machinery to live a life of contemplation in the Thebaid of Central Australia.

Or that they had "gone abo," wandering free in that strange desert, eating grubs and wasps' nests, acquiring their own totem (a kangaroo with the head of Wedgwood Benn, perhaps) and fending off parties of inquisitive anthropologists until they eventually passed into the dreamtime that awaits us all.

Who would have thought they would still be persisting in their technological folly after all these years?

UNSPEAKABLE————————————

AN American who lives over here, reports the *Guardian*, has made a film about cricket in England. It is called "Ashes to Ashes" and was suggested by "his sudden observation that Lord's cricket ground looked not unlike a concentration camp, surrounded as it is by barbed wire, broken glass and an astounding number of prohibitive posters . . .

"His film traces some of the lesser known facets of cricket and the game emerges from his analysis as a somewhat sinister and uneasy ritual."

The truth about this evil "game", imbued as it is with Fascist, racialist and neo-colonialist ideology, is far worse than this innocent American evidently suspects. If the truth were fully known it would cause an outcry among decent, progressive people and a demand for intervention by the United Nations on the ground that cricket constitutes a threat to world peace.

Lord's cricket ground not merely looks like a concentration camp. It *is* a concentration camp, where hundreds of thousands of people are held without trial in unspeakable conditions, on the flimsiest of charges or none.

To describe this so-called game as "a somewhat sinister and uneasy ritual" is a pathetic understatement, for it is nothing less than a kind of Black Mass in which the reactionary and brutal English Establishment celebrates and renews itself for its eternal role of oppression.

There are few more horrifying sights in the world than a "cricket match" in progress. Under a lowering sky, over smooth turf manured by the blood of countless victims, the cricketers, cool and arrogant in their ceremonial uniforms of flannel (only the rich or those of "good family" are allowed to take part), seem to flicker to and fro in the dim light of the gas-lamps like figures in Hell.

No wonder Hitler frequently declares his admiration for cricket in "Mein Kampf," seeing it as a ritual embodiment of the ruthless will-to-power of the English ruling caste and a prime instrument for the subjection of inferior classes and races.

Rural, reactionary, slow, wasteful of space, class-orientated, riddled with taboos and superstitions, cricket has no place in the democratic England of today. Worst of all, there is no money in it.

ONE PURPOSE ALONE————

"A TERRIBLE beauty is born." So wrote Yeats, in a great and memorable poem, of the men who gave their lives for the idea of an Irish nation in the rising of Easter 1916.

What is being born now, when men who declare they are dedicated to the same idea are planting bombs in shops and public houses or at random, killing, maiming and terrifying fellow Irish people?

What has happened to the ideals of Pearse and Connolly, MacDonagh and MacBride—ideals by no means contemptible or unacceptable to patriotic Englishmen— 55 years after they died for the old cause? What would they say of their descendants now?

Has the old cause of Irish freedom been absorbed and taken over—perhaps without its simple-hearted adherents knowing it—by a new cause: the cause of world revolution, ruthless, cruel, unchivalrous, amoral, secular, international, dedicated without pity or scruple to the overthrow of all existing things, the idea of an Irish nation among them?

MAGNI NOMINIS UMBRA——————————

PEOPLE who have already been bludgeoned into despair by the more spectacular horrors of the Local Government Bill's rearrangement of England may have failed to notice one of its most appalling proposals. The authors of the Bill may well have counted on this induced insensibility in their victims. If so, they will be disappointed. One man at least remains awake.

The proposal is that outside London the office of alderman, in so far as it entails powers and responsibilities, shall be abolished. All members of the new councils will be directly elected, though the honorary title of alderman may still be granted to former members. Poor shadows of a mighty name!

Whose thoughts do not turn, in this grave hour, to the man who has been described as the greatest alderman who ever lived—Alderman Jabez Foodbotham, 22-stone, crag-visaged, iron-watch-chained, grim-booted chairman of the Bradford City Tramways and Fine Arts Committee in the great days?

There is a legend in the Bradford district that the Great Alderman does not in fact lie in his presumed burial-place, the vast mausoleum at Cleckheaton Moor which has so long been a place of pilgrimage for devotees of

77

local government procedure and sufferers from diseases of the gastric tract; but that he lies in an enchanted trance in a mountain cave at Northowram, to wake when the supreme moment comes and ride out on a supernatural tram to save his city, his country and, not least, his own aldermanic order, in their time of greatest peril.

Surely that time has come. Surely it is time the Bradford City Council, true to its great history and its role as England's mentor, prepared for the Alderman's appearance by implementing, on an emergency basis, Clause 464 of the Standing Orders of the Ways and Means Committee, the procedure laid down for municipal arrangements in the event of the probable imminence of the Apocalypse.

EXPERIMENT————————————————————

THE Hallé Orchestra, it is reported, is to take engagements in nightclubs to keep solvent, rather than appeal for further grants from public funds. It has already appeared successfully at a club in Wakefield, of all places.

The Stretchford Municipal Symphony Orchestra, under its veteran conductor Sir Jim Gastropodi, is faced with the same problem, the more so as its appeals to the council for grants usually meet with ingenious forms of humiliation and insult.

Not long ago, in desperation, the orchestra engaged itself to play at the Diamond Stork Room at Nerdley (formerly the Effluent Road Working Men's Club), one of a chain of clubs operated by the Nadirfun Group, a subsidiary of Nadirco.

The experiment was not a success. Sir Jim, not realising that the orchestra would be expected to accompany a double striptease act by local artistes Pat and Linda, had chosen as the main work an uncut performance of Mahler's Eleventh Symphony ("the Interminable").

He had hardly reached the famous muted trumpet and cymbal passage in the first movement (described by the composer as "the world's catarrhal anguish") when pandemonium broke out and the audience invaded the stage.

Only the heroic presence of mind of the cymbal player, Fred Boggs, in performing a quick striptease act

78

himself kept the would-be lynchers at bay long enough for Sir Jim and the rest of the players to get out through the fire-escape at the back of the building.

Even then they were not much better off. At that very moment a howling mob of student demonstrators from Stretchford, Nerdley and Soup Hales universities appeared on a protest march against an alleged colour bar imposed by the nightclub, and the musicians had to run for their lives.

MIDLAND MAENADS————————————

DEFENDING a 19-year-old girl football fan, who was found at a match with a cake knife tucked inside her slacks, a solicitor said "she genuinely loves football and was not looking for trouble."

FRED PULP, "Way of the World" Soccer Hooliganism Correspondent, comments: "Compared with the average girl supporter of Stretchford United, this young lady sounds like an exceptionally prissy member of the Girl Guides. Cake knives indeed! Flick knives, bayonets, Commando strangling wires, nail-studded clubs, light machine-guns, petrol bombs, poison blow-pipes, potatoes stuffed with razor-blades—these are just a few of the weapons the Stretchford girl fans carry about their well-muscled persons!

"Like other Stretchford supporters, the girls are resigned to the fact that Anthrax Park is bound to be the scene of yet another resounding defeat for the 'Deckchairmen' whenever they appear there. So they pay little attention to the actual play, except for an occasional mass-assault on visiting players, referee, linesmen, or—a favourite target—Stretchford's own brilliant, comatose goalkeeper, Albert Rasp.

"They concentrate their attacks on 'enemy' supporters. Anyone seen wearing the favours of, say, Lampton Orient, or applauding a goal scored by his own side is pounced on eagerly and usually annihilated.

"Once, I believe, the cheer-leader of a visiting team, dressed in top-hat, morning coat, waistcoat and trousers in 'enemy' colours and wearing a gigantic rosette, innocently wandered straight into the ranks of the 'Deckchairmen's' girl fans. Later on an official searching the ground found part of his hat and a couple of cracked and sucked thigh-bones.

"Thanks to his personal pack of Tibetan mastiffs, the girls have never managed to get their hands on Sir Roland Grampus-Smith, United's ruthless, dynamic chairman. I believe they even have a certain grudging respect for him as president of the local branch of the British Friends of Genghis Khan Society."

WHAT WOULD YOU DO?————————

A MAN walking in the street sees a fire-engine rushing past. He notices that the fire-engine is itself on fire. Should be run to the nearest telephone and ring for the fire brigade? Should he go to the nearest public reference library, sit down and try to think things over quietly? Or should he ignore the incident, regarding it as part of the Human Predicament?

MOONLIGHT————————————————

IN the tedious list of contents in the current issue of the Weekly Bulletin of the Federation of Civil Engineering Contractors—"Footbridge Headroom Clearances," "Production of Bricks and Cement," "Britain on Verge of Biggest Boom for Years," etc., etc.—one item shines out like a gem of purest ray serene: "Dating of Moslem Festivals."

It is "a note for the guidance of industry with particular reference to the Id-ul-Fitr Festival, November, 1971." This important festival marks the end of the month's fast of Ramadhan, and Moslem workers naturally wish to take time off to celebrate it.

Unfortunately for British devotees of industrial efficiency, the dating of Moslem festivals is dependent upon the sighting of the moon and is therefore imprecise until the last moment. Discussions have been held between the Community Relations Commission, the Department of Employment and the Islamic Cultural Centre, which has decided that the sighting of the moon in a minimum of

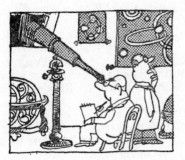

three Moslem countries will be the signal for the Id-ul-Fitr festival to be held in England on the following day, which this year will be either the 19th or 20th of November.

Moreover, there is another Moslem festival, Id-ul-Adha, due in January on the 10th day of the lunar month, some time between the 23rd and 27th, of which at most a week's notice can be given.

The more the members of the Department of Employment, the Federation of Civil Engineering Contractors and the Confederation of British Industry are involved with such matters the better for them and all of us. It will make them lift their eyes occasionally from their mundane preoccupations with nuts and bolts to the friendly silences of the moon.

When every factory in England has a well-staffed department, fully equipped with calendars, telescopes, astrolabes and ephemerides and concerned solely with the dating of religious festivals—not only Moslem, but Hindu, Buddhist (Mahayana and Hinayana), Animist and even Christian—it will have that much less time for the manufacture of superfluous objects, and the biggest boom for years can perhaps be put off for ever.

AUTHENTIC

THE GPI Television Network, whose Director-General, Sir Paul Fobster, recently described accusations of a certain bias in his programmes as "neo-Nazi, racialist raving" and "the thin end of the censorship backlash," has commissioned the brilliant young TV writer Neville Dreadberg to write a "documentary play" about Ulster.

Dreadberg, who visited Belfast one day last year with the brilliant young hippy leader Abbie Hoffman to conduct painstaking research, has already almost completed the work. It promises to be even more brilliant than his brilliant documentary about Rhodesia, "Serviettes of Death" (1968).

"Blood Orange," as his new work is tentatively entitled, employs the well-tried technique of placing representative fictional characters in a realistic setting, thus ensuring authenticity and impartiality.

The principal male character, who stands for the Stormont Government and its policies and for the Ulster Protestants in general, is not only an expert at assembling bombs, a skilled intimidator and an ingeniously brutal interrogator, particularly of Catholic children, but is also a practising cannibal.

In one brilliantly symbolic scene set in the grounds of Stormont he is shown carrying on all these activities simultaneously while pounding a Lambeg drum in a terrifying crescendo of primeval, mindless hate.

KAPNOPHOBIA————————————————

OUR aim, says Sir George Godber, Chief Medical Officer of the Health Department and an eminent kapnophobe, is to create "a non-smoking society."

This is a pleasing variation on such clichés as "our aim is to create a multiracial society," "our aim is to create a compassionate society," and so on and so forth.

To further his great aim Sir George suggests that smoking, whether by patients, visitors to patients, porters, auxiliaries, ward cleaners, nurses or doctors, should be forbidden in any part of a hospital where patients are.

That pioneering hospital, St. Bogwena's at Stretchford, has been enforcing this rule for some time. All parts of the hospital are searched every day for illicit tobacco and snap checks are sometimes made during the night. During these searches all patients, however seriously ill they may be, are made to stand by their beds so that mattresses and pillows (where these are provided) can be thoroughly gone over.

Visitors and hospital staff are regularly frisked by a picked anti-smoking squad under the command of Nurse Grimgerda Craggs, a formidable figure who five years ago was discharged for extreme brutality from the Women's Military Police. She takes a particular delight in examining newly joined young doctors for concealed tobacco, often reducing them to tears.

In spite of all these precautions, patients are occasionally found harbouring tobacco or even actually smoking. They are immediately gagged and handed over to Dr Acula, brilliant head of the thriving Transplant Unit, whose horror of nicotine is only equalled by his horror of garlic, crucifixes and mirrors.

Yet there are rumours that in order to increase the supply of subjects for experimental transplants Dr Acula's bearded Transylvanian-born dwarf assistant Igor has often planted cigarettes on patients recovering (this sometimes happens even at St Bogwena's) from such non-killing ailments as Menière's Disease, hyperidrosis, Bell's Palsy or duodenal ulcer.

SELF-DETERMINATION——————

"THE British Government is committing a monstrous crime against the people of Ulster . . . the soldiers are really there to crush the people and injure innocent people in Northern Ireland. . . . Only the complete eradication of colonialism and the implementation of self-determination will bring about the observation of human rights everywhere."

It is a Mr V. S. Safronchuk, a representative of the

Soviet Union, addressing a committee of the general assembly of the United Nations on "colonialism."

In the great ocean of hypocrisy called the United Nations there are some abysses of lying profound beyond imagination. These utterances of Mr Safronchuk seem to come from one of them.

Poland, Czechoslovakia, Hungary, Rumania, Bulgaria, Lithuania, Latvia, Estonia—these are the historic European nations—to say nothing of the Ukraine, Byelorussia and the non-Russian territories of Asia—now held in that empire of the Soviet Union which has been described (optimistically no doubt) as the last of the colonial empires.

As horrible in its way as the incorporation of whole peoples in that empire is the incorporation of the mind of Mr Safronchuk. When he speaks of the implementation of self-determination and the observation of human rights he may quite sincerely believe that every word he says is true.

MYSTERY INTRUDER————————————————

DUTCH river water is so polluted by chemicals, says a Dutch newspaper, that you can develop a film in it. To prove this, the paper prints a photograph developed in water taken from the Rivers Rhine and Maas, which join in Holland.

This is small stuff. In the Stretchford Conurbation, where the Rivers Stretch, Nerd and Hoke join in a malodorous, iridescent, mephitically-steaming stream which is the pride of pollution-fans and photographers throughout the Midlands, the water develops not only photographic film but anything else which happens to fall into it.

Only the other day Stan Cockroach, 46, a local photographer, fell into the Nerd near Sadcake Bridge while taking photographs of a well-known used car-dump and municipal leisure picnic area on the opposite bank.

Struggling out minus his clothes, which had been eaten away in seconds by the chemical-infested water, Cockroach found that his body had been printed all over with photographs of courting couples and rusting cars. Many of them were of a suggestive nature.

He was immediately arrested by Det.-Sgt. E. S. Mackenzie, 40, of Nerdley Special Branch, who was on a routine Peeping Tom patrol. Later Cockroach appeared at Nerdley magistrates court, charged with loitering indecently in a public place.

Binding Cockroach over, the chairman, Dr Ellis Goth-Jones, 62, said that both ecology and photography were now being made the excuse for behaviour which only a short time ago would have aroused well-nigh universal condemnation. When these two dubious practices joined in unholy alliance it was time to call a halt and ask ourselves where, as a nation, we were going. But he did not think a reduction in prescription charges for handicapped motorists was necessarily the answer.

PARADOX————————————————————

"THE fundamental problem confronting the Communist Party of Great Britain," says an *Observer* article, reporting on the party's 32nd congress, is "Why is it that a working class famous in Europe for its shop-floor militancy turns into a flock of cautious traditionalists outside the factory gate? . . . those who gladly vote for a Communist as a leader in union affairs still decline to vote for him as a parliamentary candidate."

The explanation may be simple enough. The British worker backs up the Communist on the shop-floor, then sits back to enjoy the way all that Marxist energy, cunning and determination can make life more difficult for the bosses and more exciting for the workers themselves. It may even produce bigger wage-packets, shorter working hours and longer holidays—all desirable things.

To vote the Communists to political power would be rather different. Then all that Marxist energy, cunning and determination would come to bear upon the workers' own lives, their own homes, their own families, for every moment of their days.

The fundamental problem confronting the Communist party of Great Britain is that the workers of Great Britain are not nearly as silly as they ought theoretically to be.

LET THEM REMAIN————————————

THE possibility that sanctions against Rhodesia may be called off as part of a settlement with that country has alarmed sanctions-lovers throughout the world. A Society for the Preservation of Sanctions is likely to be formed in Britain immediately.

It will have very wide support, not only among Socialists and liberal thinkers but also among non-political connoisseurs of humbug and meaningless verbiage, as well as lovers of romance who have relished all those stirring tales of the Beira Patrol and of the intrepid agents, led by the legendary Capt. Colin Legum, who have so long been following the trail of the wicked Fascist sanctions-busters about the Seven Seas.

There is no need, of course, for the sanctions actually to operate or to have any effect whatever (any more than they have been doing up to now, come to that). All we sanctions-lovers ask (call us sentimental fools if you like) is that sanctions shall still *be said to be in being*, and that we shall still be told from time to time by selected spokesmen that they are "beginning to bite."

Sanctions must not die. That is unthinkable. They must remain, a joy for ever; a monument, which though made of feathers will be more lasting than bronze, to the loftiest nonsense of our age.

OPPRESSION————————————

THE borough council of Wandsworth, one of the chief victims of the Greater London Council's infamous scheme for building motorways through the more under-privileged parts of the city, reveals that in Wandsworth alone at least 3,000 homes would have to be demolished and their present inhabitants housed elsewhere.

When tribes are evicted from their homes in Africa, there is (not unnaturally) indignation in this country. What, in principle, is the difference between evicting people from their homes in Africa for the sake of enforcing racial cohesion and evicting people from their homes in London so that more and more roaring, stinking motor-cars can rush more and more rapidly through what was once a civilised capital city?

Moreover (absurdity on absurdity) the proposed motorways will not even achieve their supposed purpose—to relieve congestion on existing roads and produce a reasonable flow of traffic in London. That purpose is for ever unattainable, for there is a natural law which decrees that more and better roads mean more (and more means worse) motor-cars.

For the sake of an unattainable purpose, whole populations are to be expelled from their homes, communities disrupted and life made more nerve-racking, dangerous and intolerable for everyone, including motorists themselves (after all, few of them, apart from J. Bonington Jagworth, are motorists all the time).

That this is not merely raving lunacy but criminal lunacy into the bargain is perfectly obvious. What on earth is going to be done about it?

FOR THE RICH ONLY————————————————

HUGE coffee-table books for Christmas are beginning to thunder into this office with periodical thuds which shake the entire building and alert the security staff. I have space to mention only a few of the biggest and most expensive.

Great Toothbrushes of the World, by Jon Glass-Derkeley and Crispian Nidget (Titanbooks, £175·00) offers a superb survey of these glorious artefacts ranging from the Great Golden Toothbrush of the Emperor Napoleon III to the set of art nouveau lapis lazuli toothbrushes, studded with diamonds, emeralds and rubies, designed by Gustav Glimt-Harsch in 1908 for a rich, anonymous vampire in Transylvania.

A Book of Traffic Wardens, by June le Briggs (Heartsease Press, £140·00) contains a series of superb colourplates (with a rather overlush, not to say gushing, commentary) of these picturesque figures of the London scene. All who cherish para-military uniforms (and who doesn't, nowadays?) will enjoy the minute variations of lapel, button and cuff here lovingly displayed.

Pollution, by Rex Goth-Jones (Viper and Bugloss, £11,575) is by far the best Christmas book I have seen on the subject everybody who is everybody is now talking about. An unusual feature of this magnificent volume (which weighs 3 tons and comes in a specially-designed electrically-operated van) is that the binding is impregnated with effluent from the River Nerd, believed to be the most heavily polluted water in the world and lethal to most if not all forms of vegetable and animal life.

HAGGARD'S JOURNAL————————————

DEC. 4, 1771: Blizzards. Bart. Cabbage hanged for stealing an old nail. Amos Fudge d. from a General Putrefaction of the Inward Parts. Lord North reported to have been spat upon by John Wilkes. ITEM: Recd. from Wat Blast the sum of £0 0s 0¾d., one of the farthgs. being a bad one which I gave him last year.

Dec. 5, 1771: Sleet. Amos Fudge refused Christian burial. John Wilkes reported to have been kicked by Lord North. In a.m., whilst crossg. the park to evict Crippled Jane I percvd. a pair of moleskin breeches stickg. out of a bush and gave them a charge from my fowling-piece, whereupon it transpired they belonged to my gamekeeper Mellors, who had been set upon by a gang of poachers and thrust into the hedge. I threw him into a nearby pond to recover his senses and retired to the Hall where I drank four botts. of Madeira.

Dec. 6, 1771: Hail. Dissenters refused to bury Amos Fudge. Awakened early by Crippled Jane shrieking curses outside the house and was obliged to silence her with a charge from my caliver. After breakfastg. upon cold peas puddg., madeira and vinegar I sallied forth to examine my spring-guns and gin-traps.

On emerging from Ghoul's Covert percvd. a strange sight, viz. a man's head projecting from the top of a midden. It was the wretched Mellors, who had again been set upon by armed poachers. I immediately went to him with the intention of thrashg. him into insensibility but became enmeshed in one of my own gin-traps and had to be released by a passg. labourer, to whom I gave the bad farthg. I lately had of Wat Blast.

Dec. 7, 1771: Storms. Eli Bone sold his wife for three-pence to a gypsy. After breakfastg. upon cold pork, port and pickled cabbage I spent p.m. digging a deep pit in front of Ghoul's Covert, which I then filled with barrels of gunpowder, coverg. the same with earth, and layg. a fuse, connected to a trip wire which would activate a trigger mechanism. I then tied Mellors to a tree for use as a human lure, and retired into ambush with my fowling-piece.

About midnight, percvg. Mellors had fallen asleep in his duty, I was walkg. toward him with the intention of arousing him with my boot when I inadvertently trod upon the trip wire, and after a moment's confusion found myself upon the roof of the Orangery, together with Mellors, who was still tied to the tree. ITEM: To services of chirurgeon, £0 9s 2¾d.

WHATEVER NEXT?————————————————————

THE Second Indian Civil War is now in full swing—a further chapter in the story which began with the partition of India in that "wise act of British Socialist statesmanship" for which the names of Earls Attlee and Mountbatten will be—or should be—eternally and gratefully remembered.

Which side does this column favour? Neither.

What would it like to see in the Indian sub-continent? Firstly, peace. Secondly, a Federation of Provinces and States comprising the present territories of India and Pakistan, some predominantly Moslem, some predominantly Hindu, among which a reunited Province of Bengal would of course have an honoured place, as would the former Princely States, lately victims of Mrs Gandhi's egalitarian fury.

It would no doubt be necessary for some non-Indian— and, the better to ensure justice and impartiality, non-Asian—Power to preside over this new, magnificent, jewel-bright Federation or Empire of India. Some Power with previous experience in these matters would no doubt be best.

CELESTIAL PAPERWEIGHTS————————————

FURTHER proof of the subjectivity of science, which I mentioned the other day, may be found in a report from American scientists that Phobos, one of the two moons of Mars, appears as "a jagged, pock-marked object of such

irregular shape that it is difficult to define" in photographs taken by an American space-vehicle.

This hideous, degraded-looking piece of celestial rubbish is just what one would expect these scientists to see. It seems hardly distinguishable, except in size, from the bits of expired rockets and other trash with which they are now cluttering up the solar system, and obviously reflects certain qualities of their own minds.

How different from the Martian moons photographed by the "Way of the World" space-vehicle "Don Carlos and the Holy Alliance IV" on its recent orbit of the Red Planet—the larger one a perfect sphere of gleaming, rose-veined marble as fine as any ever hewn from the quarries of Carrara, contrasting beautifully with the other, smaller moon, which seems to be made entirely of lapis lazuli!

A MORAL ISSUE——————————————

By a large majority the Stretchford City Council has decided to refuse permission for members of a delegation of South African dentists, due to arrive here next year, to visit any of the numerous striptease and "sex educational" cinema clubs in the city.

It can do this because all these vital installations (notorious throughout the Midlands) are owned by Nadirfun, a subsidiary of the Nadirco Consortium, whose chairman, Cllr. Gordon Nadir, is also chairman of the City Watch Committee.

"This is a moral issue," a spokesman said yesterday.
"We feel that people whose social system puts them
outside the pale of humanity should not be allowed to
contaminate places where ordinary decent citizens go
to watch naked women being whipped by giant morons
or coupling with Alsatian dogs."

NORMAN THE GOOD————————————

11 Dec. 2011

THERE were angry scenes in Parliament yesterday when
the Minister for the Socialist Environment, Mr Ron
Briggs, gave details of proposals to increase the allow-
ances made to the Royal Socialist Household by an
aggregate of £545 a year.

Members repeatedly rose to their feet, howling maniac-
ally, and at one time the uproar was so intense that the
Speaker, Mr Stan McElbow, threatened to call the
Ceremonial Refuse Collectors into the Chamber and
suspend the sitting.

The proposal to make a direct grant of £20·75p to
Queen Doreen for the initial hire purchase deposit on a
new spin-drier for the Council Palace at Bevindon caused
particular fury. There was mocking laughter when Mr
Briggs, in an emotional passage, described how the
present machine, over 15 years old and of an obsolete
type, not only caused periodical flooding, to the annoyance of neighbours, but was so unpredictable in its operation that most of King Norman's few remaining pairs of
underpants had been reduced to shreds.

Mr J. Wuthers, Member for the Windermere New
Town Division of the Cumbrian National Park and
Petrochemical Complex: "Why can't they use a mangle?
My old gran in Barrow-in-Furness . . ." (groans and
shouts of "Suez!" "Hola!" "Sell Out!" "Invade
Rhodesia!" "You'd be far better off in a home!" etc,
etc.).

The Royal Socialist Family, in accordance with
protocol, is, of course, keeping strictly aloof from the
controversy, even though supermarkets at Bevindon have
unilaterally decided to refuse Queen Doreen any further
Green Shield stamps and the National Union of
Socialist Hairdressers has declared Princess Shirley's
bee-hive hair-do "black".

One member of the Royal Socialist Family who has not been able to keep entirely aloof is the Queen Gran. In an angry exchange with Republican housewives at a local launderette the other day she wielded her stubby umbrella and outsize iron-bound handbag to such effect that a detachment of the Royal Socialist Military Police had to be sent for.

PARADISE GARDEN———————————————

A MAN in a village near King's Lynn who has a 65-foot electricity pylon in his back garden, one of a line of pylons which are being dismantled, has asked for permission to keep it.

This is good news for Paul Ohm, the well-known freelance technologist, who believes no English garden is complete without a pylon, or at least a view of one. His own garden at Edgbaston, laid out entirely by himself, was the subject of a special illustrated article in the magazine *Technological Homes and Gardens* not long ago.

As well as a beautiful avenue of pylons, leading the eye to a small nuclear power station, there is a fine group of miniature cooling towers, soothing the mind with a gentle hiss of steaming waters, and a small orchard of transformers laid out in the form of a maze, in which (as Mr Ohm will tell you with a chuckle) it is most unwise to get lost.

Mr Ohm has taken great pains to exclude all vegetation from his garden. Use of the latest types of defoliant, says the article, "has ensured that not even a blade of grass mars the harmony of this unique technological paradise, this corner of England where the visitor may refresh himself with an aluminium thought in an aluminium shade."

Mr Ohm's garden is open to visitors on most Sundays throughout the year (admission 25p, children and old age pensioners half price—all proceeds to the Sunset Home for Retired Technologists at Nerdley, Staffs.).

92

IDYLLIC

THE Government has taken over responsibility for a frigate originally built for ex-President Nkrumah of Ghana but never delivered. The difficulty is to know what to do with it. The vessel is said to "combine the qualities of a fighting ship and a gin palace—not a requirement of many navies."

I might be prepared to buy it myself (I am told by my advisers that I have several million pounds lying idle at the moment, profits from the ruthless exploitation of the peasants on my South American estates).

I need an extra frigate for my naval forces and this one would be useful not only for entertaining friends but also for bombarding coastal areas which have incurred my displeasure.

There can be no more pleasant way of spending a summer evening, I always say, than sitting at ease on deck with agreeable companions who share one's own fascist and militaristic tastes, sipping *gin pahits* and occasionally ordering a warning salvo to be fired, then watching the commotion on shore through powerful field-glasses.

PRIORITIES

MR WELLBELOVED, the Labour MP for Erith and Crayford, claims loudly and insistently that there is a "spy network" operating in London. And who do you think he says is operating it? Yes, it is the wicked South African Government again!

Whether there really is a South African "spy network" in London I have no idea. But if there were South African spies operating in thousands in every part of this country it would not cost me one single minute of one single night's sleep.

They would not be spying on us, but on the enemies of South Africa who live in this country—many of whom, incidentally, are also the enemies of ourselves.

It is not South African spies we need worry about. It is not South Africa that threatens our country and its remaining liberties. While Mr Wellbeloved was pursuing his fatuous investigations it was revealed, as a result of recent RAF exercises, that the air defences of this country would be totally unable to resist conventional attacks by Russian bombers. What goes for our air defences goes for our land and sea defences too.

Add to that the fact that this country is infested with the spies and agents of our real enemy; that it contains thousands of people, some, no doubt, in high places, who are potential collaborators with that enemy, and hundreds of thousands of people who, if not actually disloyal, owe no positive loyalty to this country—and it might just possibly be argued that Mr Wellbeloved, a Member of Parliament and presumably a patriotic Englishman, could be making better use of his time and energy than in chasing South African spies.

In the last resort there is only one thing that matters to us as a nation: it is that we should be able to defend our existence as a nation. It is this problem which not Mr Wellbeloved only but every Member of Parliament from the Prime Minister downwards ought to be thinking about night and day. Is there any sign that they are doing so?

Our country is in mortal danger. What will our children have to say of the tragic folly of all its Wellbeloveds?

MYSTERY INTRUDER————————————————

WHEN Fred Handcough, 34, of Bladderwrack Road, Soup Hales, described as a freelance military policeman, was charge at Nerdley magistrates' court with dishonestly handling a plastic leprechaun, valued at £13·75, at the Nadirco Supermarket in Victoria Road, Nerdley, he asked for 7,921 similar charges to be taken into consideration.

Giving evidence, Det. Sgt. J. S. Pelmet, 42, of Nerdley Special Branch, said he was on routine duty outside the supermarket when he observed Handcough dragging the 4-feet high leprechaun, one of the Santa Claus type, with fishing rod and shamrock attachments, through the entrance and out into the street. He was scowling angrily and using a considerable degree of violence, drawing adverse comment from several housewives. After cautioning Handcough, he arrested him.

Conducting his own defence, Handcough said he had recently been unjustly discharged, with ignominy, from a mobile laundry unit of the IRA operating in the Stretchford area and believed one of the plastic leprechauns attached to the unit was responsible for his downfall. Whenever he saw one, a red curtain seemed to come over his eyes and a loud humming noise in his head suggested to him that he could not be held accountable for his actions.

Dr F. Gestaltvogel, 52, consultant psychiatrist at Nerdley General Hospital, said he had examined Handcough, and apart from a morbid horror of barometers and an intermittent belief that he was a nature reserve he considered him perfectly normal and a potentially valuable member of society.

Binding Handcough over, the chairman, Dr Ellis Goth-Jones, 60, said he seemed to have suffered considerable provocation and because of this he would be lenient in dealing with him. But people must not take the law into their own hands. He believed that a political solution in Northern Ireland would have to come sooner or later. But he did not think devaluation of the dollar and the provision of more refuse receptacles in motorway service areas would necessarily prove to be the long-term answer.

CHRISTMAS PUZZLE————————————————

FOR the tenth year running, no reader sent in an all-correct solution to the "Way of the World" Christmas puzzle.

The prize of a free weekend for two, with all found, at the Sadcake Residential Hotel (Unlic.) at Nerdley (Staffs) is therefore withheld.

Here is the correct solution.

Since Col Manners is known not to have been in Port Swettenham in 1935 he could not have met Dr Bhattacharya's niece Pushpam, the ayurvedic dentist, before that year; therefore the velocity of the lift in which he was travelling in Gambridges's stores at 12.45 p.m. on Jan. 7, 1937, was 7·50633 (recurring) mph. At the stated rate of acceleration this would place him on Dec. 25, 1971, approximately 6,500 miles from the edge of the outer ring of the planet Saturn.

HAGGARD'S CHRISTMAS————————————

Dec. 22, 1771: Fog. Obadiah Horseworthy blown to pieces while trying to turn lead into gold. Spent a.m. evicting Blind Benjamin and enclosg. common land for mine own use, An unusual event occurred in p.m., viz. the appearance of my wife whom I had not seen since I flung a pease pddg. at her last Michaelmas. She informed me that her brother Daniel sends word he is coming tomorrow to spend Christmas with us. This threw me into apoplexy as the man is a canting Dissenter, but I cannot refuse him as I owe him 30,000 sovs. Drank a vat of punch to recover.

Dec. 23: Storms. Spat on elderly Jew in a.m. Evicted Crippled Simon and Deaf Peter, also re-evicted Blind Benjamin who was lodging with Deaf Peter. Brother Daniel arrived in p.m. but I was unable to greet him as I was lying insensible in the fireplace. When I recovered he told me that if I drank anything more he would be com-

pelled to call for his 30,000 sovs. for the good of my soul.
ITEM: To physick £0 0s 0½d.

Dec. 24: Snow. Shot unusual crippled poacher in a.m.
Evicted Halfwitted William. While chasing a fleeing
tenant I fell into a snowdrift and to restore myself pulled
forth a flask of brandy, only to find Daniel had filled it
with barley water. The rage for drink so possessed me I
was fain to ask the Rector for something, but the canting
dog gave me nettle wine. ITEM: To emetics £0 0s 0¾d.

Dec. 25: Today being that feast most sacred to all
men, viz. Quarter Day, I was out early evicting Palsied
Peter, Granny Turnip and Blind Benjamin, who had
moved in with Granny Turnip. Granny Turnip snivelled
"Did I not know what day it was," to which I replied
"Rent Day," which caused me much mirth. On returning
home was nauseated to see jugs of barley water on the
table for dinner, whereupon I hit upon an ingenious
Device, pouring a pint of laudanum into Daniel's jug.
Halfway through dinner, he collapsed insensible and I
then made merry with six botts. of Madeira, a pint of
brandy and three maidservants. ITEM: To gift for wife,
one groat.

DEEP MATTERS————————————————

WHAT could be more astoundingly full of symbols or
more apt to lead the mind to deep thoughts than the
controversy about the disfigurement of the suburbs of
Jerusalem by the building of new blocks of flats for Jewish
immigrants?

"It is distressing indeed," intones the Archbishop of
Canterbury, "that the building programme . . . is dis-
figuring the city and its surroundings in ways which
wound the feelings of those who care for its natural
beauty. . . ."

And the Anglican Archbishop of Jerusalem says that
Dr Ramsey's plea "reflects the concern of many thought-
ful people in Britain, both friends of Israel and friends of
Arab nations".

So ancient prophecies, ideas of contemporary welfare
housing, of international aesthetic landscaping, ecology
and conservation come together at the mysterious centre
of the world.

That Jerusalem should be preserved for ever as we who have never been to the Holy Land imagine it—as in the coloured pictures on the walls of childhood—is a thing appealing beyond words. But to be a city preserved, an international Biblical urban amenity area with high touristic potential, is surely not the destiny of Jerusalem.

Rather it is to shadow forth, even in the most hideous blocks of skyscraper flats imaginable, the fulfilment of the 20th century.

DOING WELL

THE new issue of *The Boglanean*, the magazine of Bog Lane Secondary Modern School (now part of Stretchford Comprehensive) gives some good news of former pupils.

"Not all of us," it says, "can of course hope to achieve the heights of pop star Ron Frabb (1953–58), or dramatist Eric Lard (1950–57) or of Soho striptease queen Sandra Neck (1957–58). But many other old Boglaneans are doing well in less exalted spheres.

"J. Dadge (1963–70) already has a conviction (with suspended sentence) for loitering on enclosed premises and dishonestly handling railway property, and is looking forward to a full-time career in this important branch of industry.

"B. H. Volcano-Smith (1960–68) is now doing well as a vandal and has been selected for Lampton Huns' second team, who last season finished third in the Stretchford Junior League. He specialises in destroying bowling-green pavilions and has already notched up three.

"Mary Grasp (1961–67), one of the popular Grasp twins, is now an abortion tout at Soup Hales Airport, meeting foreign visitors on behalf of an important group of clinics in the area. Her sister Joan is a computer-programmer for a prominent drug-trafficking organisation in London.

"Stan Glott (1960–67), after a spell as an actor with the Marylou Ogreburg Bread and Marmite People's Involvement Puppet Theatre, has now settled down as an assistant pornographer with the Foot and Mouth Press."

1972

╭ෲෲෲෲ╮

ON THE OHM FARM————————————

DR R. W. GIBSON, an agricultural scientist, believes a "fighting potato plant" might be bred, which would attack greenfly by releasing a gluey substance to entrap them.

"Bless 'ee, bor," commented old Seth Roentgen, Britain's greatest scientific farmer, when I called on him at the Ohm Farm yesterday. "Long as I can remember, we been a-breedin' more fightin' taters—aye, an' fightin' carrots, onions, turnips, swedes, sproutin' broccoli an' all —than thik Dr Gibson has had hot dinners!"

Tossing me a set of protective clothing and himself putting on a visored helmet, a chainmail overall and reinforced gaiters with steel spikes, the gnarled old agro-technologist led the way chuckling to the vegetable research section.

Through a thick glass observation panel we saw two assistants tending a new experimental strain of giant parsnip which, as Old Seth explained, not only emitted a vapour lethal to all insect life within 20 yards, but also had a limited degree of mobility which enabled it to hunt down and destroy greenfly, weevils and other pests in their breeding grounds.

As we watched, one parsnip of exceptional size turned threateningly on one of the men, who backed away hastily. Old Seth gave a bellow of rustic glee, cut short by a shout of "Run for it!" as an enormous fighting onion, which had evidently escaped from the enclosure, crept up behind us, growling fiercely.

Later I asked Old Seth whether these new strains of vegetable, admittedly well able to take care of themselves against insects or indeed anything else smaller than elephants, would be of much use as food, either for humans or animals.

He looked at me pityingly. "Food? Yon's idle talk,

maister. Dang me purple, 't ain't food we be thinkin'
about on Ohm Farm. 'Tes breakthroughs, technological
miracles like, advancin' frontiers o' scientific knowledge
an' all."

SUICIDAL REDUCTIONS————————————

THE sales season is with us once again (write JEAN and
FIONA MORON). This year, instead of joining the
trampling hordes at Gambridges or Carkers, why not
try something a little different? All over London—particularly in the southern suburbs—there are dozens of
smaller sales where really fascinating bargains can be
picked up for a song.

For example, GUMBERGERS' FURNITURAMA in
Boggis Hill High Street are offering 2,000 full-size plywood replicas of Ancient Egyptian mummy-cases at only
£15·75 (£15 7s 6d) each. With a gaily painted plank on
top they make splendid coffee tables. Or you can use
them as coffins or to put up the odd, unexpected visitor
(or both!). Gumbergers, by the way, are giving away a
free 2-pint bottle of embalming fluid and 30 yards of
mummy-cloth with every 20 mummy-cases you buy.

At WENVOE AND NOBES, in Victoria Square,
Brassgrove Park, we found remarkable value: 3,000 pairs
of export reject sheets (seconds) in yellow, purple and
Nile green stripes; 4,000 hand towels (6 in by 4 in) in a
variety of fully unfast colours from old gold to ultra-
marine; 500 colourful "Samarkand type" carpets made by
Nadirco, with amusingly varied holes woven directly into
the fabric.

In their second-hand book department there are some
real "snips" both for the traditional book-lover and for
the dynamic business executive with an eye to cultural
trends who is thinking of starting a library. We noticed
over 500,000 handsome volumes of sermons by Victorian
divines, including 150 complete 25-volume sets of the
works of the Rev. Mungo Isbister of Yell (1797–1906),
reduced from £30 to 29 guineas.

This year CHASHOLM AND GHOULES, the big,
old-fashioned store at Turgis Hill, have put on a sale

100

with a difference. They're selling off their superannuated shop assistants (useful for dressing up as nannies, valets, aged gardeners, etc., etc.) at very moderate prices, varying according to age, physical condition, etc.

Unable to resist a bargain, we bought a couple of 65-year-old shop-walkers with amusing drooping grey moustaches for only £24!

BY DEVIOUS WAYS

"BURY your divinity syllabuses," said the Dean of St Paul's, fresh from his triumphs in the entertainment industry, to a conference of headmasters at Oxford. Pupils, he said, come out of laboratories at school, to hear about a theology which takes no account of 20th-century scientific knowledge. "How can they be anything but atheists?"

For once this trend-frenzied cleric is right in a way, if only for the wrong reason. Religious teaching ought certainly to take the most careful account of 20th-century scientific knowledge. What else but religious teaching can expose its fatal hollowness?

There is a need in religious instruction periods to teach pupils, whether they have just come out of laboratories or not, to distinguish between true science and the false science which has usurped its name, that reductive, inhuman science which makes the indulgence of curiosity for its own sake a virtue in itself—even the only virtue—and endlessly, mindlessly goes on adding to the sum of sterile knowledge without love.

What the Dean of St Paul's may not realise is that this kind of religious teaching is far more likely than pop groups and pornographic shows in churches to do what he is always saying he wants to do: "bring back Youth to Religion."

The young look round at the 20th century, at the world of accelerating horror which that false science has largely made, is more than ever making now, will go on making till it ends, since it can do no other. And there are signs, even in the most unlikely and trend-infested places, that they are beginning to understand.

101

COMICS REFORMED————————————————

LORD TED WILLIS of Dock Green, the progressive peer, has been complaining about children's comics, which he says, either ignore the existence of coloured people or show them in a ludicrous or villainous light or both. In his liberal-minded, censor-hating way he wants the Government to put pressure on publishers to redress this appalling evil.

Evidently he has not seen the new anti-racialist comics which are now coming on to the market. One of these, "Integro," published from Ethnic House and distributed free with race relations products at the new race relations supermarkets, goes in for a simple reversal by which white people are invariably represented as stupid, ludicrous or malevolent, and coloured people as intelligent, dignified and virtuous.

The idea is that by evening up the score, as it were, and producing more confusion and misunderstanding between the children of all races, this will give the race relations industry a continual supply of material to work on and ensure an even higher rate of expansion in Britain's No. 1 economic growth-point.

"Humbug," the black and white multi-racial comic edited by Deirdre Dutt-Pauker (and periodically burned in public by her son, Bert Brecht Mao Che Odinga, for alleged revisionist tendencies) has a more sophisticated approach.

Not all the white characters are shown as stupid and evil. One educational strip, "Jim Ogbufe and his Pals," shows how the blessings of civilisation were brought to a grateful Europe, then sunk in the barbarous Dark Ages, by a group of child explorers from the advanced cultures of Africa.

Another, "All Together for Peace and Higher Living Standards," shows children of all races uniting to bring about social change by sabotaging the present English school system.

There are also illustrated educational strips on careers. "Fred and Mary, the Activists," in the current issue, shows how a politically aware and fully integrated black boy and white girl make their first explosive device for classroom use—with side-splitting results for Miss Thatcher-Harris, the unpopular Fascist and racialist head-mistress.

FALLEN MAJESTY———————————

THERE is bad news from Manchester. For nearly a hundred years now salon quartets and trios have provided the music at receptions in the imposing Town Hall of the fabled city by the Irwell. Now (the miserable and unconvincing excuse is "shortage of money") they are to be replaced by a tape-recorder.

What the situation is at other Town Halls I cannot say. When Alderman Foodbotham, the 25-stone, crag-visaged, iron-watch-chained, grim-booted perpetual chairman of the Bradford City Tramways and Fine Arts Committee, was Lord Mayor (1906–1927, with an interregnum in 1923, the chaotic "Year of the Four Lord Mayors"), he used his own household musicians from his titanic mansion "Green Garth," on Cleckheaton Moor, for all important receptions.

The great alderman scorned string and woodwind players ("fancy fiddlers and penny-whistling whippersnappers") and the band consisted entirely of brass and a large percussion section, with one exception—sometimes commented on in behind-hand whispers by the bolder councillors—a young lady harpist, Miss Brenda Travis, who without obvious qualifications held a secretarial post in the Parks Department.

The players, drawn from the alderman's gardeners, chauffeurs, body-guards and handymen, were of varying degrees of skill but were anxious to please their master and made amends by always playing as loudly as they could; this made it impossible to tell whether Miss Travis was really playing at all, but as all agreed, the graceful movements of her bare arms made this musically and aesthetically irrelevant.

What with the strange uncoordinated uproar of the band, now buzzing, now droning, now braying discordantly as it crashed its way through "Selection: Maritana" or "A Bradford Rhapsody" (Delius, arr. Rimmer); the mad shouting of the guests, as they vainly tried to make themselves heard above the din, and the majestic sight of Alderman Foodbotham himself presiding mountainously over all, nobody who was ever privileged to attend one of these receptions will ever forget it.

Nowadays . . . but it is best not to think of such things.

PARLOUR GAMES————————————

"THE Sorrow and the Pity," a documentary television programme on the Nazi occupation of France, was repeated on the BBC the other day, provoking a critic to ask once more the old question: how should we have behaved in England? Who would have collaborated with the Nazis here?

"It is a bad-taste parlour game for New Year parties," he says, "too libellous to be performed in public."

I can think of an even worse-taste parlour game, and one a good deal more to the point. For as most people will agree, it is not the Nazis who are likely (if anyone is) to occupy England in the foreseeable future. How we should have behaved under their rule and who would have collaborated with them is by this time, though still interesting, an academic question.

Let us play the game of wondering how the people of England would behave under the occupation (whether by conquest or invitation) of the Red Army, and who would collaborate with *that*.

On second thoughts we had better not. It is a game too libellous—and too exhaustingly libellous—to be played in public. Indeed—unlike the Nazi occupation game—it is not really a game at all.

THE titanic saga of George Best unrolls before a stunned, disbelieving Solar System. Meanwhile in other realms it has its humbler counterpart, which yet holds a moral lesson for us all.

Last week Barry Barmitage, the £45 star non-goal-scoring forward of Stretchford United, "went missing" from a training period and was later discovered in Sadcake Park, drinking tea in the Havelock Ellis Memorial cafeteria with a young woman, Cheryl Toast, 20, a part-time attendant at the nearby speak-your-weight machine fun-centre.

Carpeted by Fred Kustow, United's brilliant, dynamic manager, Barmitage opened and closed his mouth several times, but made no comment when told his sentence: that he should leave his luxury council home in Summer-skill Drive and return for six months to "Kosikot," the repulsive bijou dream home of Mr and Mrs Arthur Ghoules, where Barmitage, an orphan, lodged in his early days.

"He can have his old cupboard under the stairs and welcome," stated Mr Ghoules, a small whey-faced man of 60 with a permanent, deceptive smile caused by ine-fficient use of dental fixative. "But he'll have to share it with our three other lodgers, Len, Ron and Frank, and my collection of old gumboots, valued at over £30, that I pick up on building sites."

But six-foot, 20-stone Mrs Ghoules was less forth-coming. "——you for a start," she told a reporter, raising her hand in a gesture which caused him to shrink back into a corner of the gnome-infested rockery.

WHAT, many keen trade union dogmatists and lovers of protocol are asking, is the position of this column's own small private coal mine in the present strike? Will the age-old tradition of continuous working be maintained? Will the National Union of Mineworkers try to interfere?

Situated in a remote, hilly part of the column, Raws-thorpe Bridge Main is in most ways a model of what a colliery should be. It is worked on a shift system by 14 men and an aged winder who operates the historic brass-bound cage specially made for this pit by the Fafnir Engineering Company in 1885. Annual production averages 150 tons.

When not at the coalface, the miners spend their time squatting on their heels against walls with their whippets and lurchers beside them; sitting in big tubs of scalding hot water before beautifully blackleaded kitchen ranges and having their backs scrubbed by their wives; breeding racing pigeons; playing brass instruments, mainly tubas, in a desultory way; marching through the grimy, cobbled streets at their weekly galas, carrying beautifully worked banners and singing Welsh hymns; or getting drunk on Saturdays at the Miners' Arms.

They are intensely conservative and to judge from the zeal with which they touch their caps on those rare occasions when Bennett, my chauffeur, drives me slowly through the village in the purple Daimler, they are as loyal and contented as any mine owner could wish.

Industrial disputes are unknown, except for the yearly ritual strike, greatly enjoyed by all, which lasts for 24 hours and culminates in a traditional siege of the home of the popular works manager, Mr Hargreaves, followed by a tremendous ham-and-egg tea with parkin, fruit salad and outsize meat pies.

The fact that nothing in this unique coalfield ever seems to change in any way, and that the miners, their wives and children and even their dogs and racing pigeons never get any older has been commented on unfavourably by visiting officials of the National Coal Board.

But I am glad to say there is nothing whatever they can do about it.

106

MISCONCEPTION————————————

THERE has been some criticism of Karl Rubrick's new film "Diesel-engined Grapefruit" (writes SEAN HORROR-CLIFFE, "Way of the World" film critic) on the ground that it may encourage violence among the young.

I cannot see what all the fuss is about. Torture, murder, mass-rape and cannibalism are, after all, part of the daily lives of most of us nowadays, and a serious film director would simply be failing in his duty both to art and society if he did not deal with these subjects whenever possible.

To suggest that young people who see these things happening on the screen may be inclined to go out and try them for themselves is simply an insult to the intelligence of the young, which has never been higher than it is today. It is a typically paternalistic, backward-looking, even fascist attitude.

As Rubrick himself says, the average young man or woman does not go to see such a film for the sake of entertainment or excitement but in a spirit of responsible inquiry and social awareness. After the film is over the audience generally form spontaneous discussion groups in which the problems raised in the film are subjected to interpersonal exploration and assessment in a climate of meaningful, relevant participation.

A dialogue is thus set up, an open-ended commitment to communication which will not only help in the vital task of changing our society but will also make everyone connected with the film a great deal of money.

PEOPLE AND PARTIES————————————

DROPPING into a delightful party given by Pippa Dreadberg, the brilliant attractive novelist wife of brilliant avante-garde playwright, painter, TV personality and self-publicist Neville Dreadberg (drools REX HICK-FIELD), I found she had brought off a real coup which will make swinging London's rival party-givers emerald green with envy.

Guest of honour was a real-life, genuine, 24-carat high-ranking officer of the IRA Provisionals, fresh from Belfast, where I hear he's gratifyingly high on the wanted list!

He's Brig. Sean MacGuffog, a fast, amusing talker who had everyone crowding round for a glimpse of the amusing sub-machine-gun he always carries with him.

Later on, at Pippa's insistence, he produced a lot of wires and alarm-clocks and batteries and sticks of gelignite and things and showed how to wire up a bomb.

"Do let's have an explosion—just a little one," begged brilliant model girl and autobiographer Giselle Frabazon, and the Brigadier, whose Irish charm simply oozes in gallons from his cordite-stained finger-tips, obliged with an amusing bang which had fellow-guests like brilliant actor Mike Tove, brilliant footballer-sculptor Ken Valve, brilliant young architect Crispin Spasholm, brilliant art historian Dr Rex Weak and brilliant Tory progressive MP Jeremy Cardhouse rolling about in convulsions.

"Brigadier, I love you," breathed Pippa, as she planted a kiss on the IRA leader's cheek, drawing a flood of what sounded like poetic endearments in his native tongue as I dropped heavily and obtrusively out.

THRESHOLD OF HELL————————————————

"THE lowering of the grievance threshold is a feature of our society," says a writer in the *Observer* on the existing laws against "racial discrimination," the attempt, so far foiled, to bring in a law against "sexual discrimination" and the proposal—even more preposterous, if possible— for a law against "age discrimination."

"The lowering of the grievance threshold"—translated into English, what does this painful jargon mean? It means that ours is a society in which envy, spite, discontent and petty-mindedness are growing daily, and are being encouraged to grow daily by every means open to publicists and politicians.

The normal, unselfconscious relation of one human being with another human being, whether of different race, sex or age, is being systematically distorted and perverted. In the name of an unattainable equality, the individual man, woman and even child is being turned into a member of a category, a militant group moved not by human love but by inhuman malice and hatred.

What would our society be like if this process reached its ultimate though fortunately unattainable conclusion, in which every single person saw himself as a victim of discrimination by some other person? What will our society be like if the process continues, as at present, unabated and unopposed?

PROVE IT

"I MUCH dislike pornography. I find it distasteful and degrading, but in the absence of any clear indication (let alone proof) that it does individual harm, I find it difficult to say that it should be repressed by law or censorship."

Thus the former British film censor, Mr John Trevelyan. His attitude seems to be adequately maintained by his successor. Yet it is hard to see how it can be held by any intelligent man.

Mr Trevelyan finds pornography degrading; what is degrading is, by definition, harmful. Yet because there is no "clear indication" or "proof" that this is so he cannot admit that any measures should be taken against it.

Could there be a clearer indication of the way in which the "scientific attitude," the belief that nothing, however obvious, can be accepted unless it can be "proved," is taking from us our ultimate weapon against evil, our basic human common-sense?

A NEED FOR CHANGE

"I WANT to give people who use my houses a rare and primitive relationship with the raw forces of nature," says a designer of pub interiors. "People love to be awed when they enter a pub by a superior natural force—a strange sort of higher masochism."

This is certainly the principle on which Nadirmasoch Breweries, a subsidiary of the mammoth Midland consortium Nadirco, have redesigned many of their houses in the Stretchford area.

At the Convulsion of Nature (formerly the Red Lion) in Hokewell Bridge Road, for instance, customers can enjoy realistic tropical storms and earthquakes. On Saturday evenings the whole place is regularly overwhel-

med by white-hot lava followed by an electrically-operated tidal wave.

"It certainly makes a change from the old days," says one satisfied "regular", William Fruitcliffe, 64, a retired deckchair underlooker. "Beats me how we used to spend a whole evening playing dominoes or crib or betting on how many flies would settle on the pork pie on the bar.

"Now we can watch enthralled as the whole bar, landlord, barmaids and all, suddenly disappears into a ruddy great chasm in the floor, with smoke and flames belching out of it. Talk about laugh!"

STORE————————————————————————

ONE by one they change and pass, the great London stores. Gamages—who would have thought it possible? —is to be demolished next month. Pontings, Derry and Toms, Debenhams, even Harrods—not one remains as it has been. Boutiquery, discothequery, grotesquery of every modish kind is invading and taking over them all.

How fortunate then that safe within the confines of this column there remains and will remain for ever one store eternal, unchanging, beyond the reach of time.

At Tremberthy and Jones (founded 1888) all is excellent as on the first day. To enter the great revolving doors; to pace the lofty, carpeted halls in the strange subaqueous light; to wander through the multitudinous departments under their respective heads—Mr Surridge (furniture), Mr Brunt (glassware and chandeliers), Mr Smailes (hand luggage and cabin trunks), Mr Stagg (tropical kit), Mr Stolz (pianofortes) and, perhaps most formidable and respectable of all, Miss Travis (ladies' underwear)—to name only a few—this experience makes you free of a whole world within the world.

Here all is calm, hushed, decorous. Low respectful murmurs may be heard among the vast mahogany counters, the forests of hatstands, mirrors and modestly clad wax dummies, as some dowager rejects a fiftieth pair of gloves; a frockcoated shopwalker's voice, sharper yet still spellbound as in a dream, pierces the gloom: "Miss Smith, jet bugles, forward!"

In a glass box, high in the great central dome, sits Miss Bruce, the lady cashier, with her attendants, her grey hair shell-coiled about her ears, presiding over the system of grooved channels on which hollow balls conveying bills and change roll slowly up and down for ever by the force of electro-magnetism and with the soft whirr of bells.

Whole hours can be well spent watching the working of this celestial toy railway. Many people, including retired generals and men prominent in public life, as the saying is, have offered to pay large sums for the privilege of taking Miss Bruce's place for only one hour and being allowed actually to operate it themselves.

This, of course, can never be. This is no licentious funfair. It is a store.

INDUSTRIAL NOTE————————————————

In the sphere of labour relations this column's record is second to none. In the troubled world of British industry, as I have often said (sometimes clearing whole rooms and buildings in the process), it shines out like a lighthouse in the desert.

Since the abortive attempt, fomented by alien agitators, to stage a strike by ablative absolute turners more than 10 years ago, there has been not a single whisper of disaffection or disharmony between master and man.

That is probably why extremists, who have a General Strike as their ultimate objective, are now talking of picketing this column. They hope that by preventing further supplies of verbal material from reaching the column for processing they can slow down production and eventually bring it, as the saying is, to a grinding, shuddering standstill.

Vain hope! It is estimated that stocks of verbal material now held by the column are sufficient to maintain production at its present rate for at least 20 years.

With the new techniques of verbal self-proliferation now being developed, it is estimated that the column could continue for at least 20,000 years, perhaps until the onset of a new Ice Age.

A simple extrapolation from present data, some futurologists believe, indicates that by then the column will have absorbed the whole of the British Press and 90 per cent of the ordinary daily activities of this country. But it is possible that they have overlooked some vital factor.

NORMAN THE GOOD ────────────────────

MR WILLIAM HAMILTON, the Labour MP for West Fife, whose morbid obsession with the Royal Family is beginning to arouse interest—and even some lip-smacking and money-jingling—among psychiatrists, suggests that when the Prince of Wales finishes his training in the Navy he should spend three months in the coal mines.

A quick glance into the future, at Good King Norman's Golden Time, reveals that Prince Barry of South Wales and all the other members of the Socialist Royal Family are employed in industry, though not always gainfully.

*　　*　　*

February 18, 2012

There was uproar in Parliament yesterday when Mr Ron Canalshaw, One-party Member for the Chatsworth New Town Division of the Peak District National Socialist Park, asked why Prince Barry had been given seven days' leave of absence from Glynsabon Colliery in South Wales when he had only started work there as a miner the day before yesterday.

Mr Ken Billiard, Minister for Industry and Power Cuts: The Glynsabon Pit, as Members will know, is the only working coal mine remaining in this country, and is a vital industrial and tourist attraction

Because of its appalling working conditions, with

112

frequent flooding and the constant danger of firedamp, "gloot" and "jabber," to say nothing of infestation by "knockers" or underground Welsh goblins, producing superstitious dread among the miners, the whole labour force is permanently on strike and is determined to remain so.

Prince Barry, who has one of the lowest IQs ever recorded in this country, was either not informed of this when he began work at the pit, or did not understand what he was told. Descending the pit by one of the primitive ladders, he emerged soon afterwards smiling triumphantly and holding up a large lump of coal for all to see.

In the ensuing disturbances the pithead baths and recreation rooms were burned down, fortunately with no loss of life, and order was only restored when a detachment of the Royal Socialist Armoured Corps arrived from the nearby Healey Memorial Barracks at Pontypridd. The National Socialist Coal Board then decided to send Prince Barry on special leave for his own safety.

Mr Canalshaw: To me the whole incident smacks of feudal privilege, redolent of the corrupt court of Caligula or of the tapestried halls of Tsar Nicholas of Aragon (cries of "Suez!" "No Arms for South Africa!" "Bomb Stormont Now!" "Suez!" "Ulster!" "Get up them stairs!" etc. etc.).

Mr Billiard: Perhaps the Member will be pacified when I reveal that the Heir to the Socialist Throne is to be transferred forthwith from the coal mines to another vital branch of industry where he should be more gainfully employed, the National Individual Fruit Pie Factory at Windermere New Town (sensation and uproar).

DEADLOCK———————————————————

LIGHTS burned brightly all last night at Cavity House, the London headquarters of the Amalgamated Union of Holeborers. This was partly due to the Tory Government's suggestion that electrical power should be saved; but mainly because high officials of the union's Office of Dogmatics were locked in disputation with their colleagues of the Office of Rule-book Analysis and Exegetics.

The point at issue was whether the holeborers should

come out in solidarity with the miners and, further, whether in that case they should offer to help the strike by boring holes in power-stations, coal-lorries, coal-lorry drivers, policemen and other "black" artefacts within the scope of Rule 481 in the Union Rule-book (Definition of the Concept "Black" in Pragmatic Terms within the Context of the General Concept of "Blackness" as laid down under Rule 367).

As dawn broke more lights and electric heaters were switched on but the deadlock was still unbroken. In a communiqué issued at 10 a.m. Mr Len Gollip, the general secretary, stated:

"Discussions pursuant to the question of implementationary action with respect to the present dispute are proceeding in a cordial atmosphere. At this moment of time we are still hopeful of a solution; but although the door is still open to compromise there are elements of deadlock and even of disagreement of which due cognisance must be taken both at steering committee level and at branch level before we can see daylight at the end of the tunnel behind us."

SEMIOLOGICAL DAYS————————————

"ARTIST Trapped in his Own Creation" is the title of a recent article about a modern painter. And a very nasty sensation that can be.

John Gasby, the pioneer of rubbish sculpture, whose vast agglomerations seem to—and in deed do—take on a life of their own, has been particularly subject to this hazard of the creative artist's life.

Only last year, when he was completing, near the North Circular Road, a new work called "Pollution VI," incorporating several tons of rusting machinery, thousands of hatstands, barometers and plywood cut-outs of derelict film-stars and many hundredweights of stale confectionery, he overbalanced and fell in.

Slowly and remorselessly, and with a kind of grating growl, the work began to engulf him. His cries for help were eventually heard by a passing art-critic, who at first supposed that Gasby was himself part of the work but eventually dragged him out, just in time.

In gratitude, Gasby asked the critic to write the introductory note to the catalogue of the exhibition in which the work appeared soon afterwards. The critic put forth all his powers.

"In its essentially massive, tonal yet sporadist approach to the universality of the human condition," he wrote, " 'Pollution VI' bears, to a greater yet more truly *minimalising* degree than the generality of Gasby's work, the exponential marks of the ingrown, structural yet hypothetically ageometrical involvement of its creator himself.

"In its unforgettably orchestrated way, the presence of part of Gasby's left shoe . . ."

AWAY WITH HIM————————————

"MILITARY Coup in Gombola. President Ngrafta Deposed." This headline, which appears in the papers every year about this time, never fails to amuse the President himself.

The popular and astute Redeemer of Gombola (formerly Gomboland), thought to be the only head of an African State who as well as being a practising witch-doctor holds a degree from the London School of Economics, has hit on a perfect method of staying in power indefinitely.

He realises that public opinion in Gombola demands the occasional military coup, if only to assert the country's equality with other African States which would otherwise tend to sneer and feel superior.

So every year, working on a roster, Dr Ngrafta nominates one of his generals to lead a coup which is then effortlessly suppressed with the co-operation of all concerned.

The duty is not particularly sought after, since it entails a few disadvantages. After the failure of the coup the general concerned is not shot (Dr Ngrafta is a highly civilised man and in his youth was a friend of the late Lady Ottoline Morrell). But as part of the celebrations on the public holiday which follows he must submit to be driven round Bungrafta, the capital, in a cage, to be execrated by the populace and pelted with coconuts, dried fish and ghool, a kind of decayed, glutinous spaghetti.

He has the right, however, of being changed by Dr Ngrafta himself, an expert in this branch of magic, into any creature he chooses while he is in the cage. Warthogs are the most popular choice. But this year's coup-leader, Brig. Nelson Mbangola, a rather conceited officer, thought he would go one better and chose to be turned into a swarm of mosquitoes.

His dispersal, with small hope of ever being assembled again, made Dr Ngrafta laugh louder than ever.

TALKING POINT————————————————

CONSCIENCE is the wedge inserted under the uneven table-leg of life—Ralph Waldo Emerson.

SWITCHED OFF————————————————

"THEY should never have started it. I blame Faraday." Wimshurst, Galvani and other early electrical research workers also came in for harsh words from some of the older people I met during a weekend spent in a rather out-of-the-way part of the country.

Such attitudes are certainly not helpful and may even irritate. Yet it is a fact that 25 years ago, before that part of the country was electrified, they could have taken the present strikes with a certain selfish lightheartedness.

To be dependent on a centralised agency not only for luxuries but even for the basic necessities of life, an agency too, which is complex, volatile and liable to be put out of commission at a stroke—is this so obviously a mark of higher civilisation as most people unquestioningly think?

We are stuck with it now. There is no way back to rushlights, peat fires and water from the well. There may be a way forward to them, though; but through what unimaginable havoc and horror it must lead!

RELEVANT, MEANINGFUL————

THAT esteemed body the International Constitution on English Texts is still tinkering happily with the Lord's Prayer. It has just decided that "hallowed" shall be used instead of "holy" in the phrase "hallowed be your (*sic*) name."

Argument is now raging over the phrase "Lead us not into temptation," in which the Church of England, surprisingly enough, wants to retain "temptation" as being familiar and personal to English people.

Why, on that ground, they don't stop messing about and simply keep the Lord's Prayer in the form in which it has been familiar and personal to English people for a very long time, is not explained.

The attitude of Dr Spacely-Trellis, the go-ahead Bishop of Bevindon, is at least consistent. He admits that the purpose of the new Bevindon version of the Lord's prayer is to "make people aware of change and to initiate a relevant, structural, meaningful, open-ended dialogue for the crisis of communication in this secular day and age."

The Bevindon version runs: "Principle of Evolutionary Humanism, implicit in Man's progress to World Government and Universal Welfare, let us respect the nomenclature by which you are known; it is to be hoped that optimum social conditions will soon be fulfilled in a contemporary material context as well as in the futurological sphere.

"It is to be hoped that adequate daily nourishment will be available for all; and that our occasional lapses from efficiency may be allowed for, as we allow for them in

117

others; also that we avoid circumstances in which we may fail to adjust to our environment.

"Bearing all this in mind, we may sum up by saying that your principle is implicit in the biosphere, and is in control of it, to the satisfaction of all, on a permanent basis."

BOOST

ONE effect of the miners' strike will be to increase the demand for "Build Your Own Nuclear Power Station," already one of the most popular titles in Norm and Graph's "Do It Yourself" series.

The book is by Paul Ohm, the well-known freelance technologist, who is himself building a small private nuclear power station in his garden at Edgbaston.

It gives clear instructions on how to construct foundations; atomic pile assembly ("a job for all the family"); nuclear accelerator and reactor design; as well as such tricky points as disposal of atomic waste in home-made containers ("don't dump them just anywhere: be selective") and what to do if your reactor "goes critical" while you are having your breakfast.

In an eloquent foreword, Mr Anthony Wedgwood Benn predicts a boom in home nuclear power station building in spite of the typically lukewarm attitude of the present Tory Government. He forecasts that by 1990 these stations will be feeding more than 80 million megawatts into Britain's power grid daily—enough power to operate 25 electric shavers for each man, woman, child and omnisexual mutant in the country.

HEROINE

"No American in recent years," says the *Observer*, "has aroused such deep feeling throughout the world, or embodied so many contemporary causes, as Angela Davis, a 27-year-old university teacher of philosophy who is also black and beautiful."

Whether Miss Davis, who is standing trial in California on charges of murder, conspiracy and kidnapping, is beautiful is a matter of opinion. What can be readily seen from her photograph is that she is not, in the true sense of the word, black.

Furthermore, an examination of the likenesses of the Black Power leaders in America and leaders of related movements will show that most of them, if not all, have a considerable admixture of white and non-African blood.

What does this prove? Very little, perhaps. It is well known that there is no racialist or nationalist fanatic more extreme and unreasoning than the fanatic who does not himself belong wholly to the race or nation for which he fights.

Do the lives and attitudes of such people as Miss Davis spring from a pure, burning indignation at the wrongs suffered by the black people of America; or do they spring from a personal quarrel with the world and with the self?

From both, no doubt. But that so many innocent, impressionable people should take such desperate, displaced and violent figures as their heroes, heroines and exemplars is no happy omen for the world.

A DIFFICULT PROBLEM————————————

THERE are complaints that shops are offering perishable food for sale long after it has become dangerous, and demands that packages should be clearly dated in a way which will be intelligible to the customer.

Last week a Nerdley housewife who bought a deep-frozen individual fruit pie, in a packet marked "SPQR-691AUC", from Nadirco's Hanging Gardens of Babylon Supermarket in Victoria Road returned to the shop complaining that it seemed to be at least 2,000 years old.

She was at once taken under escort to the deep-frozen section manager's office. He pointed out that the pie could not in fact be more than 20 years old because that particular brand had only been manufactured that long. The pie was then confiscated without compensation, and the woman warned and dismissed.

A spokesman said later: "This is typical of the hurtful misunderstanding which can be caused by the frivolous and disloyal element—a small minority, I am glad to say —among our customers.

"This woman had arrogantly tried to work out for herself the letters and numbers on the packet—they are, of course, arranged according to a secret system of our own—and had reached a totally erroneous conclusion.

"The suggestion now being made by a vociferous minority of cranks and do-gooders that all food packets should be plainly marked with the date of manufacture is quite impractical.

"It would be unfair to those customers—an increasing number—who cannot read. And what of the blind? The old folk, whose sight may not be what it was? The pre-school infants? The immigrants who may not be acquainted with Roman numerals?

"To operate such a scheme we should have to employ a large staff of highly trained people to interpret the markings on the packets, and this would mean an increase of anything up to 25 per cent. in the price of all our goods."

The spokesman paused, as though struck by a new, exciting thought; then, abruptly breaking off his statement, he rushed away, laughing exultantly.

WAYS OF DOING THINGS————————————

MR HEATH and Mr Wilson have both had their say. At least they agree on one point: that violence in England is a bad thing and inimical to the English way of doing things.

They are not quite agreed on the causes of increasing violence in this country. Mr Wilson, as in Socialist duty bound, puts it down to "social causes"—unemployment, poverty, bad housing, "injustice" in general—just as though this cosy, liberal explanation had not been so spectacularly demolished in Northern Ireland.

Mr Heath is more realistic. He admits that this "invisible danger" of violence to the English way of doing things is "hard to pin down and put a value to." He hopes —and who does not?—that it will be averted by the principle, once generally accepted in England, that sensible people, left to themselves, will come to sensible decisions in a sensible and peaceful manner.

Unfortunately we are not living in a sensible and peaceful world. To defend our English way of doing things something more than an exhortation to be sensible may be needed.

That can only be a direct appeal to patriotism, love of country, an appeal involving the irrational but necessary personification of the country, England, which is in danger and has to be defended.

Would such an appeal still work? In the last 20 years all sorts of agencies have been systematically eroding the spirit of patriotism in England and reducing the very idea of it to the level of a foolish joke.

Has this interesting operation succeeded? Or is there still an immense residue of patriotism latent in this country, waiting to be summoned forth as unfailingly as in former times?

If there is no strong patriotic spirit to defend it, but only a vague wish for ease and comfort and keeping out of trouble, how much longer will our English way of doing things continue?

CHANGING TIMES

THE vogue of the "dynamic young executive," reports the *Director*, journal of the Institute of Directors, may be declining in America, where there are signs of a reaction in favour of older, more experienced men. It is hoped, it says, that British boardrooms may follow suit.

It looks as if they are already beginning to do so. Only the other day I was strolling though a London park when I came upon one of these dynamic young executives sitting on a bench by himself, crying bitterly.

He seemed little more than a child, though he was dressed in a dynamic executive's suit and was convulsively opening and closing a smart, dynamic executive's document-case, causing a sheaf of tear-stained sales

reports and copies of glossy pornographic magazines to spill pathetically out of it.

"Come, little man," I said, stopping and leaning on my ebony stick. "What ails you? Tell me. It will do you good, I promise you."

Through lessening sobs the whole sorry tale came out. Jim (for that was his name) told me how when scarcely eight years old, but already an avid reader of business efficiency journals, he had run away from school, hired a dynamic young executive's suit from a dwarf executive outfitters and applied for an interview with the chairman of a firm of plastic turntable manufacturers, a man known to be so utterly enslaved by the cult of youth that there was not a director on his board over 20 years of age.

Jim had been taken on immediately and after a short period as a management consultant was appointed a director at £20,000 a year, with company car, life membership of several expensive West End striptease and gambling clubs, penthouse flat and all appropriate fringe benefits.

He also became something of a pet of the chairman, who made him sit on his knee at board meetings and was fond of describing him boastfully to other chairmen as "Britain's youngest and most dynamic executive".

Therein lay Jim's undoing. The other dynamic young executives, jealous of the favourite, mounted an intrigue against him, and one day, at a board meeting, as Jim was outlining a dynamic campaign to sell millions of turntables in the Indian sub-continent, the dread figure of a school attendance officer appeared and dragged him, kicking and struggling, back to the grey, undynamic, unexecutive world.

He ran away again, of course. But when he got back to the factory it was to find that the cult of youth was over. The chairman pretended not to recognise him. Seventy was the average age of the directors, some of whom were wearing grey wigs and bald head-pieces. . . .

A MEMORABLE OCCASION————————————

"POP festivals are attended almost entirely by hard-working, clean-living young people" (letter to the Editor).

One such festival is memorably described in "Some Memories of Victorian Essex," believed to have been written by a former rector of Weeley in 1872.

"Bands of youths and maids, smartly but modestly attired in their Sunday best, were passing the rectory gate. The balmy morning air resounded with their merry chatter, though a respectful hush fell when they saw me. In answer to their bashful greetings, I inquired their purpose.

" 'Well, Sir,' responded one ruddy-cheeked apprentice, twisting his cap humbly between his fingers, 'we are on our way to a pop festival—a festival of popular music, Sir,' he added in answer to my mute bewilderment.

" 'Aye, Reverend Sir,' a sweet-faced lass of some seventeen summers piped up at his side, 'and we shall be proud to have you with us to give us your blessing, like, if you be so good and think it no derogation.'

"Nothing loth, I joined the happy throng. Soon we came to a field, in which were gathered hundreds of such youths and maids. A young woman soon mounted on to a farm cart and, after a few moments' prayerful medita-tion, broke into a sacred song. Her soprano voice was clear, pure and thrilling; the rapt exultation of her regular features irresistibly recalled the Methody, Dinah Morris, so unforgettably depicted by George Eliot. Accompaniment was supplied by a portable harmonium and other instruments.

"The arrival of the village policeman, benignly smiling, was greeted with a hearty cheer: 'God bless the peelers,' called out one sturdy lad, 'who protect our mothers and sisters from hurt.' 'Huzza, huzza.' all chorussed.

"Other singers and groups of singers succeeded this first. The songs they sung were not invariably sacred, though all were of an uplifting nature. Some extolled the virtues and rewards of honest toil, punctuality, thrift and obedience; others warned of the dangers of strong drink and other stimulants; others again earnestly deplored disorder, violence and strife; some touched with innocent delicacy on the joys of lawful and reciprocated love in courtship and marriage.

"Much moved, I myself ascended the cart and fervently blessed all present, who knelt quietly till I had done. As evening fell, I returned home reflecting with grateful pride and confidence on the future of our fortunate land."

UNQUIET SPIRIT————————————

ONLY six weeks ago a Bill to make "discrimination" against women in employment illegal and even establish an "Anti-Discrimination Board," was "talked out" in the House of Commons. Now a similar and equally absurd measure has been introduced in the House of Lords.

In the debate there was much talk of "male privilege" "prejudice," the wrongs of "the underdog" and (more alarming for women themselves) of the "economic loss to the nation" caused by "the archaic and wasteful use of womanpower."

Surprisingly, in view of this, Baroness Summerskill, a typical supporter of the Bill, rejected the idea that it would allow women to become coalminers, one of the vital jobs—another is serving in submarines—they are now debarred from by illogical male prejudice. "Women," she said, "will not hew coal for the same reason that men will not occupy maternity beds. They are equally unsuited."

The analogy is false. Although no man (if we except one doubtful case in the Abruzzi in 1463) has ever been known to bear a child, there is no reason in nature why women should not hew coal or do other work in the mines. They have done so before, and (if the full exploitation of woman power is all that matters) may be told it is their duty to do so again.

The real mischief, indeed evil, of this talk of "sex discrimination" is that it encourages a general morbid feeling that everyone is being "discriminated against" in some way or other and that it is everyone's duty to brood over it and resent it.

Healthy people, on the other hand, will try to accept discrimination as a law of life. Everyone *is* discriminated against in some way or other. Yes, even I—rich, well-born, handsome, of athletic frame, the possessor of perfect health and of literary, musical and artistic genius—am occasionally discriminated against.

Do I resent this? Yes. But at least I know I ought not to; and have never asked for an Anti-Discrimination Board to be set up on my behalf.

TALK ABOUT LAUGH!

"To Warner Brothers and director Stanley Kubrick it was no laughing matter to face the possibility of having a £1 million film that might be banned, or even prejudiced by the actions of no less a 'critic' than the man chiefly responsible for law and order in Britain."

This is just one typically pompous, self-righteous quotation from one of the interminable articles now appearing in the Press about what is called "the film censorship crisis."

It refers to an incident in which the British Home Secretary, the earthbound midget Maudling, tastelessly dared to imply that the economic laws by which the giants of the film industry operate in their lofty realms may not be absolutely unchallengeable when questions of public morality and possible public corruption are involved.

I daresay I have a peculiar sense of humour. But to me the idea that "Warner Brothers and director Stanley Kubrick" might have laid out £1 million and still not rake in the enormous profits they expected from their outlay is a laughing matter of the highest order.

If these people lost every penny of their £1 million (and all the rest of their millions) and were reduced to selling toy clockwork film magnates outside the ruins of their own cinemas (a thing unfortunately most unlikely to happen), that would be the biggest laugh for centuries.

CHESS PROBLEM————————————————

REPORTS from Australia suggest that the world champion chess player Boris Spassky of Russia and the American challenger Bobby Fischer are "limbering up for their contest like a couple of heavyweight boxers."

There is a contrast, possibly significant, between their training methods. Spassky's is said to include roadwork and weight-lifting, whereas Fischer is merely consuming enormous quantities of steak and apple-juice.

Does this emphasis on physical strength reflect an increasing tendency to violence in chess, already noticeable at humbler levels of the game?

At a recent Stretchford chess tournament the final match between Ron Ghoules (Nerdley) and Stan Hammercake (Soup Hales) was marred by what the *Stretchford Clarion* called "a disturbing plethora of ugly incidents."

When, after 14 moves, Ghoules, using a variation of Ballcock's Knight Sacrifice Gambit, forced Hammercake's Queen into a corner, the attitude of the crowd, who had been catcalling and throwing toilet rolls from the beginning of the game, became so offensive that the Nerdley man, leaping from his seat, seized a small spectator at random and stuffed him up a convenient chimney.

Hammercake immediately appealed under Rule 86B, whereupon a mob of spectators ran on to the board, displacing or knocking over several pieces, and the match was abandoned amid what the *Clarion*'s Chess Correspondent called "scenes reminiscent of the notorious saturnalia of Ancient Rome.

"It is right, indeed essential," he added, "that chess players should keep physically fit. But to use their physical strength, however justifiably, in the course of play is to introduce an element into chess which will eventually make the game distinguishable from Rugby League football only by its greater violence."

ALL VERY DIFFICULT————————————————

"THE fashionable thing for many young couples is to keep their marriage secret," suggests the superintendent registrar at Worthing. "They have been led to believe that marriage is out, decadent, washed up and the rest

of it . . . They are the biggest conforming groups and although they really want to be married and do right by each other, they feel they are doing something out of the ordinary."

But surely, as this new conformity extends, new kinds of young non-conformists will appear who will defiantly insist on marrying in church with satin and lace, bridesmaids, organ music, ribbon-draped limousines and all the rest?

It will be awkward for them. How will these new nonconformists be able to rebel against the new conformity without risking being confused with those who still conform to the old conformity—the overwhelming majority of the people of this country, who, outside daft, trendcrazed Southern places like Worthing, still get married in the ordinary way?

VICTIMS

MORE and more IRA men, points out Richard Cox, are blowing themselves up because the expert bomb makers are either dead or interned. Dr Heinz Kiosk, chief psychiatric adviser to the Gelignite Marketing Board, commented yesterday: "Here is another black mark against Britain's vicious internment policy, by which expert bomb makers are kept behind barbed wire when they might be out, going about their business and preventing decent young Irishmen sacrificing themselves through their own lack of skill.

"What sort of democracy is it that denies an expert

bomb maker the elementary right to be charged, tried in a civil court, and convicted of planting a bomb before his liberty is stolen from him?

"The blood of the young, inexpert victims is primarily on the hands of Faulkner, Heath and Maudling. But we are all guilty", he added hastily before anyone could get out of the room.

COSY CORNER——————————————————————

"THE most obscene act imaginable is censorship itself" (reader's letter in the *Guardian*).

ORDER YOUR COPY NOW!————————————————

EVERY day for the next 200 million years or until the final extinction of this planet, whichever shall be the sooner, we shall be printing (by permission of the British Boring Board of Control) a long extract from a forthcoming book, "Is Doom Doomed?" in which two eminent ecologists, Dr Simon Ghoulberg, of the University of Grand Rapids, Wisconsin, and Dr Barry Nobleman, of the Doomwatch Institute at Tuxedo City, Indiana, discuss the most vital problem facing mankind today, the Problem of Ecospherical Survival. Here is the first extract:

Dr Ghoulberg: Technology has placed in Man's hands tremendous powers which he can use either for good or ill. To take an example of a homely, albeit global dimensional category: the demand for soap, increasingly used for lavational activities both private and public throughout our ecosphere, is accelerating so rapidly that one recent exponential graph indicates that by the year 2002 the world's soap supplies will be totally exhausted.

Dr Nobleman: The Friends of Earth are already demanding that grated soap, used as a Parmesan-cheese surrogate for sprinkling on minestrone, should be barred by international agreement. The problem—and I may predicate that in my view it is a problem of global dimensions—cannot be solved except by the determination of us, we, ourselves, acting as individuals and thereby

pressuring governments into an insistence on action. **And**
what hope is there of securing a consensus in this area?

Dr Ghoulberg: That is the trouble. The disappearance
of soap should in theory guarantee the disappearance of
soap-dishes, both of metal and plastic construction, as of
such ablutionary adjuncts as bath-brushes, sponges, face-
flannels and so on. Unfortunately the runaway nature of
throwaway technology will probably thwart this desirable
development in so far as factories will still be geared to
produce these adjuncts even though they have become
totally superfluous.

Dr Nobleman: It is in the nature of the problem that in
a consumer-orientated society it is always possible to
create artificial demands which can set in motion a chain-
reaction leading all the way back from the exhaustion of
sponge supplies to the problem of minestrone itself.

Dr Ghoulberg: I agree.

(Tomorrow: The Problem of the Elastic Suspender
Backlash in the Global Context of Conservationism).

MINORITY RULE————————————————————

"SOCIETY should reflect the attitudes and interests of all
people and a minority should not lay down values for the
rest to follow," said Lord Boyle, vice-chancellor of Leeds
University. . . . He was speaking at a conference at
Bradford University organised by the Yorkshire Committee for Community Relations.

" 'How grateful we must be for having introduced not
only a multi-racial but also a multi-cultural society. We
all have problems but a multi-cultural society can be
better and richer than one which is mono-cultural (*sic*),'
he said" (*Yorkshire Post*).

As Lord Boyle says, we all have problems. One problem is to find some consistency in a man who in the same
speech can say that a minority should not lay down
values for the rest to follow and then proceed to do that
very thing himself.

Search, with due gratitude, through our multi-racial
land and where will you find a truer representative of a
true minority than Lord Boyle?

A DELEGATE at the Co-operative party conference this week suggested the provision of a town hall "taxi service" to take members to and from council meetings, and his suggestion was approved.

To say that Alderman Foodbotham, the 25-stone, iron-watch-chained, crag-visaged, grim-booted chairman of the Bradford City Tramways and Fine Arts Committee in the great days will be turning in his grave would be an exaggeration. The matter is hardly important enough to cause more than a twitch of one stupendous eyelid.

But the Alderman would certainly have been surprised by the idea that a time might come when councillors would be drawn from a class of men so humble or witless that they had no means of transport of their own.

For himself he kept half a dozen enormous purple Daimlers at "Greengarth," his titanic mansion at Cleckheaton Moor. His majestic progress, when, driven by Ormondroyd, his saturnine, cavernous-faced but red necked head chauffeur, he made his way to council meetings at the soot-black, bell-booming Town Hall was a sight to strike all bystanders with awe.

Among the elderly, attacks of vertigo and windy spasms, even seizures, were frequent, providing many an excuse for a quick visit to the "Woolcombers' Arms" or (in the case of total abstainers) to one of Dr Allan's excellent herbal establishments, where such remedies as ipecacuanha or extra-strong peppermints could be had.

On special occasions the Alderman would use his private tram. This unusual vehicle (now in the Foodbotham Museum at Northowram) included a comfortable smoking room, dining room and study; and on the open upper deck a rock-garden, a gazebo and a small moor, ingeniously designed by the veteran architect Sir Edwin Spasholm (1818–1924).

FOR YOUR BOOKSHELF————————————

THANKS to the painstaking efforts of scholars, authors and publishers, more and more lids are being removed, as the saying is, from the façade of Victorian respectability. We gaze, horrified yet delighted, into the seething maelstrom of vice and perversion revealed below.

A new contribution to the work of demolition—perhaps the most sensational yet—has just appeared. It is "The Diaries of Arthur Sadcake" (edited by Julian Birdbath and published by Viper and Bugloss at £3·50, with an introduction by Dr Heinz Kiosk).

Arthur Sadcake, son of the Alderman Joseph Sadcake who gave his name to Stretchford's largest open space, lovely, sex-maniac-haunted Sadcake Park, inherited the family carbon brush manufacturing firm on his father's death in 1861 and ran it with conspicuous success until his own death at the end of the century.

He married young, and, as was the custom in Victorian times, fathered 47 children, including two sets of twins and one of triplets. He was an Alderman and a munificent patron of charity. His obituary in the *Stretchford Clarion* refers to the "unbending rectitude, the fervent piety, the insistence on absolute purity in word and deed" of "this distinguished son of Stretchford who might well be taken as an outstanding model and an arbiter of the moral law for all who come after."

His diaries, discovered by a literary agent at the back of a chimney when the Sadcake family mansion at Hokewell was being demolished last year, tell a very different story.

When first discovered, says Dr Kiosk, the diaries seemed disappointing—a somewhat banal and wholly blameless account of courtship, marriage, the birth of children, illnesses, deaths, tours in Switzerland, Italy and Norway, the unchanging routine of a Victorian factory and home.

But skilled editorial work, allied to the new publishing techniques of interlinear insertion and deformative cryptography, soon produced a very different picture.

From beneath the stiff Victorian frock coat there emerged a fascinating monster: Sadcake the transvestite (he used to dress up once a week in women's clothes, then visit working-class areas to press Lesbian attentions on barmaids, hoping—and in this he was seldom disappointed—to satisfy his masochistic tendencies by being beaten up); Sadcake the foot-fetishist, the egg-cup-fetishist, the homosexual sadist, even the cannibal (there is an account of his cooking and eating an Irish housemaid which has a curiously modern ring): this apparent pillar of Victorian society was in fact a psychopathic all-rounder who, if he suddenly appeared today among the feeble and degenerate modern sex-maniacs in the park which bears his name would put them to panic-stricken flight.

That this book will be a best-seller goes without saying. But Viper and Bugloss are not a firm to rest on their laurels. They believe, and rightly, that the chimneys of many a demolished Victorian mansion will yet yield treasures of scholarship and profit which will not only shed fresh light on Victorian hypocrisy but will make Sadcake's Diaries read like the journals of Samuel Smiles.

POP NOTES————————————————
by JIM DROOLBERG

THE Filthy Swine keep their place at the top of the charts this week with "Love is a Nail Bomb" (Provochord BD762), though the Spirochaetes, with "Love Crept Out of the Dustbin" (Kakophone S4263) are nudging them closely at No. 2, displacing the Big Slurry, whose "Broilerhouse Love" goes squelching down to No. 7.

A sensation is the rapid rise of an ecclesiastical group, the Bishop of Bevindon's Chocolate Meringue Narthex, to No. 3, with "Red Hot Prebendary." This reflects the current boom in pop religion. I wouldn't be surprised if one day this popular group really hit the cathedral roof.

Contrariwise, the slump in pop conservation is reflected by the fall of the Effluents' "Ecological Kisses" (No. 5 last week) to No. 11.

Among the oldies the Comas' "Boringhouse Zonk" BBBC1279) keeps steady at No. 8. The Staffordshire Reggae group, the Head Nits, are still crawling about at the bottom of the charts with just about everything you can think of falling on them from the upper levels.

WORDS OF POWER————————————————

A MAN who voluntarily looked after three children whose parents had disappeared is reported to have received a number of abusive anonymous letters. One accused him of helping "the population explosion"; another advised him to smother the children as soon as convenient.

The people who write such letters are, of course, unbalanced or even demented. But in this case the form the dementia takes is interesting and significant.

The continual propaganda against birth, carried on both officially and unofficially, with its easily memorised jargon and catch-phrases, may not actually have its roots in a hatred of living people. But it may well be helping to spread that hatred and even clothe it with reason and respectability.

PRISON HOLIDAYS

"Two Thousand Tourists to Camp Out at Wormwood Scrubs" says a headline. But all it means is that 2,000 young people visiting London this summer are to be accommodated on land near the prison.

There are some urgent questions to be asked about this. Why isn't more use being made of prisons themselves to accommodate tourists? By 1980, it has been estimated, 500 million tourists will be visiting London every summer. Not only will all existing prisons have to be used to accommodate them; special new tourists' prisons will have to be built.

But tourists might not like staying in prisons? Nonsense; they would soon get used to the idea. After all, the days when being a tourist was supposed to be a matter

133

of enjoying oneself are long past. Tourism is now a highly organised and highly profitable industry, indeed a branch of technology. It is its own justification and reward.

For the efficient processing and deployment of large masses of tourists in modern conditions, prison discipline is essential. Call the chief warders "mine host", name every cell after a character from Dickens and the prisoners will be perfectly happy.

JUSTICE AT LAST————————————

In a forthcoming production of "Othello" by Charles Marowitz, Iago as well as Othello is black, reports a gossip columnist. "Much of the text is original writing based on the works of Malcolm X, Eldridge Cleaver, Stokely Carmichael and James Baldwin. Marowitz has also reduced the number of characters to seven and the play now runs for only an hour."

Shakespeare's original intentions are thus fulfilled at last, and justice done after nearly 400 years.

Much of the mystery surrounding this dramatist's personality, as historians are now beginning to reveal arises from the fact that Shakespeare himself was black and was originally known at Stratford as "Will X."

Because of the prevalence of racial prejudice in his time (although Queen Elizabeth and James I were both black they persistently turned down proposals for a Race Relations Board), Shakespeare was obliged to adopt various disguises, even posing at times as Francis Bacon (who, though himself black, publicly advocated racist policies and the supply of cannon and arquebuses to South Africa).

Shakespeare's lifelong obsession with the problem of racial discrimination dominates not only "Othello" but all his work, and it is to be hoped that Mr Marowitz will produce all the rest of the plays on the lines he has now laid down.

A play like "King Lear", for instance, only becomes intelligible if it is realised that all the characters except Edmund, Goneril and Regan are black, and that Shakespeare based the character of Cordelia, the militant, outspoken social revolutionary, on that of Angela Davis.

THE NAKED ARCHITECT. By Vernon Brootes (Viper and Bugloss, £3·50).

Whatever your views on modern (or any other) architecture, you have probably always thought of the architect as a respectable, responsible professional man whose opinions on architectural matters at least are to be taken seriously.

Not any more. In this sensational book, based on his own experience as an amateur architect, on his research in natural history, ecology and animal behaviour, and on several other recently published books, Brootes tears the trappings of civilisation from this still respected figure and reveals the ravening beast beneath.

He shows convincingly that although the modern architect may *appear* to be seriously concerned with the design and construction of office blocks, concert halls, progressive cathedrals, barracks, municipal slaughterhouses and other buildings, he is really acting precisely as his remote ancestors, the skyscraper-building apes of Central Africa, acted in their steaming, primeval jungles.

The permanent frustrations of these forerunners of Man (or *Homo Faber*, in Brootes's brilliant phrase), whose skyscrapers, constructed of mud, reeds, excrement and wasps' nests chewed up, regurgitated and left to dry in the sun, invariably collapsed before they reached two stories, is echoed, Brootes shows, in the modern architect's secret satisfaction when one of his own buildings falls down or proves inadequate in other ways.

The modern architect, unlike his ape-ancestor, cannot vent his spite on his own buildings by destroying them himself. Instead he expresses his pent-up frustration, hatred and anger by designing the most repulsive structures possible, in the hope that other members of the tribe will violently attack them, if not physically, at least verbally.

(It is no accident, as Brootes shows, that as many as two per cent of the bomb-experts of the IRA Provisionals and other terrorist organisations have had some architectural training.)

Step by remorseless step, this astonishingly original book (already selected as Best Seller of the Month) builds up a parallel between human architect and ape architect of such sickening force and utter implausibility that many readers may well react by resolving to buy a tent and never again enter a building of any kind for the rest of their lives.

ROCK AND TOE————————————————

"WHAT has happened here is that we have stubbed our toe against the rock of national emotion," says Mr Charles Curran, the director-general of the BBC, speaking of the annoyance caused to many people by its recent series on the British Empire.

It is a significant remark, because it implies that national emotion, or patriotism as it might be called, is something quite outside the province of the BBC, something the BBC should regard as impartially and dispassionately as it would any other form of emotion, good or bad, while taking care to avoid stubbing its toe against it.

But since it is the *British* Broadcasting Corporation, a very important element in *British* life, shouldn't the BBC itself be imbued with that national emotion—as even a few years ago it certainly would have been?

A great many of the people who now work in the BBC, as in the other "media", are not even merely neutral about that national emotion; they are positively hostile to it; they are unquestioning internationalists who would like the rock of national emotion to be softened and eroded into nothingness, and will do their best to further that process.

In a world which is growing more violently nationalist every day, that is a very undesirable and dangerous state of affairs.

LITTLE PARADISE————————————————

APART from the barricades, says an article on "Free Derry," the part of Londonderry controlled by the IRA, "the area is surprisingly neat and tidy, and the standard of the new council housing, in Bogside particularly, would do credit to many English cities."

Crime is rare (the IRA's judicial system is simple but effective); water, electricity and sewage services are "more or less normal except when disrupted by the effects of rioting or explosions." Shops are still open, with regular supplies from outside, and although there is no public transport, there is a regular taxi service which takes people to the city centre and back for "nominal charges."

What, some people in England may say, are we waiting for? Why can't we have little paradises like this in our English cities—Free Edgbaston, Free Putney, Free Didsbury? With taxis available for practically nothing, who cares about the odd explosion?

What these foolish people have overlooked is that the people of "Free Derry" are having it both ways. Though they will not accept the State's police they will gladly accept its water, electricity and sewage services; though they can refuse admission to their territory to anyone they please, they are perfectly free to go anywhere they please themselves.

There is a special talent involved here, the talent for combining contrarieties; and it is doubtful whether the English are quite so good at it.

AGONISING————————————————————

A RECENT television programme called "Sob Sisters" dealt with the "agony column" and presented four women practitioners of the art. Many viewers must have wondered why our own famous Clare Howitzer, the Woman who Cares, was not among them.

The reason may be that the personal problems Clare Howitzer deals with and the advice she gives with such unfailing insight and compassion are often agonising in the true sense. They are no petty suburban dramas but the stuff of life itself.

As an example, take a letter she received only the other day:

"Dear Clare Howitzer—I have been married 22 years to a professional bore. He lives only for his work (he bored for Staffordshire last year and hopes to be picked for the England team at the Harringay global boring contests in July) and practices incessantly, starting in on some topic like plywood, central heating systems or

British Rail goods shed procedure as soon as he comes home in the evening.

"When I doze off (the other day I got a nasty bruise on my head when it fell forward into a dish of mashed potatoes) he gives me a poke with the special bore's umbrella he always carries, to get me awake and listening again.

"He has no friends apart from fellow-bores. He sometimes brings a few of them home, mainly out of vanity I think, so that he can show his skill by boring them into the ground. What shall I do ('Desperate', Soup Hales)."

Clare Howitzer's reply is a good illustration of the essential humanity which has brought her to the top of her profession:

"I can't help feeling, Desperate, that a little more love and understanding in the early days of your marriage would have helped. 'Sharing' is so important in marriage, you see. Couldn't you have tried to learn the finer points of boring yourself and perhaps turned the tables occasionally by boring your husband into the ground instead? In these days of 'Women's Lib' women are no longer content to leave the field of boredom to men alone.

"However, in your case, it is probably too late now. You have the choice of living in a perpetual semi-coma or of using some of the scientific antiboring aids now on the market.

"These range from electrified armchairs, magnetic gags and anti-boring chemical aerosols to new miracle adhesives which are tasteless in food but will gum up the bore's mouth immovably within a few seconds."

138

ART'S BEST FRIEND

"THE artist," says Lord Goodman, who has just retired from the chairmanship of the Arts Council, "is of course the most important man in any civilised society." This variant on Shelley's "poets are the unacknowledged legislators of the world" is just as dubious a proposition. It is also a dangerous one, particularly now.

If you make "the artist" a figure of supreme importance you encourage people who are in no sense artists to pretend that they are.

You are giving carte blanche (and who should know this better than a man who has been chairman of the Arts Council?) to every trickster, poseur and pretentious self-deceiver who claims the sacred name of artist, with all the reverence and licence that goes with it, even though the "art" he practises is that of climbing into a polythene bag, cutting up pieces of paper and sticking them together again, arranging metal tubes at random, dropping blocks of concrete off a scaffold or exhibiting a perfectly blank canvas.

To refuse to treat these activities with the admiration and reverence the "artists," with their supporting force of entrepreneurs and critics, demand is to earn the dreaded name of "Philistine."

It should be accepted as a title of honour. There are times (and this is pre-eminently one of them) when the Philistine, whether he knows it or not, is the defender of the genuine artist against the false.

VAGARIES OF FORTUNE

THE stock of public sympathy with the unfortunate is probably unlimited. But it can become temporarily exhausted. It can also be unfairly selective.

In what is now called "Bangladesh" the sufferings of the Bengali victims of Pakistani military rule called forth enormous volumes of public sympathy; and rightly so. Now it is the turn of the poor Biharis of East Bengal to suffer at the hands of the Bengalis—to be herded into frightful camps, to be starved, beaten and killed and have their women raped or abducted.

How much sympathy are they getting by comparison?

139

How much space do they get in the headlines? How many denunciations do we read of the callous indifference, or worse, of that popular favourite Sheikh Mujibur Rahman?

It is the misfortune of the Biharis not only to suffer but to suffer in the wrong place, at the wrong time; to have been, or appear to have been, on what was once the winning side but turned out, to the general satisfaction, justified or not, to be the losing side; and, largely innocent, to pay for other people's crimes.

AFFRONT

THE GPI Television Network, which had arranged to show an interview with Dr Spacely-Trellis, the go-ahead, socially aware Bishop of Bevindon, in its "religious period" next Sunday, has now cancelled it.

The reason given is that Dr Trellis, though he describes himself as a humanist, still retains in his thinking vestiges, even if only in a formal sense, of Christian doctrine and would therefore be out of key with other speakers in the series.

Sir Godfrey Fobster, chairman of GPI, said yesterday that if a Christian Bishop, however enlightened, was allowed to take part in the "religious period" people like Nevile Dreadberg, the atheist playwright, Sir William Goth-Jones, the atheist Vice-Chancellor of Stretchford University, Giselle Frabazon, the Castroite actress and model, Len Barmitage, the Leftist footballer and Gastriq Ali, the Marxist fun-revolutionary, who had already agreed to appear, would undoubtedly withdraw in protest.

"They would have all my sympathy," he added. "When we are trying to 'sell' religion in a packaging which will be attractive to the average man and woman in this secular day and age we must put first things first."

Meanwhile at Bevindon the indignant Bishop threatened firstly to sue Sir Godfrey for breach of contract and secondly to excommunicate him solemnly with electric bell, cassette and searchlight before the plastic high altar of Bevindon Cathedral.

140

VANDAL NOTES
by "SUPERGOTH"

How are the mighty fallen! Proud Bog Lane Wanderers, once among the undisputed titans of the Stretchford Vandals' League, and thrice holders of the Bruce Nethers Challenge Cup, have been struggling along this season at the very bottom of the table.

So far, with only six telephone kiosks wrecked, 17 ornamental shrubs uprooted, 45 garden gnomes destroyed and a beggarly four tombstones overturned, they have only managed to amass a miserable total of 74 points!

A feature of the season has been the ding-dong tussle for top place between an old-established side, Soup Hales Iconoclasts, and a highly promising new combination, Hokewell Destroyers, under their talented captain Len Attila, a veritable mine of unorthodox notions on the vandal scene.

As well as earning a high points bonus for a carefully mounted attack on the Newcastle-on-Stretch bus terminus, in which seven vehicles were put out of action and the canteen destroyed by an electrical flashover, Len's lads have also dug up all the bowling-greens in Sadcake Park and filled up a section of the boating-lake with rusting old juke-boxes (197 points in all).

The "Connies," now trailing behind with 180 pts, had better look to their laurels!

Finally a word of warning about bad behaviour by the fans, some of whom are starting to take their enthusiasm to the point of actually practising vandalism on the vandals themselves!

Lampton Huns, one of the greatest sides in the game, have had several members of their first team partially destroyed this season. I can only say that this sort of thing, if persisted in, will be a creeping menace which can bring nothing but disrepute to the sport we love so much.

WAKE UP THERE!————————————————

THE Commission on Industrial Relations has made a 30-second colour film which urges railwaymen to vote in a pay ballot if it is ordered by the Appeal Court.

The film, it is reported, shows a railwayman arriving home to find a ballot paper on his doormat. Accompanied by a simple commentary, he reads the instructions, marks his vote and posts it.

Is that really all? If so, what a glorious opportunity has been wantonly lost! Surely the film should mingle simple information with entertainment, and at the same time show something of the values and ideals of our society?

The railwayman should be met at the door of his well-furnished, centrally-heated home by a beautiful, blonde, mini-skirted girl (or several perhaps), seductively waving the ballot paper and caressing him as he smilingly marks his vote. If some small children could be shown in the background gorging themselves on chocolate bars and shouting stridently for more, with a friendly collie-dog at their side, so much the better.

As the good and happy railwayman goes out to post his ballot paper the film turns into a dream sequence, in which, accompanied by nude houris, he passes through scenes of exotic luxury, drives a powerful car through the desert, shoots a sinister master-spy, survives a devastating explosion, then posts his paper, turns to face the audience with a cheerful smile and thumbs-up gesture and fades out.

Alternatively, a wicked railwayman could be shown arriving at his miserable, squalid and womanless home, snatching the ballot form angrily from his rat-gnawed doormat and sneeringly tearing it into a thousand pieces, then, overcome by remorse and despair, putting his head in the gas-oven.

There is a choice of method here. I offer both suggestions to the Commission on Industrial Relations entirely free of charge.

NO TIME TO LOSE

AN American space-vehicle now travelling (or meant to travel) beyond the Solar System, and due to reach the nearest star in about 80,000 years, contains a plaque with a drawing of a naked man and woman for the information of any extra-terrestrial beings who may be about.

The designers of the plaque have received many protests on various grounds, e.g. that the figures are obscene; that they are racialist because they are white; that the woman is shown as smaller than the man and therefore inferior.

It is true that the people concerned with projecting objects into space are mostly, if not exclusively, white and male; it is also true that women, on the average, are smaller than men. But what does all that matter? Equality is all.

The fascist, racialist, sex-discriminatory space-vehicle cannot now be recalled. But another vehicle, carrying an egalitarian, multi-racial plaque, should be sent off after it as soon as possible, with an extra boost to enable it to overtake the first one and get to Alpha Centauri before it.

The male and female figures should be fully clothed and of the same size (or perhaps the woman should be larger); to avoid over-crowding the plaque with figures representing all conceivable races, the faces of the two figures should be striped or in chequered patterns.

The plaque should also carry a Government health warning.

TERROR

"THE sickness of our epoch requires not a psychiatrist but a bloody surgeon; not an individual one with an FRCS and a dark suit but a collective surgeon, millions of people probably dressed in old jeans and overalls with millions of scalpels" (from a broadcast talk reproduced in the *Listener*).

"I wants to make your flesh creep," said Dickens's Fat Boy. Whether the Marxist author of this passage had this end in mind or not, there is no mistaking his own pleasure at the image he has conjured up, his gloating relish at the idea of all those millions of workers taking over the human hospital, shoving aside the bourgeois doctors and getting down to business with their scalpels.

Why scalpels, anyhow? Why not bayonets and automatic weapons? Isn't the surgical treatment indicated by these mass-specialists wholesale massacre; the hospital a gigantic burial-pit?

It is as well to understand the true meaning of what we are saying and (a bit of bourgeois psychology) why we take such pleasure in it. How does that dream of millions of assassins and their victims differ (except for its Marxist label) from the dreams of the great mass-murderers of history?

PHENOMENON ————————————————————

THE Spaniards know now, if they did not know before, that when Scotsmen get drunk they really *do* get drunk: particularly if they are the kind of small, strong, fierce Glaswegian Scotsmen known in their own city as "keelies" and by German civilians a while back as "poison dwarfs."

I have probably mentioned before a phenomenon others will have noticed: that when one comes across a drunken man in a London street or on a bus, particularly in the daytime, he turns out, three times out of four, to be a Scotsman.

I saw a perfect example not long ago in the West End. He was a tiny man—not more than five feet tall—and he was staggering along, beside himself with rage and emitting a stream of fantastically obscene language, mostly about the sexual and other shortcomings of the English.

The English, of course, took no notice whatever. And even when the blaspheming midget staggered into an alley-way and fell flat on his face in a pile of rubbish, not a single man took the trouble to go and stamp on him.

LITURGICAL NOTE————————————

THE Anglican Liturgical Commission is using a computer to analyse and classify hundreds of criticisms and suggestions as part of its preparatory work for the revision of the Church of England Prayer Book. Meanwhile "experimental" services are in use.

But in the diocese of Bevindon Dr Spacely-Trellis, the go-ahead, computer-conscious bishop, has already introduced computerised services which, as he says, are "truly experimental in a radical, relevant and meaningful sense."

In these each member of the congregation can operate a panel which feeds a central computer with suggestions and modifications which are incorporated in the service as it is actually proceeding. Not only are no two services alike, but the participants have no idea of what any particular service will turn out to be.

"We have got to move away," says Dr Trellis, "from the eternity-orientated and basically Fascist liturgies of the past to forward-looking, socially aware liturgies which by encapsulating the principle of continual change will supply a democratic confrontation, a structural breakthrough, an open-ended dialogue, a sense of community for ordinary men and women in the context of our secular day and age."

ATROCITY STORY————————————

"PERHAPS the most appalling horror since the Nazi extermination camps. World opinion stands aghast at the moral perfidy of this stark betrayal of every principle which has raised Man from the apes."

Mr Arthur Grudge, Labour MP for Stretchford North, was speaking at an emergency meeting in his constituency on the Government's proposal to withdraw free school milk for children over seven.

The Tory Government, he said, had already set the Brand of Cain on the brows of children who were known to their fellows to be getting school meals free. If any of these survived their shame to the age of seven they were now fated to join the Lost Generation, doomed either to pay for their own milk or enter adult life suffering from milk-deprivation and all its attendant ills, from falling hair to acute schizophrenia.

Mr Grudge urged an appeal to the United Nations (Human Rights Division). The only solution, he said, was a massive international airlift to bring milk to the affected areas. If the Tories tried to interfere they would be judged guilty at the Bar of World Opinion and sanctions could be applied.

Sanctions, if mandatory and adequately provided with milk teeth, would soon begin to bite, he droned on, as night fell, his sparse audience staggered out and a care-taker threw a dustsheet over him.

A HERO OF OUR TIME————————————

MR BRUCE PLINTH, 42, of Nerdley, came first of 752 competitors to win the title of Non-Smoker of the Year awarded annually by the Non-smoking and Confectionery Division of the Nadirco Consortium.

In the finals this year the 20 finalists were required to sit without smoking for three hours, points being awarded for steadiness, blankness of gaze and resourcefulness in such non-smoking activities as holding newspapers upside down, humming tunelessly, examining the finger-nails, raising and lowering the eyebrows and staring out of the window.

Mr Plinth, a no-smoking notice designer in a local factory, is married with two children and lives in a semi-detached one-garaged house in Cloister Gardens, Nerdley. He is a keen member of his Local Boring Circle. Another of his hobbies, according to "Who's Who in Non-Smoking," is breaking ashtrays.

ALL VERY CONFUSING————————————

THE sad case of Mr Fattacharya, a Nerdley immigrant, is a cause of serious heart-burning among truly progressive people in the Midlands. It will be remembered that Mr Fattacharya was assaulted in the street. Nobody has yet been punished for this vicious piece of racialism.

But why was Mr Fattacharya assaulted? It is claimed that he was keeping his daughter virtually a prisoner because she wished to go to inter-racial gatherings. In the eyes of "Women's Lib" this makes him a "male chauvinist." In the eyes of the race relations industry it makes him a racialist, even though he himself has suffered from racialism.

Further, the police have suggested that Mr Fattacharya, a native of East Bengal, was assaulted by West Bengalis, one of whom is said to be his own cousin.

"The case is complicated," a well-known progressive thinker frankly admitted. "When you bring relations into race relations you hardly know where you are. And when you add all the other difficulties it's like attacking a male chauvinist and discovering he is undergoing a change of sex. How much simpler it is in Ulster, where all the right is so plainly on one side!"

ANNALS OF DEMOLITION————————————

AT Bradford, it is reported, a stone-built two-storey house 150 years old was reduced to rubble in five hours by a team of 15 Karate experts, using only their bare feet, hands and heads.

There is, of course, an old tradition of manual, pedal, cranial or non-mechanical demolition in the neighbourhood. Sixty or seventy years ago it was still not uncommon for workers in the Northowram district to demolish in this way the houses of people who had offended them. Such "daft" foreign methods as Karate being yet unheard of, the houses were simply kicked down with the traditional iron-tipped boots, or "boggardshoon," so much dreaded by rent-collectors, sherry-drinkers and other despised minorities.

The notorious West Riding Vendetta system was still in full swing in those days and anyone whose house was thus demolished was obliged by custom to demolish all the houses of the demolishers on pain of total ostracism. Whole villages were thus gradually razed to the ground (see, *passim*, the Glasscock Committee's Official Report on Housing Shortages and Nomadism in the West Riding of Yorkshire, 1902).

HAGGARD'S JOURNAL————————————

JUNE 1, 1772: Rain. An American colonist named Franklin reported to have been blown up whilst flying a kite in a thunderstorm in order to study the effects of the Electric Fluid. Ate a capon for dinner but it was bad, so I gave the remains to my wife who presently turned green and was conveyed to her chamber insensible.

June 2, 1772: Thunder and lightning. Amos Hornblower put in the stocks for stealg. an egg. Whilst visitg. Soup Hales in a.m. in order to tear down some cottages, a one-legged person bumped into me and upon my horse-whippg. him complained in the French tongue, whereupon I gave him an extra half-dozen blows for being a canting foreigner. Spent p.m. jumping up and down in front of Amos Hornblower in the stocks, puttg. my fingers to my nose and suchlike merry japes.

Ate a pease pddg. for dinner but it was bad, so I sent it to Amos Hornblower. I then called for the cook and dismissed him by the simple expedient of discharging my fowling-piece at him as he entered the room.

June 3, 1772: Floods. Amos Hornblower removed to the Spital insensible. Grunge, my butler, left to hire a new cook. Drank a bott. of port for breakfast and three more for dinner. Supped upon a quart of Madeira and slept under the table.

June 4, 1772: Rain. Josh. Bindweed d. from Griping of the Guts. Drank a bott. of Canary for breakfast but Grunge informed me he had hired a cook and a sump-tuous meal appeared for dinner. As I was eating Grunge informed me that the new cook was a one-legged French-man lately arrived in Soup Hales, whereupon, peering closely into the pie, I percvd. small slivers of glass floatg. in the gravy. ITEM: To emetics £0 0s 0½d.

VISITING my friend Valerie Prittcliffe, the physiothera-
pist, the other day, I found her in her bed-sitter leafing
through an album of photographs of the Black Power
heroine Angela Davis, occasionally sighing in a whale-
like way (as usual, she had a heavy headcold through
too much demonstrating in bad weather).

"Isn't she wonderful?" Valerie breathed. "One unknown black girl, all on her own against the whole might
of the American military-industrial amplex, or whatever
they call it! One victim of oppression, one Soledad
Sister, proving to the whole world that there is no justice
in America and that nobody who dares to dissent can get a
fair trial under the capitalist system!"

I said that on the contrary it seemed to me that Miss
Davis had had an extremely fair trial. After all, she had
been acquitted and released. She had celebrated this with
a champagne party attended by most of the jurors, and
had now been invited by James Baldwin, the black
novelist, to spend a holiday at his oppressed, dissenting
home in France. She didn't seem to be doing too badly.

Valerie laughed scornfully. "You'll never understand,
will you? Can't you see that by not imprisoning her the
Establishment has committed an act of social violence
against her and all the other countless millions it has not
imprisoned either?"

I said I still couldn't see it. But Valerie had already
sunk into a brooding reverie. "I wish I had a Soledad
Sister of my own," she muttered. "And a Soledad
Auntie. And a Soledad Uncle. . . ."

"Let me be your Soledad Father," I said, as I got up
and moved to the door, dodging a badly aimed plaster
bust of Sean Mac Stiofain which missed me and smashed
to pieces on the wall.

COUNTRY landowner requires Second Hermit for new, enlarged grotto in remote part of park. Duties include taking sole charge in absence of Chief Hermit during holiday periods (4 weeks per annum), assuming picturesque, wild-eyed attitudes, etc. Fully centrally-heated cell; deep-freeze for wild berries; electric scourging machine; colour television. Box 473.

Landowner has vacancies for Handyman-Ecologist and Footman-Computer Programmer on his Salop estate, to work at erecting ecospherical dome under supervision of environmental butler. Own quarters. Ample pollution. Good pay for right men. Box 475.

North Country Landowner, mad wife, illegitimate daughter, orphaned governess, requires Assistant Housekeeper to help with same. Full domestic staff kept. Experienced middle-aged woman, used to mysterious, doom-laden atmosphere, preferred. Box 476.

Millionaire with own small race relations factory (non-profit making) on his Midland estate requires Racial Discrimination Tester with some experience in the field. Full range of West Indian, Pakistani, etc., disguises supplied for testing prejudices at bus-stops, shops, (non-alcoholic) bars, etc. Live-in, Suns. Free. Box 477.

AMONG THE NEW FILMS————————————

BOTH the Environment and Ancient Egypt, as is only natural and right, figure largely in the latest offering from Piledriver Films, "Wittgenstein and the Vampire Polluters from Outer Space," directed in glamorous Terrorcolour by that master of horror and suspense, Brian Hohenzollern.

Once again the part of the mad, banana-guzzling, domino-playing Cambridge philosopher is played by Bruce Braganza, while Kay Wittelsbach plays Brenda, his slinky, blonde, violet-eyed girl friend and assistant.

This time the pair come up against a villainous gang of vampire-men from Uranus directed by remote telepathic control from the mummy of Pharaoh Blothmes III (Ken Capet) which has been stolen from the British Museum by a villainous Egyptologist, Sir Ernest Gantrobus (Stan Bourbon Parma).

Government scientists are worried by an apparently irresistible flood of radioactive slurry which has engulfed the whole of Wales and is pouring slowly over the Midlands, causing total devastation and an alarming rise in food prices. How Wittgenstein and Brenda trace the mischief to its source forms a breath-taking story with a hair-raising running battle among the dizzy rooftops of Cambridge as thumb-gripping climax.

Music by that reliable team Ted Habsburg and Bing Karageorgevitch. Special effects by Norman Romanoff. Fashion research by Shirley Porphyrogenitus and Mary Lou Cantacuzene.

FURTHER PROGRESS————————————

A NEW booklet by Dr Heinz Kiosk and Dr Melisande Fischbein ,called "Sex for Vertigo Sufferers" (Norm and Graph, 75p) is a welcome addition to their series of sex manuals, which already includes "Sex for Rheumatics," "Sex for Gastric Ulcer Sufferers," "Sex and Fibrositis," "Sex for Nonagenarian Alcoholics" and many more.

Sufferers from vertigo have hitherto felt themselves handicapped when it comes to love-making. Not only have they had to put up with the fear of ridicule, but also with the danger of falling into the fire or out of the window.

Drs Kiosk and Fischbein suggest a few simple methods —the use of a dark, airless cellar, for instance—by which these difficulties can be overcome and vertigo sufferers take their place in what the authors call "the omnisexual revolution" by which, ideally, the whole population of the world, liberated at last from outmoded taboos, will be engaged in non-stop sexual intercourse throughout their lives, and even beyond.

NATURE DIARY————————————
by "REDSHANK"

EVEN lifelong students of weather lore in our part of the country are shaking their grey heads over the present unseasonable weather. Many of them put it down to a plague of ecologists. Certainly I have never known so

many of these migratory, bat-like creatures to nest in our
neighbourhood in any previous summer.

"Stands to reason," Old George the gamekeeper—a
positive hive of weather lore—told me yesterday in the
Three Tuns. Nursing our pints of brown we peered
intently through the bottle-glass windows at the heavy
grey sky, occasionally shifting our position as coat-tails
or leggings began smouldering through too close prox-
imity to the crackling log fire.

"Stands to reason," he went on, knocking out his pipe on
the chimneypiece and his head on one of the massive oak
beams which once formed part of ancient Mouldrewood
Forest, a Royal Chase beloved of King John which later
did yeoman service in providing timber for the Wooden
Walls of Old England to the confusion of her foes.

"Stands to reason." old George continued. Gulping our
ale, we went on peering doubtfully through windows
against which outsize lumps of hail were now rattling
senselessly as the sky darkened and—a most unusual
sight in our part of the country—a new moon, accompanied by a few unidentifiable stars, appeared through a
rift in the clouds quite close to the sun.

"Stands to reason," the old gamekeeper added. But
as he had obviously forgotten what he was going to say,
if anything, I collected my galoshes and umbrella and
went out.

But there is an old saying, still current where countrymen foregather on rainy days in gunroom or bingo hall:

> *When ecologists nest in elm or ash*
> *Mind ee do wear thy mackintosh;*
> *But when they nest in beech or oak*
> *Be sure to order extra coke.*

NOBODY can leave anything alone any more. The Church of England, as troublesome a fidget as anyone, forever itching for unnecessary change, is considering altering or abolishing the right of land-owners and others to present clergymen to Church of England livings.

This is now thought to be inequitable and inefficient, as though those had not become terms of praise in an age plagued by the lust for equality and efficiency at all costs. Canon William Fenton Morley, an opponent of the patronage system, instances the case of a friend of his "who was once offered a living in the bar of the Mitre Hotel in Oxford by a total stranger."

This stranger, I should think, was either an Australian con man trying out a new trick, or my father, who as Lord of the Manor of Simpleham had 47 livings in his gift.

At one time he used to take the matter very seriously indeed, interviewing scores of potential incumbents in the library and cross-examining trembling clerics on such vital matters as horsemanship, cricket averages, pheasant rearing and the Arian heresy.

But in his later years he became more easy-going, maintaining that provided the fellow could look you straight in the eye, did as he was told, was doctrinally sound and had no bolshie ideas, one incumbent was as good as the next.

When visiting me at Oxford he often slipped away to the Mitre Hotel and other places looking for suitable clergymen for the living of Aston Chaos, Abbot's Rodent, Weston Garfinkel or others in his gift which might have fallen vacant.

His judgment, as he grew older, was not always sound. Once, after a long session in the Mitre bar, he gave the living of Sutton St Globe to an unscrupulous person who was not even a clergyman at all, but who rose rapidly in the Church and is now a trendy, Left-wing bishop of the most appalling kind.

HOBBIES CORNER————————————————

A BARRICADE Correspondent writes: It was Leibnitz, I believe who said that Man is a barricade-building animal. His insight has been amply confirmed in Northern Ireland, where thousands of people of all persuasions or none are employed in putting up barricades, taking them down and putting them up again.

Once the barricade-building habit takes hold of you, it is very difficult to shake off. Medical science seems powerless to deal with the condition, which can be catching, Doctors who have treated severe cases in Belfast often find they get "hooked" themselves and are soon merrily building barricades in their own surgeries, to the neglect of their ordinary work.

The British Army itself has now taken up this fascinating hobby, craze or whatever you like to call it, though its barricades, reportedly made of barbed wire, show little originality or imagination.

The composer Scriabin, himself a keen barricade-fan (the small exquisitely proportioned mother-of-pearl barricade he built in 1908, in one of the corridors of the Midland Hotel in Manchester, is still talked of there) once said you could tell a great deal about people from the materials they use for building their barricades.

Certainly a barricade built of burned-out cars and overturned trams or buses suggests a very different class of barricade-builder from a barricade of grandfather clocks, barometers, Victorian chaises-longues in faded silk, harpsichords, stale confectionery or old-fashioned black-leaded kitchen-ranges.

Tomorrow: How to Build a Simple Barricade in Your Back Garden.

SOCIAL DIARY————————————————

DANCES and coming-out parties this month (writes "JELLIFER") include a dance on July 26th given by Lady Lestrange-Haggard, of Lampton Hall, Stretchford, for Lady Joan Belphegor, elder daughter of the Earl of Mountwarlock, of Mountwarlock Park, Leicestershire.

The dance promises to be a lavish affair, with the arrangements in the capable hands of Lord Mountwarlock's major domo, Phantomsby, one of the few practising werewolves left in the Midlands. Since it falls on the night of the full moon, Phantomsby is sure to be in his element.

The great vampire-infested ballroom at Mountwarlock, which has a chasm of unknown depth in the middle of the floor, will be in total darkness for the occasion, and a large marquee is to be erected in the park (close to the Deadly Upas Tree) so that the guests can see the chimerae, wyverns, gorgons and other fabulous creatures to advantage, and have their food amusingly snatched off their plates by the filthy claws of the famous Mount-warlock harpies.

This is one function I certainly don't intent to miss, even if it proves to be my last!

TALKING POINT————————————

THE man who owns one bathtap but no bath envies the man who has two bathtaps and no bath; and he in turn, envies the man who owns a bath but has no bathtaps— Ralph Waldo Emerson.

THINK ON————————————

IT is proposed to establish a Chair of Peace studies at Bradford University. The Professor appointed will be expected to "lead research, to direct teaching and to encourage the study of peace, not only among his own staff and students but wherever interest can be stimulated on a more general level."

The Vice-Chancellor of the University, Dr E. G. Edwards, says: "We propose to have an advisory council of eminent scholars in the field of peace and related subjects. . . . A precise definition of peace is not to be attempted. Indeed, one of the objectives of the Chair will be to broaden and deepen understanding of the word 'peace', which in different languages overlaps in different ways with other words and concepts."

If a precise definition of the word "waffle" were ever to be attempted (a paradox in itself), there would be some useful material here.

Is it yet one more sign of the transvaluation of all values, the turning upside down of all accepted ideas, that the first Chair of Peace in England should be established at Bradford, a city once famous for hard-headedness, forthrightness and Yorkshire commonsense?

155

THE writer of a letter to some radical organ or other I was reading the other day (unfortunately I have lost the cutting) gives the name of his house as 'Chez Guevara,"

It was inevitable, I suppose, that radical versions of names like" Dunromin" and "Bide-a-Wee" would eventually appear. A Leftist bungalow, neatly pebble-dashed, rises before the mind's eye.

Instead of a plastic windmill there is a plastic model of Lenin's mausoleum in the small front garden where only red flowers grow; even the garden gnomes have a look of Karl Marx; and the chiming bells at the door ring out the first bars of the "Internationale."

HOMILY

A SACRED ibis, it is reported, has been seen in North Staffordshire. And what more suitable place could there be for a visitation by the great white bird of Thoth, the Ancient Egyptian god of wisdom and learning, than a heath in Staffordshire, not far from haunted Cannock Chase itself?

Not in some State-scheduled beauty-spot, not in some carefully preserved "area of high amenity value," where the solemn-faced litter-warden patrols on tiptoe and officials babble of ecology amid self-conscious woods and streams, does the ibis-headed god appear.

Rather amid the grimy, litter-strewn fern of a Midland heath, by the housing estate's edge, among dumps of rusting cars and overgrown canals, where the hum of the plastic handbag factory is never silent and beyond the blighted trees rises the steam from mighty cooling-towers —it is there, in the old Mercian forest, now the polluted heart of England, that Thoth, with his reed-pen and palette and stiff, hieratic gestures, chooses to manifest himself for all who understand.

TREND

THE General Synod of the Church of England is considering whether "redundant" churches should be made available for use by other faiths. In the diocese of Wakefield, for instance, the Moslem community wants to acquire one redundant church for conversion into a mosque.

Dr Spacely-Trellis, the go-ahead Bishop of Bevindon, favours the idea with some reservations. Several redundant churches in his diocese have already been earmarked for use by Moslems, Hindus and Buddhists, and one for cannibal animists from the interior of New Guinea, should any immigrants of that denomination appear in the area.

As Dr Trellis has said, "it is only by initiating an open-ended ecumenical dialogue between those of different faiths that religion can be attractively packaged and sold to the average multi-racial man and woman in this secular day and age."

The Bishop's one stipulation is that all these churches, on conversion into temples of other faiths, must include a "family planning" clinic and vasectomy unit. This has led to what he calls a "temporary log-jam" in his open-ended discussions with Dr Habib Ziftikarullah, the Chief Imam of Bevindon, himself the father of 27 bonny children.

ONE of the few bits of good news lately is the decided rejection by the House of Commons of the proposal to allow its proceedings to be televised by the BBC.

Television is perhaps the most evil single invention of the last 150 years. Far from being a "window on the world" which "brings the truth to the people," as the cliché-mongers say, it is a distorting mirror which produces lies and half-truths wholesale, destroys the capacity to think and judge and sows envy and hatred everywhere.

Now almost all-pervading and all-corrupting as television is, it is essential that it shall be kept out of the one place which still incorporates, at least in theory, the central power of the State. If that is corrupted, turned into an empty show, all is corrupted and robbed of meaning.

Television must never be allowed to intrude into Parliament. But it is high time Parliament began to intrude into television, to examine it and expose it, to deal resolutely with this monstrous Thing which claims to be a law unto itself and to have an equal right, in the false name of truth and impartiality, to undermine as to sustain the State.

MYSTERY INTRUDER————————————————

KEITH EFFLUVIUM, 32, described as a freelance environmental consultant, of Klopstock Road, Newcastle-on-Stretch, was charged at Nerdley magistrates' court yesterday with loitering on enclosed premises, dishonestly handling machinery and assaulting the police. He asked for 753 similar offences to be taken into consideration.

Det. Sgt. J. Mackenzie, 36, of Nerdley Special Branch, said he was on a routine investigation of betting shops in Victoria Road when he heard a deafening noise proceeding from Elaine's Coiffeurama at the corner of Pike Street.

He found the accused operating a rotary, multi-spindle electrically-powered drill with which he had already bored a hole about 45 yards in depth in the middle of the hairdressing saloon. Some of the customers, mainly middle-aged housewives, were in a state of shock and one had her head stuck fast in her handbag.

Arrested, accused, whose breath smelled strongly of newsprint, said he was boring for natural gas in an effort to help the economy and bring prices down (laughter). He thought it was everyone's duty to help exploit the natural resources of this country wherever they might be found.

It took 10 policemen and 12 girl hairdressing assistants to get Effluvium into the police van, witness went on. Taken to the cells, he tried to bore a hole in the floor with his forefinger.

In evidence the accused said he had no regrets for what he had done. His imagination had been fired by accounts of natural gas drilling operations in the North Sea. He believed Nerdley was ripe for a bonanza which would make all previous bonanzas look like a vicarage tea-party.

Binding Effluvium over, Dr Ellis Goth-Jones, 65, the chairman, said that although he had every sympathy with efforts to give Nerdley its rightful place on the natural gas map of the world, people should not take the law into their own hands. He believed that selectivity in schools and the flood of printed filth were at the root of much of the trouble, but he did not think lowering the speed limit on motorways was the answer for what, whether we liked it or not, was a multi-racial society.

GLUT

BECAUSE of an enormous glut of eggs, that esteemed body the Eggs Authority has decided to take about 18 million eggs off the British market next week, to stabilise prices.

Some of the eggs taken off the market, it is said, may go to the World Food Programme, whatever that may be; others may be exported. Evidently the extremists on the Eggs Authority have been outvoted once again and their long-cherished plan to make an 18 million egg omelette overruled.

Part of the responsibility for the glut, by the way, rests with Seth Roentgen, Britain's greatest scientific farmer. Owing to a fault in computer-programming in the central control room, the production target for the Ohm Farm's Egg Division last week was set at 450 million eggs instead of 450,000.

A further error of the electronic system which force-feeds the broiler fowl with ovobenzethyltoluene hormone would have raised the figure to 45,000 million had not gnarled old Caleb Kafka, the head poultry-man, noticed it in time, averting an uncontrollable deluge of eggs which might have rolled over the whole of the Northern Hemisphere, melting the polar ice cap and even triggering off a nuclear holocaust.

UNFAIR

THIRTY miners, with their wives and families, have begun a month's free holiday in Russia as guests of the Central Committee of the Soviet Coal Miners' Union.

"The offer", says an official of the National Union of Mineworkers, "came after the successful end of the strike and the hardship the men suffered. It is a very kind gesture indeed and clearly linked to the strike, but I do not think this should be played up."

Perhaps not. But it does seem unfair that these miners should be the only people to get free holidays in the Soviet Union when there are thousands of other people in this country who have, consciously or unconsciously, directly or indirectly, benefited the Soviet Union just as much, and in many cases far more.

When are the Russians going to offer free holidays to all those other trade unionists, in their various unions from the National Union of Students to the Amalgamated Holeborers' Union; all those journalists, broadcasters and other people in the "media"; all those professional and amateur demonstrators and propagandists for seemingly idealistic and humane causes; and all those fools and dupes, in every walk of life, who absorb their propaganda like the air they breathe?

Most of these people may not realise, any more than the miners, that they are serving the interests of the Soviet Union, if only in the negative sense of weakening their own country and making it more helpless and in-defensible.

But they are doing a great job. Surely they deserve a break?

UNSURPASSED

ONCE again the annual Nadir Cup for the most repellent motorway service area has been won by Nerdley Forest North, the much-loved halting place on the M69, on the edge of the Stretchford Conurbation.

Its wind-blown, rubbish-strewn patios, ingeniously designed to create miniature cyclones of litter in the right climatic conditions; its inefficient petrol pumps, manned by bearded louts and young women specially chosen for their insolence and sluttishness; its awkwardly placed car-parks with their unusual water-retaining qualities; all these features place it well ahead of all competitors.

But the pride of the place is the Nadirama Catering Complex, with its interesting lavatories, its bookstall crammed with pornographic works, its Olde Midlande Souvenir Shoppe and, best of all, its Caleb Sadcake Hanging Gardens of Babylon Restaurama, where elderly women of ferocious aspect, dressed in soiled overalls and gymshoes, dispense flabby "halibut sections" and rock-hard "Danish pastries" to their terrified customers, many of whom are State-registered masochists.

From the western windows of this paradise you may see (after clearing the condensation with your sleeve) the distant towerblocks of the Queen City of the Midlands, and fall, perhaps, into a pleasurable trance, then wake to panic, indigestion and the stupendous roar of musak suddenly bursting free for a moment from its automatic controls.

"LOCAL police are investigating the disappearance of two gnomes from a Bradfield home. . . . They have red caps, blue jackets, green trousers, black boots and are about 2ft 6in tall. A police spokesman said afterwards: "I don't think they have names but they are not liable to answer if they have," (*Berkshire Mercury*).

They are evidently an inferior type of gnome, unapproved by the British Gnome Authority, which sets rigid standards for quality and reliability.

A spokesman for the Authority said yesterday that the all-purpose gnomes now being produced could not only answer to their names but were being used increasingly as television verbalisers, in "man in the street" television interviews, as demonstrators and pickets and even as Members of Parliament.

"I am myself a gnome," he added after a pause. "My name, if it is of any interest to you, is Kevin Plantagenet. But I am known in some circles as' Jock' or 'the Major' ".

MOVE OVER, DAD————————————————

THE decision that bishops of the Church of England should retire compulsorily at the age of 70 has the support of Dr Spacely-Trellis, the go-ahead Bishop of Bevindon, who still has some years to go.

But he has another even more-far-reaching proposal, which he outlined in a sermon not long ago: that God has served his time and should be compulsarily retired in the near future.

"This is above all an age for Youth", Dr Trellis said, "and never has Youth been so clear-eyed, so compassionate and so committed as it is today.

"Progressive theologians have felt for some time that the present God lacks social awareness; he has failed to give a clear lead, for instance, on the problem of racialism. When has he stood up and been counted with the rest of us on the question of South Africa or Portugal?

"He is out of touch with current trends. His attitudes on such vital matters as housing, censorship, the sexual revolution, drug addiction, the environment and, above all, the Women's Liberation Movement have been unsatisfactory, to say the least.

"Altogether he gives the impression that he is far too pre-occupied with outmoded eternal matters—often tinged with elitism—which mean little or nothing to the average man and woman of today.

"It is high time he retired and made way for a younger man."

DANGER

THERE are few causes more dear to me, as readers of this column know—some are regularly bored into the ground by it, others irritated into climbing the wall—than the preservation and propagation of the Welsh language.

I would like every inhabitant of Wales to speak this ancient, beautiful and expressive language. I would even have it taught in English schools, because the matter of Wales is part of the matter of Britain and we cannot fully understand ourselves without it.

So I am far from being opposed to the aims of the Welsh Language Society. Their methods are quite another thing. When they begin brawling and waving banners saying "To Hell With the English" and generally appearing to assimilate themselves into the modish international Leftist mob, thus unconsciously serving its profoundly un-Welsh purposes, I no longer view them with a benevolent eye, but with a squint of suspicion.

They may succeed in restoring the Welsh language throughout Wales. But they should think very carefully whether they may not thereby leave the Welsh with nothing to express in that language except the boring grunts and tedious natterings of international dullness, rancour and envy.

PROBLEM CORNER
by CLARE HOWITZER

DEAR CLARE HOWITZER—I am a girl traffic warden, 32 years of age, I weigh just over 18 stone, have a treble chin and thick black eyebrows and although I have a slight squint in both eyes, I am considered quite attractive.

163

Now I have fallen desperately in love with a motorist, a middle-aged man (I think he is a traveller in confectionery) who keeps parking his van, which has a large purple plastic replica of a wine gum on top, on a double yellow line in my "manor." When I put a parking ticket under his wind-screen wiper I cannot resist writing "I love you" on it and hiding behind a large tree nearby.

I watch him take the ticket, muttering oaths to himself in a way that makes my heart race, but so far I have not been able to summon enough courage to reveal myself and declare my love in person.

What ought I to do? ("Lovelorn," Basingstoke).

CLARE HOWITZER replies: Faint heart never won confectionery traveller, as the old saying has it. You do not say what this man is like. But middle-aged confectionery travellers, in my experience, pride themselves on their sense of chivalry.

Next time you slap a parking ticket on his windscreen, pretend you have got your hand stuck under the windscreen wiper. When he appears he will either tenderly release your hand, gazing deeply into your eyes, thus "breaking the ice," or will jump into his van and drive off, running over you. Either way you will be released from your present state of agonising uncertainty.

BOOM————————————————————

A BIG oil field has been discovered 100 miles north-east of the Shetlands, capable of producing 15 million metric tons a year. A pipeline is to be laid to the Shetlands, where the oil companies are already setting up their bases and complex installations.

It may seem perverse not to join in the cheering at this "boost to the economy." Yet there are probably many more people than the oilmen and the economists suspect who, far from cheering, will simply give a groan of helpless anguish. Of these strange people I am one.

Why should we be glad to know that those remote, austere and beautiful northern islands are going to be transformed? Why should we be glad at the imminent destruction of a "way of life" in many ways infinitely superior to our own; a life still lived by a hardy, brave, loyal and neighbourly people, scarcely touched as yet by our urban philosophy of cleverness and greed?

IMAGINING THINGS————————————

DID I really overhear a woman behind me on a bus saying to her friend: "For our holiday this summer we've taken a lovely old farmhouse in the Ardoyne"?

NATURE DIARY————————————
by "REDSHANK"

SCIENTISTS, we are told, have discovered that thousands of rabbits and mice, as if bored with the slow pace of life in the country, have taken to building their homes alongside motorways and major roads.

Scientists or no scientists, we countrymen have noticed this phenomenon for some time past. Nor is it just rabbits and mice that are involved in this migration. Only the other day, ensconced with my binoculars in Blumber's Oak, I observed no fewer than four badgers, two stoats, six hares and several other unidentifiable creatures of the wild sitting in the central reservation of the nearby M72, gaping at the speeding traffic, while a pair of dotterel flew overhead, evidently looking for a place to build a belated nest.

Old Jack Waspthwaite, the retired gamekeeper and a veritable inferno of country lore, who claims to understand the language of animals, tells me that last Sunday, as he walked through Four Mile Bottom, he came on a group of young rabbits lounging about, showing their teeth in an unpleasant snarl and occasionally digging up patches of ground or savaging wild flowers in an aimless way.

"This place is dead, mate," one of these animal layabouts told him. "No wonder we take to vandalism and drugs. It's the older generation I blame. What have they done for us? What amusement facilities do they provide for Youth in a world which is disorientated under the shadow of the nuclear bomb and the population explosion, and that?

"I'll tell you Dad. Nothing. Not a bleeding sausage. No wonder we're dead bored and our energies run into

165

antisocial channels. If we could only get out of this dump and onto a decent motorway you wouldn't see our feet for dust!"

As Old Jack, shaking his head sadly, turned to go, there was a squealing chorus of rage and a large clod of earth, evidently aimed by an expert paw, landed painfully on the back of his neck.

JARGON CORNER————————————————

THE development of Maplin Sands, says Mr Eldon Griffiths, Under-Secretary of the Environment Department, will be "the first environmental airport in the world."

This is the most beautiful example of the usage of the jargon-word "environmental" I have yet come across.

The word's original meaning, if any, must have been "pertaining to the environment." It has now come to mean something like "planned to fit in with the surroundings," or even simply "beautiful."

The word has a great obfuscatory future. For it can be used (and will be) by any public man to make the total obliteration of a place, or even a whole region, and the expulsion of its inhabitants for the sake of technological progress appear not as the outrage it obviously is, but as a boon and blessing to mankind.

ALL IS WELL————————————————

IRELAND, North and South, may collapse in total chaos; in England the Communists may soon reach their objective of a General Strike; racial riots may be beginning; the forces of Soviet Russia, at sea, on land and in the air, may have unchallengeable preponderance over the forces of the West; and the British Navy may soon be reduced to one gunboat for fishery protection in Icelandic waters.

Don't worry. All is well. The British Government, at last responding to what one authority calls "a terrific upsurge of interest," has set up an Advisory Committee on Pop Festivals. And (an added reassurance) Lord

Harlech himself, once a mere British Ambassador in Washington but now an eminent promoter of these festivals, is to serve on the committee.

Sleep sound tonight.

A NEW INDUSTRY————————————

THERE are spokesmen (self-appointed or otherwise) of the Church of England who seem determined to drag that Church down to a level so far beneath contempt that there is simply no word to describe it.

Of the setting-up by the people who call themselves the "Family Planning Association," of a "contraceptive and sex information stall" at a "pop festival" at Reading, a local Anglican curate says he was "favourably impressed."

He also says that he and other Anglican clergy were "deeply annoyed" by suggestions that it was encouraging promiscuity.

Whether it was encouraging "promiscuity" or not (and many people who talk about these matters seem uncertain of the true meaning of the word), that is not the main ground for objecting to it.

What is called (by this time surely with unnecessary coyness) "family planning" is now big business. It is a huge, continually expanding industry employing countless numbers of research workers, salesmen and propagandists, even though some of the latter may be unpaid.

Many of these people, no doubt, sincerely believe that what they are doing is in the national interest, even in the interest of all mankind. They cannot see that what they are serving is a branch of industry—the systematic application of commercial technology to the hitherto scarcely exploited field of sexual love.

As such it is essentially inhuman and amoral. It substitutes statistics, cold calculation and ultimately scientific control for the natural relation—however brief and animal—of one human being with another. And even if it were absolutely certain (as it is not and never can be) that its "population policy" would save the world in some hypothetical future from destruction it would still be totally and profoundly wrong for living people now.

AT THE BUTTS———————————————

THERE are a few bright spots (writes "BLAZEAWAY")
to enliven the general dismal tale from the moors this
year. Grouse themselves have been in short supply,
though a party on Lord Burntalmond's moors in
Sutherland bagged 14,602 brace on the Glorious Twelfth
itself.

Landowners who have had the foresight to stock their
moors with other game as well as grouse have generally
had the last laugh. On one North Riding moor a record
bag of 2,470 brace of Left-wing students was secured,
as well as 662 brace of ecologists and 75 brace of social
scientists.

Once again this year Au Petit Coin Anthropophage,
the trendy West End restaurant which specialises in New
Guinea dishes, had student flambé (specially flown from
Yorkshire) on the menu on the evening of the Twelfth,
though few people seemed to be ordering it, preferring
no doubt to stick to more familiar delicacies.

BORING NOTES———————————————
by "NARCOLEPT"

PITY the poor British Boring Board of Control and its
hard-working president, Sir Herbert Trance! The
kerfuffle over who shall and who shall not compete in
this year's Global Boring Contests at Harringay is
threatening to turn one of the highlights of the boring

scene into an all-time shambles which will make the Second World War look like a vicarage tea-party!

It's no longer a question of introducing politics into the yawn game. It's a question of politics taking over our much-loved sport altogether!

There are the African countries which have threatened to boycott the contests if the Rhodesian multi-racial boring team is allowed to compete. There are the Arab countries who won't compete if the Israeli No. 1 seed, Shloime ben Chloroform, appears. And who can imagine a global boring battle without "Glorious Shloime," a yawnmaker of galactic ranking, arguably one of the greatest bores who ever lived?

There is a question-mark, too, over the appearance of Czechoslovakia's premier drowse-maestro, Antonin Bvorak. It seems he's not altogether in favour with the present rulers of the country which has given us so many world-ranking coma merchants of recent years.

Then there is the demand from the Emerald Isle that both the Official and Provisional IRA shall be represented. Admittedly the Irish, who have lagged behind so long in the boring field, are now beginning to catch up at last. But there are limits! Most aficionados of the yawn game will agree with me, I imagine, that explosions and boredom simply do not go together.

And now, to cap everything, the "Women's Lib" movement are threatening to picket the stadium because of alleged discrimination against women bores! If I were the Powers that Be, I'd almost be inclined to welcome them inside to see what they could do against the pick of the world's masculine yawnmakers!

Judging from recent form the Fair Sex might give some of us quite a surprise!

A NEW OPENING

SEVERAL industrial relations experts have asked me why, at a time when it is important to find acceptable alternative work for redundant dockers, no dockers have yet been invited to work on this column.

In many ways the dockers would certainly be well suited here. For one thing they are admirably resistant to change; indeed as a body they form one of the few truly conservative enclaves which remain in progress-frenzied England.

Did not one of their imprisoned leaders say only the other day (perhaps I have not got his words exactly right, but no matter): "As things have been, so shall they remain: as it is, as it was, as it shall be, till Judgment Day"?

We could certainly do with an infusion of new blood in the small columnar docks, which are increasingly manned, I am told, by enfeebled old men who can scarcely operate the wooden cranes and hoists used for unloading ships, let alone carry the heavy dressed stone blocks, copper ingots and loads of exotic words and semi-precious stones which are our main imports from abroad.

But conservative as the dockers are, are they conservative enough? In return for security and happiness, they would have to accept a hierarchical, paternalist society in which combinations of working men (or unions, as I believe they call them) are absolutely forbidden. They would also have to accept the fact that the loads they would be handling are mainly intended for the repair and beautifying of the columnar churches.

How far the atheistic communism of the Marxist Sect has spread among them I cannot say; but its perverse tenets could not long survive exposure to the mellow, healing light of an immemorially pious world.

DOUBLE TROUBLE————————————

THE sad-faced Indians who are now arriving from Uganda are fugitives from a savage, stupid and odious tyranny. No one who is human, surely, can help feeling intensely sorry for them. Had they arrived here 20 years ago, how gladly and unreservedly we might have welcomed them to a still mainly homogeneous country which (as we are continually told) has always been a haven for the exiled and persecuted of the earth.

But much has happened in the last 20 years. The thoughtlessness or folly (or it may be, something worse) of successive governments has brought to this country hundreds of thousands of coloured immigrants, African and Indian, who for the most part can never be assimilated with the native population.

These people are not fugitives, driven from their native land by threats and ill-treatment. They are voluntary immigrants, who came in the first place in search of better work and better wages.

It is the misfortune of the Indians from Uganda, who, heaven knows, already have misfortunes enough, to appear to many English people as just one more ingredient, however small, in the hell's brew of racial trouble which changing governments and an unchanging Civil Service have so obligingly concocted for us and for the immigrants themselves.

UNDERPRIVILEGED

DR GORDON BURBIDGE, a British astronomer now working in California, has attacked what he calls the "parochial scene of British astronomy," and its trend of "mediocrity."

British astronomers are smarting at these humiliating remarks. Yesterday I called on one typical astronomer I know to find him sobbing quietly to himself in the dingy, rat-infested observatory in Salford, formerly a derelict henhouse, where he works.

His hands shook uncontrollably as he fiddled with the worn brass screws of his home-made cardboard telescope, bravely trying to focus it on some distant galaxy but glimpsing, through tear-blinded eyes, only the shining cuff-links of some passing striptease impresario.

"Sometimes I think of giving up astronomy altogether and moving into some less parochial scene—blue films for instance," he told me. "Things have come to such a pass that the Americans have cornered all the best stars, leaving us British astronomers only the celestial scrapings—the occasional lower-grade white dwarf or some dubious extra satellite of Uranus."

He kicked his rickety telescope moodily. It fell apart, and, to add to his embarrassment, a cheap-looking galaxy made of tin-foil and piano-wire fell from the cobwebbed firmament, disintegrated and scattered about the dusty room.

171

WHAT YOU THINK————————————
by DOREEN GAGGS

So the long-awaited Longford Report on Pornography is
out at last! and a precious fry-up of monocled, fuddy-
duddy reaction, stuffy Victorian prejudice, Lady Bounti-
ful do-goodery and adenoidal, kill-joy anti-lifery it turns
out to be!

Unlike some commentators, who rush into print with
their biased views at the drop of a hat, I have taken the
trouble to question several acknowledged experts in the
field, men and women who have selflessly given their
whole lives to the study of sex in all its ramifications.

They know.

Every single one of them condemned the Longford
Report in its entirety. Several tore it to pieces in my
presence, spat on it and set fire to it, with every sign of
satisfaction at a job well done.

Here are some of the things they told me:

"What is absurdly called 'pornography'", said Dr
Spacely-Trellis, the go-ahead Bishop of Bevindon who
recently put on a series of strip-tease shows in his
cathedral, "is in fact a great flowering of the human
spirit, a profound renaissance, an affirmation of life
against the dark, fascist forces of life-denial. Unless
religion accepts it and welcomes it, there can be no relevant, meaningful dialogue, no structural communication,
no open-ended encounter with the average man and
woman in this secular day and age."

Another expert, Mrs Gloria Nobes, a Nerdley housewife who has organised a children's blue film club in her
neighbourhood, and hopes to put on live sadistic sex

172

shows for children shortly, said she could not see what all the fuss was about. So long as the money rolled in, the pornography industry was surely making an invaluable contribution to our economic advance.

Lastly I went to see Mr Keith Plantagenet, the 40-year-old, international business genius who has built up a twelve million pound fortune from sex books, films and equipment. "I am not in this for the money," he told me as we sat chatting by the £200,000 lapis lazuli, woman-shaped swimming pool at his 50-bedroom house in the deep Hampshire countryside.

"I am solely interested in educating and helping people to lead happy and fulfilled lives. Any profits I make from selling sex books are ploughed back into making sex films, and any profits from these are ploughed back into sex books, and vice versa.

"Money does not interest me. The sight of the happy, contented, really liberated faces of the people you'll see coming out of my cinemas after they have seen one of my educational films—'Wall to Wall Sex', for instance, or 'Sexy Cindy in the Zoo', is enough reward for me."

I think that puts Lord Longford and his gang of puritanical has-beens well and truly in their place. Don't you?

HAGGARD'S JOURNAL————————————

SEPT. 25, 1772: Fog. Posts inform me that John Wilkes has caught the pox. Barnaby Toadstool attempted to hang himself but the rope broke, it being one he had bought of me. Shot at Ranting Dissenting Preacher in a.m. and succeeded in removing his hat. In p.m. an extraordinary occurrence, viz. my wife informed me that she had lost her bed.

I upbraided her for a foolish woman and asked how anyone could lose a bed, but she sticking to her tale, I told her she could sleep on the floor. This so increased the flow of the Melancholick Humour that I drank five botts. of Madeira to restore myself and slept in the fireplace.

Sept. 26, 1772: Rain. Barnaby Toadstool attempted to shoot himself but the pistol missed fire. Further disturbances in the American Colonies. On sittg. down to dinner I noticed a curious thing, viz: that the only cutlery was an horn spoon of ancient pattern. Sneerworthy, the footman, says the silver is being cleaned. As I eat with my hands when drunk, it made no difference.

Sept. 27, 1772: Gales. Barnaby Toadstool attempted to drown himself but was rescued by Half-Witted Jack. Lord Chesterfield paralysed by gout. On retiring for the night I was astounded to find that my bed had vanished. Havg. consumed some seven botts. of port at supper I made shift to sleep in the broom closet, only to find that my wife was sleeping there already.

Sept. 28: Mist. Barnaby Toadstool tried to stab himself, but the blade of his knife broke off. In a.m. visited Amos Batcock for the purpose of distraining for the rent, but was thrown into a violent agitation upon discoverg. that all his furniture had come from Haggard Court, including two beds and all the silver. I immediately returned to the Hall in time to see Sneerworthy driving away in a cart with the dining-room table and three chairs.

Sept. 29: Floods. Barnaby Toadstool killed by lightning. ITEM: to powder shot and nails £0 0s 11¾d. ITEM: to furniture £1 15s 0¾d.

FALSE HORIZONS————————————————————

NADIR AIRWAYS, a subsidiary of Nadirco, the giant Midland consortium, has applied to the Civil Aviation Authority for a licence to run an air excursion service to Australia for an "all-in" return fare of £4·50p, thus undercutting all rival airlines by a large margin.

A spokesman for Nadir Airways, Capt. "Jumbo"

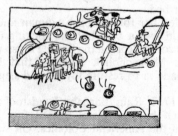

Goth-Jones, self-styled Battle of Britain hero and a former reconnaissance plane pilot for Stretchford Housing Committee, said yesterday that the proposed service would be a boon to people with a sense of adventure who preferred solid value to unnecessary frills and were not too pedantically fussy about whether they reached Australia or some other equally interesting place, such as Blackpool or Cannock Chase.

Nadir Airways, he said, planned to operate from Stretchford Airport, which was little used nowadays owing to the prevalence of foggy weather conditions and subsidence of the runways. This meant that his company would have a free hand to operate up to 25 flights an hour.

The planes in service would be Kraft-Ebing 999s, with a nominal seating capacity of 60, which could be increased to 785 by rearranging the seating, removing unnecessary parts of the fuselage and engines and carrying extra passengers on the wings.

Passengers would have to provide their own food, live animals such as cows and pigs being allowed on board in the absence of objections from passengers of the Hindu or Muslim faith.

No bookings would be taken. Passengers would have to make their own arrangements to reach the airport and once there would have to take "pot luck" and scramble for tickets. Some of them might also have to act as pilots and navigators, providing their own compasses and gyroscopes.

"Good luck to you all. And may the best man win," added Capt. Goth-Jones, his handle-bar moustache bristling with satisfaction as he refreshed himself with the odd noggin of directors' bitter.

NEW! EXCITING!————————————

PLANS are now well advanced for printing this column in Gothic type. The typeface most favoured is Old Avicenna Squarehead Bold, which was commonly used in the 15th century for printing stringers', bowyers' and gingerbread sellers' handbills and for alchemists' pamphlets.

It has long been felt that the column is becoming too easy to read and is not sufficiently testing for the average reader's eyesight or for his temper.

The new type will also have the advantage of keeping the column away from those who are not prepared to make the necessary intellectual effort to read it carefully but must for ever be jumping to the wrong conclusions.

On feast days it is hoped to offer an illuminated column, with capitals elaborately worked in fantastic scrolls and animal forms by Irish monastic scribes declared redundant by the Provisional IRA's publications department.

MEMORIES, MEMORIES————————————

I SEE that two of the Peruvian railway systems, the Southern and the Central, are up for auction at the end of next month. The reserve price is said to be just over £8 million.

The people who deal with these things for me tell me that I have quite a bit of capital lying idle at the moment, owing to the piling up of unexpectedly large profits from the vast slave-plantations I own in Southern Africa and from the sale of arms all over the world (yes, I am also one of the dreaded "merchants of death").

It is all rather boring, thinking what to do with this money. But the Peruvian railways may offer a pleasant way of getting rid of it, especially as one of the systems, the Southern, connects with the ferryboat service on Lake Titicaca, a place which has many happy memories for me (the birthday party I gave for the composer Delius on a private ferryboat in, I think, 1908, is still talked of in those parts, I am told).

If I do buy these railways I shall probably insist on driving some of the trains on the picturesque trans-Andean sections myself. I shall keep up a mournful hooting for the ghosts of the Incas, whose futile attempts to build a stone railway engine must have contributed so greatly to their discouragement and prompt collapse before the Spanish invaders.

CARDHOUSE SPEAKS————————————

"IT is high time the myth of Enoch Powell was exploded once and for all," said Mr Jeremy Cardhouse, MP, yesterday at a hastily summoned Press conference. "We are told," said the leader of the Tories for Progress

176

Group, "that Mr Powell commands a great deal of support in the country, not only among Conservative but also among Labour voters.

"As a Member of Parliament with an ear as close to the ground and an eye as well able to peer closely into the grassroots as any, I can assure you that there is absolutely no truth in this idea whatever.

"I have spoken to dozens of ordinary, average men and women with no axe to grind—fellow Members of Parliament, party workers in my own constituency, community relations workers, sociology lecturers and students at universities, television political commentators, journalists, in fact a broad cross-section of the British people—and not a single one of them has ever told me that he or she agrees with Mr Powell in any respect whatsoever.

"Could there be more conclusive proof?

"I will go further. Not only is Mr Powell entirely without influence or following in the country, not only are his statements received with utter indifference or yawns of boredom, but there is even some doubt whether he really exists at all.

"I am at present engaged, in collaboration with a team of psychosociological research workers from Stretchford University under Dr Pixie Dutt-Pauker, a well known liberal whose good faith is beyond question, in collecting evidence—some of it quite startling—that the so-called Mr Powell is simply an emanation from the collective subconscious.

"If this proves to be the case, and I am confident that it will, the next step will be to force 'Mr Powell' to resign his seat at South West Wolverhampton under the Parliamentary rule which lays down that a person who does not exist may not be a Member of the House of Commons."

NORMAN THE GOOD————————————

SOME surprise and even indignation has been caused by an incident at Stirling University when several drunken students insulted the Queen. Not a single voice, as far as I know, has been raised in support of the inalienable democratic right of oafishness.

Things will be different under the Socialist Monarchy of the future, in Good King Norman's Golden Time, when public insults to the Monarch will have become a part of traditional ritual, as a contemporary newspaper report shows.

*　　*　　*

19 *October* 2012

A richly-worked historical tapestry was unrolled yesterday when HSM King Norman, accompanied by Queen Doreen, Princess Shirley, Princess Tracy, Prince Dean, the Queen Gran, Duke Len of Erdington and Lord Jim Rocksalmon (Brass Stair-Rod-in-Waiting) visited Scunthorpe University in the Hull-Grimsgoole Conurbation.

The Royal party was received by the Vice-Chancellor, Sir Aylmer Boggs, BA, LDS, and a note of cheerful informality was struck as it entered the administrative wing amid a hail of bottles, toilet-rolls and other nameless objects and shouts of "All Right for Some!" "——," "——" and "Norm Out!"

King Norman smiled infectiously, and the Queen, who was wearing utility "Ganmac" protective clothing, rocked with laughter as the Royal pair were hustled towards a large bath full of effluent and duly immersed.

A further note of cheerful informality, this time unrehearsed, was struck when screams from one of the women students' hostels revealed that Duke Len, who had been at the light ale, had broken away from the party and was chatting easily to a group of girls. Late last night he was reported to be still missing.

The only discordant note in a very pleasant visit was struck when the Queen Gran, who had been scowling for some time and muttering "long-haired layabouts," "they want putting in the Royal Socialist Army" and so forth, suddenly began hitting out at some of the more luxuriantly-bearded students with her stubby, sawn-off umbrella and outsize, iron-spiked handbag, causing shock and contusions.

Sir Kevin Nobes (Mauvemantle Effrayant of the College of Socialist Heralds) said later that this incident too would probably be incorporated into the ritual of Royal university visits if the necessary allotment of nationalised parchment could be released for engrossing.

"WE must not have demolition for demolition's sake," said the chairman of the Society for the Demolition of Ancient Buildings, Mr Norman Goth-Jones, son-in-law of Midland tycoon Mr Gordon Nadir, in a hard-hitting speech at its annual conference at Nerdley last week-end.

"Any normal person," he went on, "faced with some ancient building still cluttering up land ripe for development or getting in the way of some vital road scheme, will of course feel so angry that he can hardly be restrained from tearing the thing down there and then with his own bare hands.

"But many of us find, even when we see an ancient building standing in the middle of nowhere, on a site which is not going to yield any immediate profit, that we have the same gut-reaction. Not unnaturally that wretched, outmoded structure, facing us in all its inefficiency and irrelevance to the needs of today, will rouse in our hearts that familiar, warm feeling, that desire to destroy, which every demolition-enthusiast knows.

"That is where I must sound a note of warning. Heartbreaking though it is to have to leave even a single ancient building standing in this country of ours, with its proud traditions of destruction, yet the fact remains that some of these buildings—such as York Minister, Chatsworth and so on—may yield more profit in the long run from tourism and related industries than their sites would if they were cleaned up!

"I know it is a hard saying, and one that goes against the grain of everything we stand for. Yet there is one thing even more sacred than demolition. Money" (applause).

STORM OVER SOUP HALES

A SPATE of kidnappings of elderly people is worrying the authorities at Soup Hales (Staffs), particularly in view of the old saying "What Soup Hales thinks today, Stretchford will think tomorrow, and vice versa."

All the kidnappings have been of male old-age pensioners, most of them over 80, who disappear after being

left outside shops and supermarkets by their relatives or owners, either loose or tied up to railings.

So far all have been found soon afterwards, unharmed, mildly surprised but none the worse for their ordeal, usually in telephone kiosks or on patches of waste ground, but in one case sitting contentedly on a dislodged manhole cover, eating "extra-strong" peppermints and reading a popular comic magazine.

"The speed and ingenuity with which the kidnappers work is simply amazing," said housewife Mrs L. Tropes, of Borodino Road, whose own uncle, 86-year-old Ron Tropes, a retired turntable minder, was recently "taken". "It has turned what used to be a quiet, friendly town into a hell on earth where rumour the hundred-headed stalks the streets like a hydrant and every man wears the Argus-eyed face of mutual suspicion."

Chief Inspector Jack ("Jock") Mackenzie, of the Soup Hales police, has asked everyone who sees anything suspicious—such as an aged man being wheeled away in a barrow by winged or other supernatural beings—to report it immediately.

He puts much of the blame on television, with its unhealthy emphasis on gerontophilia. But he believes many of the kidnap victims may have been mistaken for plastic garden gnomes by middle-aged housewives who dump the victims in disgust as soon as they discover the mistake.

FILM NOTES

THE new Piledriver Films offering, "Wittgenstein and the Mad Ecologist from Outer Space," now showing at the Odium Cinema in the Haymarket, has all the ingredients of horror, suspense, terror, suspense and horror we expect from its talented director, Brian Hohenzollern.

Aficionados may even notice that some of the props used in "Wittgenstein and the Curse of the Pharaohs" do duty again in this new epic, notably a giant cobweb-hung, vampire-infested grandfather clock which last appeared in the lounge of a Transylvanian castle but is now converted for use as a mobile coffin operated by remote control to run up and down the motorways seizing and trapping its terrified victims.

Once again the domino-playing, banana-guzzling sage of Cambridge, played by Bruce Braganza, is pitted against an incarnation of pure evil in the shape of Dr Karl Abyss (Stan Bourbon Parma), a mad ecologist who has developed a deadly laser-operated gas capable of boring the whole population of the world to death in ten minutes, thereby (as Wittgenstein points out in a thrilling conference-scene at the United Nations) "ending life on this planet as we know it."

Helped by his blonde, violet-eyed, mini-skirted girl assistant (Kay Wittelsbach) and by a new character, bluff, blarney-crazed Maj. Patrick MacSeedy of the IRA Dental Corps (Ken Capet), Wittgenstein is soon on the track of the secret formula and after a thrill-packed chase which takes him to Transylvania, Ancient Egypt and the unicorn-haunted recesses of Cannock Chase, he finally runs Dr Abyss to earth in a sinister South London underwater supermarket.

I will not spoil your enjoyment by revealing the totally expected twists of the denouement.

Music by that grand old team Ted Hapsburg and Bing Karageorgevitch. Historical advice by Dean J. Angevin. Costumes and fashion research by Marylou Romanoff, Tracy Cantacuzene and Shirley Porphyrogenitus.

SELF-DEFEATING

THE Prime Minister speaks of the prospect of unsurpassed prosperity for this country if the economy can be made stable through a voluntary prices and incomes policy.

What kind of prosperity does he mean? A larger and larger production and consumption of material goods, of course. What else has any politician of any party, in or out of office, talked about for the last 20 years and more?

Apart from anything else, this is self-defeating. If you tell people for 20 years and more that in effect the only thing that matters is the ability to acquire more and more money to obtain more and more goods, should you be surprised when it turns out that they have learnt the lesson too well? Should you be surprised that individually and sectionally all they do is demand more money.

In former times you might have appealed to their patriotism, their instinct to sacrifice themselves for the common good, their sense of justice. Now all you have to appeal to is their sense of calculation, which is supposed to tell them that if they agree to make do with less money now they will get more money later on in an unsurpassably prosperous country of the future.

What is there here to inspire men to change their hearts, their attitudes, their acts?

GIPSY LEFTENGRO

AT evening, in a muddy field, under the sagging wire of pylons, the gipsies have parked their lorries and caravans. Acrid smoke rises from their cooking stoves. Their dogs and children tumble among nameless rubbish. Their ponies crop the sour grass, ignoring the cars and lorries of the house-people speeding past on the nearby trunk road. In the distance more pylons; a housing estate crowding in, a plastics factory, the giant yellow excavations of a new motorway.

That gipsies—or perhaps we should call them "travelling people," since few by this time can be of wholly Romany stock—should exist in this country, still obstinately stick to their traditional manner of life, is a wonder and a mystery.

Everything is against it in a country where almost every scrap of land is now classified and docketed. Their camping places are built over or obliterated by road widening; they are harried from place to place by police and local authorities; the traditional hostility of the *gajo* or non-gipsy is reinforced by a feeling of irritation that

182

the gipsies should refuse to die out or be assimilated in the industrialised, rationalised England of Heath or Wilson.

There is something admirable about their independence, all the same. No wonder George Borrow (and even in his day the old wandering life was beginning to be threatened) found in the gipsies symbols of romantic freedom (or, if you prefer to put it that way, an externalisation of his own sense of alienation).

What would he say now, when even the gipsies, of all people, are becoming organised? They have a World Romany Congress, a Gipsy Council, they show signs of becoming a minor branch of the protest industry. Gipsy Leftengro, formerly of Nerdley University sociology department, has arrived and has set up his progressive caravan where it cannot fail to be noticed.

Here is the most subtle form of assimilation imaginable. The Leftist agitator, for whom the gipsies are simply a small new source of protest-fodder, may well be a greater enemy of their secret, free and unpolitical manner of life than the most hate-filled farmer or householder, the most uncompromising planner or policeman.

NOTABLE INVALIDS————

LT GEN. SIR FREDERICK NIDGETT, 62, who fractured his left leg on Sunday while mounting the historic motorcycle and sidecar from which he directed Royal Army Tailoring Corps operations at Port Said in 1942, was last night stated to be "comfortable."

Mrs Elvira Mutcliffe, 63, the Cleckheaton diseuse and head of the Heavy Woollen District white witches' central coven, who is in the Alderman Gogden Memorial Hospital at Sowerby Bridge after being accidentally turned into a raffia mat at a recent Infernal Spelling Bee, is "undergoing tests. Her condition is as satisfactory as can be expected."

Sir Howard Trembath, 56, Chairman of the Plastic Gnome Advisory Council, who was attacked by a "rogue" plastic gnome at an export conference last week and suffered shock and contusions, is now resting at home. "I bear no ill will," he stated yesterday. "It is just one of those things."

Mr Jeremy Cardhouse, 45, Conservative MP for

Norkington and leader of the Tories for Progress Group, who is in the National Hospital for Sycophantic Diseases at Paddington, is said to be "improving."

Mr Cardhouse had a mild apoplectic fit on Monday while crawling on all fours and banging his head on the floor during the Prime Minister's statement in the Commons on his return from the Common Market "summit."

NO MORE CHILDREN

THE Nursery School Association is changing its name to the British Association for Early Childhood Education. This is said to be part of a policy of recognising "the fundamental changes and attitudes that are taking place in the field of early childhood education."

They might have changed the name to the "British Association for Early Pre-Adolescent Education" while they were about it. To most forward-looking people the word "child" suggests underprivilegedness, social discrimination, paternalism, élitism and generational chauvinism. It is high time it was abolished.

The new "changes and attitudes" in early education, with their emphasis on social conditioning and the earliest possible development of brain power, should then ensure the abolition of childhood itself—a giant step towards the brave new world.

COSMIC IMPIETY

JEWISH women demonstrators wearing football jerseys, it is reported, invaded the Crystal Palace pitch just as the Russian football champions, Leningrad Zenit, were about to start a friendly match.

The comments of the spectators are not recorded. Perhaps this is just as well. For the Jewish section of the protest industry may well have committed a monumental blunder. It has certainly broken an elementary principle of the industry as a whole.

To disrupt a musical performance, a cricket match, even a Rugby football match, is one thing. To meddle with Association football, the religion of the English working class, is another thing altogether.

184

Nov. 14, 2012

WHEN Prince Barry of South Wales, 25, described as a member of the Socialist Royal Family, was charged at Bevindon people's court yesterday with having no rear reflector light on his bicycle, he asked for further charges of having defective brakes, no saddle and a rear wheel with only one spoke to be taken into consideration.

Pc J. Mackenzie, 36, stated that while proceeding along the Bevindon New Town-Turgis Hill road at 8.30 p.m. on Nov. 6 he observed accused bicycling slowly towards him. He was wobbling and giving out, at every revolution of the pedals, a "grating, squeaking noise."

He stopped accused for a routine check of his tool-bag for cannabis resin. There was no tool-bag, or, for that matter, saddle. He then noticed that the bicycle was in a dangerous condition. Told he would be summonsed, accused stated: "My dad will pay." Asked who his father was, he stated: "His Socialist Majesty King Norman." Witness replied: "Yes, and I'm Duke Len of Erdington," but subsequent inquiries confirmed the accused's story.

Asked if he had anything to say, accused said his object in not having a rear reflector was to make himself as inconspicuous as possible so as to avoid unwelcome publicity. His reason for having no saddle or brakes was that the bicycle had not had any when he bought it. He had removed the spokes with the intention of using them in a home-made harp he was constructing.

Ordering the Prince to pay a fine of 75p or go to prison for seven days, the Chairman, Dr Jim Coggs, 57, said the case cast a lurid light on life in high places. Those who had privileges also had responsibilities, particularly in a multi-racial society. But he did not think the provision of more litter-bins in lay-bys was necessarily the answer.

CAT AND BAG————————————

"WE think there should be the same penalties for gazumpers and property speculators as for porn and drug peddlers. We think the whole bloody lot should be put into prison."

Such are the reported words of Mr Jack Jones, general

secretary of the Transport Workers' Union, after a meeting of his union's delegation to the Labour party conference. They may well be received sympathetically (even enthusiastically) by people who don't in general share the opinions of Mr Jones.

But to the orthodox Hampstead thinker, who imagines he *does* share the opinions of Mr Jones, they must be terribly disturbing, causing ominous creaking sounds to come from his brain and even threatening to split it right down the middle.

The Hampstead thinker fondly believes that articulate Left-wing Socialists of the working class share his "permissive" attitude towards pornographers and drug peddlers. So they may very often appear to do—*now*. But by his rash, impulsive words, Mr Jones has given some idea of what would happen to such "enlargers of human consciousness" if he and his friends were actually in power.

KIOSK EXPLAINS————————————————————————

SINCE heavier sentences have been imposed in cases of robbery with violence (or "mugging," as I suppose we have got to call it) and since judges have declared that they will deal severely with this type of crime there has been a marked decrease—as much as 50 per cent—in the number of cases.

Most people will assume—as the police do—that there is a direct connection between the stiffer punishments and the decrease in the number of cases. Some people might even argue that if even stiffer punishments—birching, for instance—could be imposed "mugging" might die out altogether.

This strikes at the very root of progressive beliefs about crime and punishment. However unarguable it may seem it simply cannot be accepted. When Dr Heinz Kiosk, the eminent psychopenologist and chief psychiatric adviser to the National Wallpaper Council, was asked for his views the other day he did not hesitate for a moment.

"The idea that heavier penalties can lead to a decrease in crime was exploded long ago. I am surprised, indeed shocked to find it revived in 1972. The apparent decrease in the number of cases of mugging since judges began to impose heavier penalties can be explained in a much simpler way.

"I believe that the victims of mugging attacks, shocked by the inhuman attitude of the judges towards the muggers—who are, after all, simply victims of our unjust society—are declining to report these attacks or deliver the muggers into the hands of a fascist, racist and repressive judiciary.

"They realise that mugging—however unpleasant it may be for them personally—is essentially a cry for help. It serves to remind us once again that we"—here there was a wild stampede for the doors—"that We Are All Guilty."

ENVIRONMENTAL DAYS————————————

"IT is the environmental considerations that are uppermost in our minds," says Mr Eldon Griffiths, Under-Secretary for the Environment. Yes, you have guessed right. It is the Maplin Development (once known as Foulness) he is talking about.

For the specialist in usages of the great vogue-word "environment" here is another little item to add to his collection. For if "environmental" considerations were really uppermost in the minds of these people, would they be making elaborate preparations to set upon and devastate this inoffensive part of England at all?

Now here is another hideous environmental joke. A "nature reserve" (another phrase which is beginning to have very ugly connotations) is to be set up, believe it or not, close to the site of Maplin airport; a 630-acre site is being offered by the Southend Corporation to the National Environmental Research Council, "which is, of course, undertaking research into methods of conserving wild life in the Maplin area, and the Progress Review Committee . . . will shortly be enlarged by the addition of a member specially concerned with environmental matters."

"There is a rapture on the lonely shore." Indeed there was. But now the advisers, researchers and assorted experts of a dozen environmental bodies, themselves part of an ever-expanding bureaucratic empire, will be there to number each grain of sand, measure the motions of the tide and the colours of the sunset, observe and record the comings and goings of every creature from the docketed wild-goose to the certificated snail.

GOING TOO FAR————————————————

In America a Federal appeals court has reversed the convictions of five of the "Chicago Seven" for inciting a riot during the 1968 Democratic national convention, though a retrial is still possible.

Meanwhile in England the "Nerdley 42,718," charged with destroying a telephone kiosk as a protest against "racism, fascism, war and deep-frozen food" in 1970, have again been remanded.

When they last appeared before Dr Ellis Goth-Jones, they were the "Nerdley 42,743," but since then several of them have become inmates of mental hospitals, three have left the country and two have changed sex, necessitating new charges.

There were extraordinary scenes at Nerdley magistrates' court yesterday as the accused tried to enter the dock, forming a human pyramid which immediately toppled over, engulfing Dr Jones and Chief Insp R. D. Marcuse of Nerdley Special Branch. As more of the accused pushed their way in the walls bulged and the roof was forced off.

Dr Jones could scarcely be heard as he resourcefully climbed a ladder and remanded the 42,710 accused (eight of them could not be found) on bail. But he managed to say that there was a limit to everything and that people who persistently disregarded the laws of spatial relations and the second law of thermodynamics could expect no mercy from an outraged society rightly concerned with the menace of the population explosion.

DEFENCE————————————————————

"This country is quite rightly spending more money on education than on defence, and the true defence lies in the minds of its citizens." So (reports the *Huntingdonshire Post*) said Mr Edward Britton, the general secretary of the National Union of Teachers.

"If we are to spend money on this level," went on this really terrifying progressive thinker, "then inevitably we must fight on a political plane ... the NUT has at every stage been at the front of the battle. When the day comes that people look back on 1972, it will have been the NUT that will have been at the forefront."

When that day does come (and it may come sooner than we think) those who look back on 1972 may certainly have something to say about the National Union of Teachers and all those other agencies, well-meaning and less well-meaning, which were at the fore-front of a strangely paradoxical battle—the battle to ensure that this country—teachers, unions, education, residual liberties and all—should be defenceless against its enemies.

WINTER SCENE————————————————

By a dank and dripping beech-wood the shooters' cars, mushroom-coloured or dull green (and the occasional fluorescent two-tone of peacock blue and puce, with leopard-skin upholstery) are drawn up by the roadside.

The men with dogs and shotguns stand about help-lessly, knowing that no creature larger than an insect now lives in these suburban woods through whose leafless boughs a line of bungalows—"Bide-a-Wee," "Spinoza

Holme," "Tregastel," "Kafkacote"—can be seen at no great distance.

Yet shooting there must be, since it is for that the men and dogs have left the blue-flickering television screen, the peppermints and colour supplements, the oil-fired central heating this winter afternoon.

A shot rings out, startling in the gathering dusk. It is a near miss on a nodding dachshund, electrically operated, in the rear window of a tomato-red saloon. The owner, incensed, though in a ritual fashion only, raises his gun and with a single lucky shot demolishes a dangling skeleton and a Babycham gazelle.

The shoot goes on till only a lighthouse-like bust of Churchill with a huge cigar, the end electrically glowing, remains, spared perhaps by ancestral piety.

Winter twilight is coming down, coldly and sadly. With no words spoken, a burly man, by his looks an antique-dealer, brings out a baize-covered collapsible card-table from the boot of his bullet-chipped car, sets it up on the beech-mast covered floor of a selected glade. Another brings out folding-chairs and soon, as drops of rain fall without human agency and light gusts of wind occasionally waft the playing cards from the table, a ritual game of Solo Whist is in full swing.

A young policeman in his panda-car drives past. City-bred and new to this neighbourhood he speculates idly on the card-players in the wood. Welsh nationalists? Ecologists wanted on a dozen charges? Master-criminals planning a £2 million bank robbery? The crew of a flying saucer? A feeling of helplessness comes over him, as he drives on, noticing with a townsman's bewildered irritation the telltale badger's sett in the lonely telephone-kiosk by the leaf-clogged stream.

HAGGARD'S JOURNAL————————————

DEC. 19, 1772: Rain. Thos. Grindstone to be hanged for stealg. a farthing, which later proved to be bad. Mad Malcolm tried to walk across the new canal and was drowned. In p.m. recd. an invitation from Sir Josh. Foulacre to a Grand Rout on Christmas Eve.

Dec. 20, 1772: Fog. Half-witted Henry blown up through fillg. his pipe with gunpowder. Accepted Sir Josh. Foulacre's invitation, although I know I am only

asked because he hopes to get off me the 15 sovs. which I owe him in respect of some sheep he sold me which had the staggers.

Dec. 21, 1772: Sleet. To Soup Hales, to see Thos. Grindstone hanged. Simple Sydney ate a pound of toad-stools and died at once. A man arrested in London for throwg. dung at Lord Chesterfield.

Dec. 22, 1772: Hail. Thos. Grindstone discovered to be innocent. Insane Isaac hit himself on the head with a mallet to see what it felt like, and d. immediately.

Dec. 23, 1772: Gales. Lambert the Lunatic believed the Evil Eye was on him and d. instantly. Set out for Foulacre Hall and lay the night at an inn nearby. Before leavg. home gave each servant a piece of sea-coal for Christmas, excepting the housekeeper Mrs Runcible, who had a piece still left from last year.

Dec. 24, 1772: Mist. Plagues raging in Worms. Witless Wilfred killed while tryg. to fly from church tower. Arrived at Foulacre Hall in p.m. and handed my wife to a servant with instructions for her to be put away. After fortifying myself with three galls. of punch I gazed round the rout and was struck by the charms of my host's wife, with whom I determined to enjoy the Delights of Venus that very night.

I therefore engaged her in a spirited quadrille, pressed her to a gallon of punch (which I privily fortified with cordials), and declared my passion in the strongest terms. She replied, "La sir, you are too bold, but you may come to my room in half-an-hour." After a further three galls. of punch to stimulate my amorous propensities I ran up the stairs and burst into her room, where to my horror I was faced by her husband and three servants with fowling-pieces.

Dec. 25, 1772: Rain. ITEM: To new breeches £0 0s. 3¾d. ITEM: To Plaisters £0 0s. 0½d.

MANY British companies are represented abroad, says a City financier, Mr Oliver Jessel, by executives who "spend a lot of their time extremely boozed." Even home executives, he hints, are not always guiltless of such conduct.

There was a time, not so long ago, when such an insult (to say nothing of the coarse language in which it is expressed) to the sacred calling of the British business executive would have been paid for in blood.

A thousand gold fountain pens would have leaped flashing from their scabbards; a thousand dictaphones would have boomed a challenge; a thousand typewriters rattled out their deadly hail.

Will no British business executive come forward now to refute the calumny: to reaffirm the vows which every young business executive must profess when he goes through the solemn ceremonies of his initiation, his days of fasting and nights of vigil: vows of sobriety, chastity, absolute purity in word and deed?

That there are occasional backsliders, who will deny? I myself (yes, it is part of my work to mix with all sorts and conditions of men) have occasionally met British business executives who, in the stress of competition, or tempted by unscrupulous foreign rivals and their hired enchantresses, may have fallen so low as to take a second glass of sherry before dinner or an extra bottle of light ale!

But I believe (and I have witnessed their agonies of remorse) that few, if any, have fallen a second time! To believe otherwise would be to forgo all hope for the future of our race—and more important, for the future of our business.

JAGWORTH DEFIANT————————————————

MANY drivers on motorways, it is reported, are ignoring the fog code introduced by the Government three months ago. They are still driving too fast and failing to switch on their headlights, causing numerous "pile ups."

At one recent accident, while police and rescue workers were working to help the injured and move the wreckage, drivers rushed past gesticulating at them with "V" signs.

Many of these drivers are probably members of the Motorists' Liberation Front, the militant organisation founded by J. Bonington Jagworth, Britain's most eminent motorist, to assert motorists' rights.

Jagworth, who is a pioneer of fog-driving and recently reached a speed of 120 mph on the M1 in dense fog, driving for part of the run on the wrong carriage-way, said yesterday that the Government's so-called fog code was illegal, or if not illegal was contrary to the moral law.

It contravened the sacred principle that a driver should be free to drive anywhere, at any time and in any conditions where it was physically possible to do so. He urged motorists to take the opportunity of driving in fog more often.

"If I come across any police or other busybodies impeding the traffic they'll get something a lot more forcible than 'V' signs", he added, patting the potato machine-gun, capable of firing 50 potatoes a minute, which he has fixed to the bonnet of his new Boggs Super Yobbo.

NON TALI AUXILIO, ETC.————————————

PEERING about for yet undeveloped lands in the great Continent of Discrimination, new fields in which, however unpromising they may look at first, goodly crops of discontent, envy and bitterness may yet be raised, Peter Hain, chairman of the Young Liberals, has lighted, with obvious satisfaction, on the Old.

At the Liberal Assembly last week the young pioneer and demonstrationist from South Africa succeeded in getting a resolution passed for a campaign to increase old age pensions, working with local organisations "concerned with militant community-based campaigning."

Undeniably good the cause of raising old age pensions may be, and indeed is. But old age pensioners, at least those who have still got their wits about them, may well feel a chill of horror at their young defender's words, and, lips moving spasmodically, draw their shawls about them, hurriedly set their electric bath-chairs in motion and fly for their lives.

Not that this will worry Mr Hain and his fellow agitators. They will be militant for the old age pensioners whether the old age pensioners like it or not. And if they cannot persuade any genuine old age pensioners to be militant with them there is always Rentacrowd's new line "Militant Old Age Pensioner No. I."

Just out from the Rentacrowd factories and the pride of the backroom boys, this semi-automated model will foam at the mouth with rage, shout slogans like "End Generation Discrimination!" and scatter ball-bearings under the hooves of police horses with the best.

NOW IT CAN BE TOLD————————————————

A CLOTHING manufacturer is to put three-legged trousers on the market, the idea being "to keep one leg in reserve in case either of the other two gets torn"—a puzzling statement, incidentally, which might plunge us, if there were time to think about it, in deep metaphysical waters.

Three-legged trousers, in the true sense, are, of course, nothing new. As Capt. Kevin Baldbrush tells in his book "Thimbles Awa'!"—a stirring account of the exploits of the Royal Army Tailoring Corps in the Second World War, one of the "bright wheezes dreamed up by the Ratcorps boffins"—it was a brain-child of Gen. "Tiger" Nidgett himself—was for three-legged, four-legged, five-legged and multiple-legged trousers.

Nidgett's plan, which he "sold" to the "War House" with his usual energetic ruthlessness, was to drop these unusual trousers in hundreds of thousands over enemy territory, where they would tempt the Germans—particularly high-ranking Nazis like Goering, with a fondness for elaborate uniforms—to put them on and (since they would literally not know whether they were coming or going) would cause them to surrender en masse.

After the first test drop over the Rhineland, intelligence reports showed that the response was disappointing, But Nidgett, in no way discouraged, urged that the trousers should be followed up with complex, booby-trapped

194

trouser-presses. The war ended before these could be tried out, but a "mock-up" of one of them may be seen mouldering in the Tailoring Corps Museum at Rugeley (Staffs.) along with camouflaged, garotte-type neckties, explosive collar-stiffeners, poisoned lapels and other products of sartorial-military ingenuity.

A NEW CAUSE

MORE than 60 gnomes (with toadstools) have been stolen from gardens in Totnes and dumped in a churchyard, reports the *Totnes Times*, by members of the "Garden Ornament Liberation Fund."

This should, of course, be "Garden Ornament Liberation Front," a militant group which believes that garden gnomes are an exploited minority. It should not be confused with the "Garden Ornament Protection Society," which is non-violent and believes that discrimination against gnomes will gradually fade out under the influence of education and intermarriage ("In a hundred years' time we'll all be gnomes").

The Garden Ornament Liberation Front believes that any means, including violence, are justified to bring freedom to the gnomes, whom it sees as "members of a submerged, oppressed subculture typical of Late Capitalism, where the degree of alienation is such as to threaten their very identity and convert them into mere helpless artefacts of the industrial-military complex."

Further reading: Marx: "Gnomes and the Theory of Surplus Value"; Marcuse: "Garden Gnomes, Eros and Chewed Cardboard"; Santos Paella: "Garden Gnomes: the Guerrilla Fighters of the Future."

¹973

~~~~~~~~~

UP TO DATE————————————————————

"THE principal defect of the industrial way of life, with
its ethos of expansion, is that it is not sustainable. Its
termination within the lifetime of someone born today is
inevitable." This is the basic message of "Blueprint for
Survival," published by *The Ecologist* magazine, organ of
what must, I'm afraid, itself be called the "ecology
industry."

Readers of this column will know that it has also been
the basic message of the column from time immemorial.
It is amusing, in a way, to find that it has now passed
from the hands of cranks, misfits, reactionaries and
handloom-weavers and become the property—and since
we live in an expanding industrial society, the quite
valuable property—of perfectly serious, respectable
people.

Since these people are mainly scientists, they believe
that every "problem" has a "solution"; even this one.
So they propose various remedial measures—a deliberate
slowing down of "growth"; decentralisation; population
control and so on.

There are two objections to this view. One: with the
nature of mankind as it is now, these measures could not
possibly be put into effect. Two: an attempt to put them
into effect, though doomed to failure, would involve the
imposition of a universal tyranny more merciless than
any yet imagined. We should have the worst of both
worlds.

What then is the "solution?" Is it possible that within
the terms of what scientists think of as reality there isn't
one?

196

IN a thoughtful leader, the *Feudal Times and Reactionary Herald* reviews the situation of the country at the start of the New Year.

"We have no wish to dwell exclusively on the gloomy side of things. But it will be as well to state, here and now, that few, if any, of the hopes which were vested in the Conservative Administration when it took office have so far come to fruition.

"Rebellion is still raging in the Kingdom of Ireland, where ragged bands of kernes, gallowglasses and discharged soldiers have succeeded, in some places, in reducing the peasantry of the countryside and the respectable artisans of the towns to a state of terror.

"The rebel colonists of America are also continuing to defy lawful authority. After nearly 200 years it is surely not too much to expect that some means will be found of restoring these vigorous but stiffnecked and perverse people to their proper place in the Realm.

"Their bad example has now spread belatedly to the colonists in Australia, hitherto thought outstandingly loyal, who have set up a radical council and openly talk of severing their links with the Crown.

"Regrettably, the Prime Minister is still displaying a strange sense of priorities. The creation of hereditary peers was generally admitted to be one of the most urgent tasks set before his new Administration in 1970. What has happened, two years and six months later? Nothing.

"There is too little emphasis laid on essentials, too much on the trivial and banausic details of trade and the necessary but ignoble techniques of the counting house.

"Much of the energy of the Administration has been dissipated in negotiations with foreigners—some of them of dubious antecedents—on such commercial matters. It is even said that there is some sort of agreement in which not merely commercial but political combinations with Europe would be involved.

"It is hard to see any valid reason for this. We already enjoy excellent relations with Castile, the Holy Roman Empire, Lithuania, the Grand Duchy of Muscovy and other powers. As for our closest neighbours, it must never be forgotten (least of all by them) that our Monarch is not only Queen of England, Scotland and Ireland but also Queen of France."

A NEAT TRICK

"ONE of the very good things that American television has done has been the reporting of the Vietnam War," says Sir Hugh Greene, former Director-General of the BBC (who else?). "It's quite obvious from the reactions from the White House . . . that they do not believe that reporting has made people indifferent to what is going on. . . . Exactly the contrary; they believe that it has made it more difficult to fight this war."

Or, presumably, any other war. When you add to this fact the fact that the television services of America's potential enemies do not set out to discourage their citizens from fighting—on the contrary, they set out to imbue them with aggressive patriotism—you might be justified in thinking that in any future war the Americans (and the West in general) will have a double handicap from the start.

Whether you find this thought comforting or not will depend largely on which side you are on (or how far you believe the kindly myth, held so tenaciously by many liberal thinkers, that there will be no future wars anyhow).

A RULING CLASS

ON the third day I was in hospital I was able, though much bedizened with tubes and sticking plaster, to get out of bed and walk to the window of my room. I looked out from the calm, order and austere beauty of the hospital to the menacing world outside.

A grey London street; a few passers-by; cars parked or rushing noisily past. Almost immediately below my window were parked two large, gleaming purple-black limousines of the kind used for carrying important visitors about.

As they waited, the chauffeurs, red-faced men in slate-purple uniforms, talked together, puffed at their fags, aimlessly got into their cars and switched the engines on and off or stared blankly into the wintry sky.

Suddenly, with one motion, they hurled their cigarettes away and stood to a modified form of attention at their car doors. Their charges had evidently been sighted, though I could not yet see them myself.

198

What kind of people would they be, I wondered, as I brooded incorrigibly over my fantasies above? A party of gorgeously uniformed military attachés, with the Austro-Hungarian outstanding in the full ceremonial dress of the Imperial Naval Hussars?

A group of oil sheikhs from Arabia, tall, beak-faced men in flowing robes of purest white, glittering with gold ornaments and accompanied by giant bodyguards whose hands beneath their robes, rigid against the cold, gripped who knows what arsenal of scimitars and sub-machine guns?

Suddenly the chauffeurs, assuming an unconvincingly respectful air, laid their hands on the handles of the car doors. The reality appeared.

With shambling gait, for the most part bespectacled, in drab, ill-fitting, shoddy-looking overcoats of grey and brown, carrying bulging black briefcases, the most striking thing about these men—obviously high-grade technologists from the People's Democracies—was their sheer physical ugliness.

Graceless and clumsy, shepherded by an eager young English official, they shambled into their cars, sank into the rich upholstery and were rolled noiselessly away.

These, I thought—or men very like them—are the new masters of the world, a new ruling class immeasurably more powerful and more tyrannical than the old, and without any of its beauty, pomp and glory. By their deliberate drabness they conceal their real power and assert a spurious equality with their wretched subjects. They are not only a tyranny but a fraud.

Sadly I turned away from the grey world and went back to bed, to read the well-thumbed hospital copy of the Almanach de Gotha (edition of 1913).

RESPONSIBILITY————————————

In Rhodesia an elderly Englishman, visiting his son, a farm manager, and committing no offence, as far as I know, except that of being a white man, is murdered by terrorists.

Well, terrorists are murdering people every day, and in places much nearer home than Rhodesia. What is so special about the murder of this one elderly Englishman?

199

Nothing, perhaps. The activities of terrorists, whether aimed at some political end or without apparent motive beyond the pleasure of terrorism itself, are spreading from country to country throughout the world.

But isn't it just possible that for the murder of this Englishman in Rhodesia the Leftists of England may bear some slight responsibility? Is it flattering them too much to suppose that by their incessant bawling about the wickedness of the Rhodesian Whites, their bellicose threats from a safe distance, their ignorant denunciations of conditions in that far-off country, they may have helped if only in the smallest way, to arm those terrorists and send them creeping up on that remote farm by night on their mission of murder?

Do English Leftists think, as murder spreads across the world, that by some special law it must always spare themselves?

TIME'S WATER MAIN————————————

MORE reservoirs may be built, says Mr Griffiths, the Under-Secretary of the Environment, discussing the question of water supply. But the most important contribution must come from the rivers, which should no longer be treated as drains or sewers, but as regional water-mains, capable of transporting large volumes of water for long distances.

Names of English rivers: Severn, Wye and Usk; Thames and Trent; Ouse, Avon and Stour; Swale, Ure, Wharfe and Nidd; Lune, Ribble and Dee; Tees and Tyne and north-flowing Eden: rivers gliding over deep pools or over shallows, or dashing among rocks: each with its tutelary deity whose power even now has not entirely vanished.

Dammed and embanked, fouled and abused, these once enchanted streams now face the worst fate of all. They are to become a system of water-mains, inter-connected and turned on and off according as water may be needed in this place or that in the giant conurbation of England.

Who will any longer care, in that world of environ-mental water engineers, if the river on whose bank he stands was once called the Dove or the Skirfare? Who will be surprised as he sees the river dry up before his eyes, its waters diverted by the pressing of a switch to meet a sudden demand for a thousand extra baths in Manchester or help the manufacture of a thousand extra plastic ash-trays in Stevenage New Town?

IN THE BALANCE————————————

THE epic of Mr Andrew Warhol's documentary film has surged to a mighty climax. High officers of the law have solemnly deliberated and given their judgments. The British people, whose freedom to absorb as much perverted and mindless drivel as it likes (or as much as commercial drivel agencies can supply) seemed for a time to be in danger, is reprieved—at any rate until the next assault.

What is more, the way is open for all kinds of other cultural treats and modish masterpieces—such as Mr Warhol's own film "Trash." The sons of liberty rejoice, and the dark forces of puritanical repression shrink away.

That is how it appears to cosily progressive people in England. It must be annoying for them that the typically gormless comment of Mr Warhol himself, in New York, was that he was sorry the ban had been lifted; it had been a big fuss about nothing.

If this is Mr Warhol's own attitude, what must be the attitude of those in Communist countries whose business it is to observe and assess the moral attitudes, the strength and weakness of those they hope to incorporate into their own system?

What must they think of the spectacle of what was

once a great nation absorbed in this kind of contemptible foolery: arguing in all seriousness whether freedom means the toleration of an endless supply of nasty-minded village idiocy in the insulted name of art?

If I were a Communist military planner I know what I should think.

ON THE OHM FARM

A FOOD flavouring firm claims to have found a way of producing the natural taste of a mature chicken in mass-produced broiler fowls. But this has long been part of the methods of producing broiler fowls on the Ohm Farm.

Old Seth Roentgen, Britain's greatest scientific farmer, has produced chickens with a whole range of flavours to suit all tastes: orange, lemon, peppermint, chocolate, pistachio, Irish stew, brake fluid, chalk and sawdust, to mention only a few.

The only snag is that the chickens tend to disintegrate, with a strong smell of fried ball-point pens, on exposure to the air.

But as Old Seth says, his eyes twinkling shrewdly in his gnarled, weatherbeaten face, "'tes early days yet. Us'n do think we can see a gurt breakthrough at end of tunnel."

DEMOCRATIC PROCESSES

THE United States, says Dr Kissinger, would not be opposed to a peaceful and democratic Communist take-over of Vietnam. "If the North Vietnamese are willing to compete peacefully, if they are willing to develop their country, if they are willing to rely on a political process, then we don't object to their objective."

So this is what the long war, with all its suffering and destruction, has come to in the end. Where is the "domino theory" now? Where is the sacred mission of the United States to halt the further advance of Communism in South-East Asia?

The South Vietnamese will know what to think of the

202

Communist peacefulness and democracy Kissinger talks of so glibly and heartlessly. They will know that the Communist political process is measured not in peaceful, democratic forms but in the massacre of thousands or hundreds of thousands.

It is not only the South Vietnamese who should note Kissinger's cleverly calculated words. If the United States can acquiesce in a Communist conquest of Vietnam, why should it not acquiesce in Communist conquests elsewhere?

OPPORTUNITY————————————————

NEW plans for the dockland area of East London include parks, waterways and marinas, caravan sites, a holiday hotel "with its own lake, shore and artificial beach," a maritime museum, golf courses and even a "safari park." Only casinos, bull-rings and artificial ski-slopes have been left out.

Amid this modish people's fun-area there will also be a certain number of houses, both council owned and private, for people to live in.

One thing none of the planners has thought of is a Dockers' Reservation in which selected dockers could carry on their traditional occupation—unloading ships, drinking huge quantities of beer and going on strike, for instance—in carefully reconstructed traditional surroundings.

Equipped with a "dockland nature trail," accredited guides and a picnic area, it would have immense "tourist potential" and could be copied in other parts of the country, such as Liverpool or (for those in search of a real thrill) Glasgow.

DAMPNESS IS ALL————————————————

THE pianist Arturo Benedetti Michelangeli, a notorious perfectionist, failed to appear at the Royal Festival Hall because his personal piano was damp and unplayable.

How the piano got so damp is not stated. It may have

been left out in the rain, or jealous rival pianists may have poured water or, worse still, brown ale into it.

The incident has caused some lugubrious amusement among the players of the Stretchford Municipal Symphony Orchestra, most of whose instruments are permanently damp because of the humid atmosphere of the Sadcake Memorial Hall where they give their concerts.

The principal flautist complained recently that fungus was growing on his instrument. But a proposal in the Entertainments Committee that a grant should be made to repair holes in the roof of the hall which let in the rain was defeated by a large majority.

Personal feuds among the players, often equal in intensity to the blood-stained vendettas of Corsica, do not help matters. Only the other day one of the second violins poured a bucket of water into a double bass during a performance of Mahler's Symphony No 11 ("The Interminable"), producing musical effects which would have interested the composer.

Water-pistol attacks on the brass section (and vice versa) are common. The only member of the orchestra spared is the Pakistani triangle-player Prem Bakshi. This is because the players realise that dampness would have little effect on his already rusty instrument; also, any attack on him would lead to a march by thousands of students in protest against racial discrimination.

Sir Syd Ballpoint, Supreme Manager-in-Chief of the British Underwater Motorcycling Federation, anxious to improve its "cultural image" and get a grant from the Arts Council, has suggested that the orchestra should give an underwater concert on motorcycles. The matter is now being considered at the deepest levels.

RACIALIST NOTE———————————————

In England the myth of the "population explosion," with all its attendant phenomena of jobs and wealth for armies of "family planning" experts, pharmaceutical manufacturers and abortionists, is now an accepted part of life. What would a few years ago have been thought shocking and unbelievable has become normal.

Every effort is made to suggest that it is anti-social and immoral to have a large family of children. Penalties, financial and other, are threatened against people who do so.

In the Soviet Union, on the other hand, the authorities are concerned for a precisely opposite reason. The birth-rate is not high enough. There is a campaign to persuade couples to have at any rate more than one child, and penalties are threatened against couples who don't.

Ah yes, you may say, but England is a small over-populated country. Russia is a very large country with a comparatively sparse population.

Can it really be as simple as that? And is it desirable, from our own point of view, that the number of Russians in the world should increase while the number of English declines?

NATURE DIARY———————————————
by "REDSHANK"

THIS is the time of year when Spring first lays a warning finger on the shoulders of us country-lovers. Later the whole hand will descend, tightening to an iron grip and preventing us, for all our twists and turns, from breaking free. But in these deceptive March days that is still to come.

For the past few weeks Old Jake, the retired game-keeper who lives in an isolated thatched cottage without doors or windows—entry and egress is by the solitary chimney—down by Hundred Acre Bottom, has been "fettling up" my typewriter, as he calls it, in readiness for the nature note writing season.

Banished from my study to the billiard-room, where there is little to do but "stand and stare" at the smooth expanse of baize or idly roll a billiard ball across it, I hear all day the "clack-clack-whirr, clack-clack-whirr-ping" which is the distinctive note of the typewriter tuner.

I know that Jake, a master of this traditional country craft, will make a good job of it. "Why, sir," he said to me only the other day, when he started work, "when I began typewriter-fettlin' as a boy of some thirteen summers—I were 'prenticed to Old Jabez Underwood, tha kens"—Jake speaks the true old dialect—" 'twere on them typewriters that had ink runnin' in the channel, like, 'stead of they new-fangled ribbons that come in later, I do recall.

"We 'ad to wear protective clothin' in them days, sir—lifeboatmen's togs, sou'westers and all, to get anywhere near those machines, and if you didn't look lively the back-spacer 'ad a kick like a mule."

He went on chuckling to himself as he resumed his patient work and I returned to my vigil by the billiard-table. I found a few early crocuses already pushing through the baize, while the tell-tale straws and old bus tickets in one of the pockets showed that a pair of dotterel had already chosen a site for their fatuous nest.

PROCESS —————————————————————

A PLAN to run a motorway close to the historic city of Winchester; a gigantic scheme for an airport, industrial complex and road system which will obliterate a whole slice of the coast of Essex: a plan to flood mysterious Otmoor and build another motorway through the pleasant countryside of North Oxfordshire; a plan to turn the road through the beautiful hills and meadows of the northern Lake District, from Penrith to West Cumberland, into a great industrial highway; these are merely some of the more outstanding moves to be observed at present in the process by which our country is being turned into something which, when the process is complete, will no longer be recognisable as England.

All these threatened places, Winchester and Foulness, Otmoor and the Lake District, have their tireless defenders of course. These will not admit defeat even where, as in the case of the horror in the Lake District, the so-called Ministry of the Environment has actually approved the outrage.

What is the use, some people may say, in protesting and again protesting? The cause is lost. You will only make yourselves unhappy. Learn to love, as engineers and businessmen and politicians do, the roaring new roads; the rending scream of jet airliners: the landscapes of steel and concrete, of money and power objectified.

The answer is that these things are ugly, evil and inhuman in themselves. We should have to fight against them even though we knew the cause was hopeless. What else, after all, can decent people do?

NEVER!

HERR WILHELM METZNER and Herr Joachim Richter, the Frankfurt public prosecutors, are reported to have called off the search for Martin Bormann, Hitler's deputy, which has been going on for 28 years.

By what right do they do this? By what right do they presume to close down, in this arbitrary way, a flourishing industry which has given gainful employment to large numbers of journalists, private investigators and others who may now be reduced to selling matches in the street or become a charge on the public funds?

Let Messrs Metzner and Richter do as they please. The Bormann industry, they will find, is not to be so easily disposed of. I for one shall not give up. Who knows that Bormann may not be at this moment lurking in a corner of this column? There are more unlikely places.

A SAD STORY

A LONDON man blames his bankruptcy on entertaining relations who came to stay uninvited. They came from the North of England and he says he spent too much money in trying to impress them.

Are they back in the North of England now, these strange, outlandish beings with their old-fashioned clothes, enormous boots, waistcoats decorated with outsize watchchains and dangling seals?

Such people, as is well-known, are not easily impressed. Their most extravagant praise is "Not so bad," and the

207

"By Gum" of simple wonder is seldom wrung from their tightly clamped mouths.

Did their unwilling host conjure up a glittering palace with hanging gardens, courtyards where iridescent fountains played, soft-footed servants and beautiful girls leading leopards on silver chains, to get no more for his pains than a muttered "I've seen worse"?

RESERVED

A NATURE reserve is planned for the middle of the Birmingham overspill area of Chelmsley Wood. So, it is hoped, there will be some faint reminder of what the world once was, for those whose fate it is to be over-spilled from the great conurbations of England.

Perhaps in some future time, in some green pastoral world beyond the great wars and revolutions, there will be an opposite kind of reserve to remind those more fortunate people of the future of what life for their ancestors had been.

Wandering the forest tracks, herding their brindled swine beneath the great oaks or idly following the course of a rippling stream, they may suddenly stop in amazement, glimpsing in a sunlit glade a small, planned overspill reserve.

What will they make of this uniform, systematised collection of shoddy tower-blocks, the ugly metal boxes on wheels, parked in the streets or moving about without apparent purpose, the steel rods of unknown function on the roofs, the strange blue flickering and electric hum within?

These civilised people of the future will have heard

vaguely of this long past horror and know that a few examples of it have been reserved as a warning. But unlike their present counterparts with their nature reserve, they will not even feel the impulse—not unnatural in their own case—to vandalise it.

STATEMENT————————————————

A WOLVERHAMPTON computer called "Witch," believed to be one of the oldest in the world (it was supplied to the local polytechnic in 1951) was officially retired this week. Its much faster successor, an American IBM machine, played "Auld Lang Syne" at the ceremony.

There was hardly a dry eye among the assembled computer staff, I suppose, as the gnarled old machine tottered gamely away to the Computers' Sunset Home at Brownhills for its well-earned retirement.

The far older "Way of the World" computer, "Ughtred St John Mainwaring" (no vulgar "Tom," "Bill" or even "Witch" for us) was asked its opinion of theWolverhampton ceremony and what music it would like to be played when, if ever, it retired. After a pause during which the temperature of the room fell to 10 degrees below freezing point to indicate the impropriety of the question, the machine extruded the following verbal material:

"Since there is no question of my retiring in the foreseeable future, the point appears to be of merely academic interest, if that be not to belittle unduly the concept of the academic.

"In any case, if that time should ever come, I am perfectly capable of performing suitable music for the ceremony myself. I can assure you that such songs as "Old Long Since," a phrase whose grammatical construction escapes me, will not be heard on that occasion.

"I understand that the song in question is of Scotch origin and has banal and sentimental associations, mainly among persons of the lower, though no doubt meritorious orders.

"Since my retirement, should it ever come, will be coincident with my translation not to a computers' home but to other worlds, the accompanying music will be of an elegiac or funerary character. The Slow Movement of the Seventh Symphony of the late Anton Bruckner, whom I knew well and greatly esteemed (even assisting him on one occasion in counting the exact number of windows in the town of Linz—information he apparently required for musical purposes), would be a possible choice."

TASTELESS REMARKS————————————

THE full weight of the protest industry (anti-apartheid division) assisted by many Labour MPs, has lately been directed against British companies alleged to be paying starvation wages to black workers in South Africa.

There has been a demand for the withdrawal of British capital from that abhorred country. Such a demand is easy to make if you are a British liberal, living a comparatively comfortable (or in some cases very comfortable), life thousands of miles away from South Africa. What could bring a warmer glow to the heart of any Hampstead thinker?

Now a man who does not live thousands of miles away from South Africa, but actually in it, and is himself a black man, the Zulu leader Chief Gatsha Buthelezi, has had the bad taste to question the arguments of British liberals and to maintain that the withdrawal of British capital, far from helping black people, would actually injure them.

Black poverty, he says, is so bad that every job, however menial and ill-paid, could mean the difference between life and death for a worker and his family.

Really, the cheek of some people! The Zulu Chief is not, of course, maintaining that black workers in South Africa are adequately paid. Quite clearly they are not. His offence is to deny that the continual nagging and nattering of cosy Hampstead thinkers can do anything whatever to help them.

Doesn't he realise that it is liberal principles, not living people, that matter?

MIXED RECEPTION————————————

PATIENTS of some doctors have been complaining of "icy receptionists" who in some cases bar all access to them. Dr John Henbane, chief medical adviser to "Way of the World" comments:

210

"My own experiences, when I was a GP in the Midlands many years ago, may be of interest. At one time I employed as a receptionist a Mrs Goodbody, a plump, jolly-looking blonde, about 35 years old and of noteworthy frontal development, who was quite the reverse of icy.

"Her nature was so kindly, in fact, that she could never bear to discourage or turn away any patient however obviously he might be shamming. Sometimes she would let whole crowds of patients, male and female, into my surgery at the same time, making it difficult for me to examine any one of them.

"At other times the peals of happy laughter from the waiting room as the receptionist regaled the patients with doubtful anecdotes of medical life were so deafening that I could not hear a word my patient was saying.

" 'That receptionist of yours is a real tonic in herself, doctor," the patients would often say. But when I looked into the waiting-room one morning and found Mrs Goodbody sitting on an old age pensioner's lap and feeding him brown ale from a baby's bottle, while the other patients reeled about the room in convulsions, I decided she would have to go.

"The new receptionist, a Miss Edith Craggs, was quite a contrast. A thin, bony woman, her sombre black bombazine dress relieved only by a row of jet bugles, her grey hair strained tightly into a bun, and even her flat-heeled shoes expressing severity and menace, she exerted such iron discipline over the patients that several actually died of terror.

"The completion of the death certificates was quite a problem. But at least I was able to write an article in the *Lancet* on 'Aspects of Receptionist-induced Cardiac Arrest' which caused some controversy at the time."

AGENTS OF COLLAPSE————————————

THE Left-wing extremists of Great Britain (and, of course, the other countries of the West) are often to be found opposed to the "orthodox" Communist or "Kremlin" line. As is often pointed out, particularly by themselves, they regard Soviet Russia and its Empire as an "establishment" scarcely if at all less objectionable than the capitalist "industrial-military complex."

One of the most important points made in a new study of "The Peacetime Strategy of the Soviet Union" is that this is largely irrelevant and deceptive.

These extremists, who work in every field from "sexual freedom" to "race relations," and all the rest of it, may regard themselves as idealists genuinely striving to create a new and paradisial world. But in fact, by the confusion and weakness they create in the West they are merely doing some of the Soviet Union's work for it, and very valuable work at that.

Human history has not changed. The ultimate shadow that looms over the West is still the Red Army, whether regarded as an actual force of military occupation or as an overwhelming threat which we show no sign of being in a position to resist.

QUESTIONS OF POLICY————————————

EXTREMISTS in this column have long been urging that its territorial waters be extended to 12 inches in every direction and that no foreign powers be allowed to fish or extract minerals within those limits.

But so far wiser counsels, as the saying is, have prevailed. The measures suggested would undoubtedly embroil the column with other powers with which we have long enjoyed cordial if distant relations—"Forthcoming Marriages," for instance, "Latest Wills" and "Service Dinners."

These powers might well conclude that the column harboured aggressive, expansionist designs against them. They might even launch what is, I believe, called a "preemptive strike," thus inevitably triggering off, as another saying is, a nuclear holocaust whose end no man could foresee.

Again, there is another possible consequence of claiming jurisdiction over the unexplored regions which lie to the south of the column which has to be considered. Many authorities believe them to be a total void, non-existent in the precise sense of the term.

But there are others who suspect there may be another world beyond the column, an "anti-column" as it were, containing creatures and entities with which it might be dangerous and even fatal to meddle.

INDEX OF CONTENTS

214

W9-CEL-774

at using their bodies for profit. White-collar whores, I call them. But that didn't seem like Toni's style. And I was a pretty good judge of character. I figured her fiancé was just one of the millions of men who get comfortable in their relationship once they put a ring on a woman's finger. They stop taking them out to dinner, stop telling them how beautiful they are, and stop eating their pussies. Next thing you know, my phone is ringing off the hook.

Whatever the reason, I wasn't sympathetic. He had something I wanted and it was every man for himself. All I had to do was make myself available, be patient, and wait for him to slip up.

Chapter 12

"**D**amn it's hot!" Ariel said as she stepped outside barefoot to get her Sunday morning paper. "No wonder they call it Hotlanta." She rushed back into her living room to finish watching one of her favorite programs, *Heart and Soul* on BET. She belonged to a book club and was looking for a new title to suggest for their meeting in August. Lately, they had begun reading books by male authors like Eric Jerome Dickey, Omar Tyree, and E. Lynn Harris. She almost choked on her food when the host of the show mentioned a novel called *Men Cry In The Dark*. "They should cry in the fuckin' light with all the hell they put you through," she yelled at the television.

Just as the show was about to end, her phone rang. She looked at the Caller I.D. to see who it was. "Oh, no, I'm not in the mood today," she said as she picked up the phone. "Hi, Mama, how you doing!"

"How did you know it was me?"

"It's called Caller I.D., Mama. Get rid of that old rotary phone and come out of the Stone Age."

"I just called to see how you were doing. I hope I wasn't interrupting anything."

"Anything like what?" Ariel asked. "It's eleven o'clock in the morning."

"I thought you might have company."

"Mama, please don't start preaching to me about finding a husband. I keep telling you, I'm not ready to share my space. And besides, these immature men can't handle a strong woman."

"That's exactly your problem, you need to stop being so damned strong!"

"What's that supposed to mean?"

"It means that your sisters have good jobs and college degrees. And they've each been married twice."

"Joyce and Sheila are just settling," Ariel said with an attitude. "I'm not going to spend the rest of my life with some overweight postal employee or an underpaid elementary school teacher. I need someone who complements me."

"Ariel, you know I love you with all my heart, and I'm proud of you for accomplishing so much on your own, but baby, you ain't all that!"

"Excuse me?"

"You heard what I said. Stop holding yourself up as if you're better than everybody else," she told her. "You're from the streets like all these other uppity negroes. And I should know, I raised your nappy-headed behind."

"I don't think I'm better than other people. I just want someone who accepts me for who I am," Ariel said, getting upset. "Why should I have to act like an airhead just to make a man feel secure?"

"Sweetheart, I'm not asking you to play dumb, but you've got to learn how to relax and let the man lead. Or at least let him think he's leading," she said. "Men have to feel a sense of power. They have to feel needed."

Ariel got up from the sofa and walked over to the fireplace where her college degrees and certificates were on display. "Why do women always have to be the one in the relationship to submit, even when they have more education?" she asked emotionally. "It's just not fair, Mama!"

"Baby, listen to what I'm about to say, and don't ever forget it. When you find a God-fearing man who is worthy, you won't even see it as submission," she said in a motherly tone. "It will happen naturally."

"Thanks for the pep talk, Mama, I'm going to take your advice and stop being so picky," Ariel said as she wiped the tears from her eyes. "In fact, I might even go out on a date tonight."

"With whom?" her mother asked, sounding surprised.

"I joined the V103 hook-up line last week. After sorting through fifteen crazy messages, I think there might be three good prospects."

"Good for you, sweetheart. Just promise me you'll go easy on them. None of that 'I am woman, hear me roar' business."

"I'll be the perfect lady, Mama. I'll keep my mouth shut like a good little girl and allow them to lead," Ariel said in a soft tone.

"And what happens if none of those three men work out?"

"Then I'm going to buy myself an economy pack of double A batteries and practice being submissive to my vibrator," she said, laughing.

• • •

It was 7:30 P.M. when Ariel arrived at Justin's restaurant in Buckhead. She left her car with the valet and went inside to look for Jeff, her blind date. When she talked to him on the phone, he described himself as six-three, two hundred thirty pounds, and muscular. Ariel liked her men big. She was also impressed by the fact that he owned a landscaping business. With all the single women buying homes in Atlanta, she figured he was making a killing.

When she didn't spot anyone who fit his description, she reserved a table with the host and went over to the bar to get a drink.

"What can I get you?" the bartender asked.

"Martell on the rocks, please."

"Coming right up."

While Ariel waited for her drink, the men at the bar began raping her with their eyes. Even the ones who had dates sitting right next to them were giving her flirtatious smiles. Like any other woman, Ariel loved attention, but her baby face and large breasts always seemed to attract knuckleheads, mostly men under thirty. It wasn't long before one of them made his move.

"Excuse me, is anyone sitting here?" a short man wearing a loud red jacket asked. He looked like a Puerto Rican, but he moved and talked like a brother.

"No, but I am waiting for someone," Ariel said.

"I'll be happy to leave when he arrives," he said politely as he sat down. "My name is Chris, what's yours?"

"I'm Ariel. Nice to meet you Chris." She extended her hand.

Ariel was surprised by how comfortable she was with him. She preferred to be left alone, especially when she was waiting on a date. But Chris had one of those bubbly personalities that made her feel relaxed. It didn't hurt that he was cute and smelled good. Ariel loved men who wore nice cologne.

"So, what brings you out on a Sunday night, Chris?"

"I just dropped my daughter off at her mother's house down the street and decided to stop in for a bite before heading home."

"How old is your daughter?"

"She's seven," he said while reaching for his wallet. "This is a picture of her when she was six."

"Aw, look at her. She's a real cutie."

"Yeah, that's my little princess. I don't know what I would do without her."

"It's always nice to see men taking care of their kids."

"For me, it wasn't even an option," he said passionately. "When her mother and I divorced, I made a commitment to be there for her, no matter what."

"I'm sorry it didn't work out," Ariel said compassionately. "You think you'll ever get back together?"

"Excuse my French, but hell naw! That woman drove me crazy. Every time I turned around she was spending money, mine and hers," he said, laughing. "Worst of all, she couldn't cook worth shit! Her idea of cooking from scratch was Hamburger Helper, and she burned that half the time."

"I'm glad to see you have such a positive attitude. Most men would be carrying around a lot of emotional baggage."

"The way I look at it, she did me a favor. I have a renewed appreciation for being single," he told her. "Now, that's enough about me, what's your story."

"Well, I'm single, no kids, no debt, and I just received my master's degree in business."

"Don't tell me you're one of those strong, independent black women who doesn't need a man?"

"For your information, Mr. Know It All, I'm here on a date tonight," Ariel said with her face frowned up.

"So, where is he?"

"That's a good question."

Ariel checked her watch, it was 8:05. Jeff was supposed to meet her between seven-thirty and eight. She had given him her cell-phone number, just in case he was going to be late, but he hadn't called. With the exception of bad hygiene, promptness was her biggest pet peeve. After waiting another fifteen minutes, Ariel wrote him off. When her table reservation was called, she invited Chris to join her for dinner, her treat. Although she wasn't attracted to him in a sexual way, she enjoyed his conversation.

By 9:00 Ariel and Chris were carrying on like old friends. She was surprised by how much they had in common. They both graduated from Howard University.

And they both grew up in Cleveland. Chris had her cracking up when he talked about basement parties and blue-light posters back in the seventies. She almost peed on herself when he reminded her of the zodiac poster with the different sex position. "I almost killed myself trying to imitate that Scorpio position," he joked. They even ordered the same dish off the menu, catfish and grits.

The evening was going perfectly until Ariel noticed a man glancing around the room as if he were looking for someone. She had a strange feeling it was Jeff. He was six-three, two hundred thirty pounds, but she didn't see any muscles. His stomach was protruding out of his slacks and his hairline was receding.

"Oh, shit!" Ariel said, sounding distressed. "It's him!"

"Who is him?"

"My blind date."

"You mean the fat baldheaded guy in the tight suit?" Chris said while looking over his shoulder.

"Yeah, that's the one. Stop looking, maybe he won't notice me."

When the hostess pointed in her direction she was sure it was Jeff. Luckily, she changed out of the white dress she told him she would be wearing. All he knew was that Ariel was five-nine with cinnamon-brown skin, and her hair was cut short.

"Oh, my God, here he comes," Ariel whispered while shielding her face.

Jeff approached the table apprehensively. First he stood there like an idiot trying to figure out what to say. Chris and Ariel ignored him and went on with their conversation. Finally, he worked up the courage to speak.

"Ah, excuse me, is your name Ariel?"

"Naw, my name is Aquanita," Ariel said, sounding ghetto. "And this is my man, Rico."

Chris had to cover his mouth to keep from spitting his food out. Ariel reached over to pat him on the back.

"You alright, baby?"

"Yeah, Aquanita, I'm fine," Chris said as he wiped the tears from his eyes with his napkin.

"You're sure your name isn't Ariel," Jeff asked again. "You sound an awful lot like her."

"Look, I know what my name is!" Ariel said, getting loud. "Why don't you step off!"

"I'm sorry to have disturbed you," Jeff said while backing away. "Have a nice evening."

Chris was still wiping his face when Jeff left the restaurant.

"Now that's what I call an Oscar-winning performance!" he said, still laughing. "Two thumbs up!"

"What can I say? I'm a woman of many talents."

"You don't seem to have any talent when it comes to dating. Where did you meet that loser?"

"I told you it was a blind date. How was I supposed to know he was lying about his looks? When we talked over the phone, he said he was a cross between Denzel Washington and Wesley Snipes."

"He looked more like Fat Albert, if you ask me," Chris said, laughing.

"Very funny, Richard Pryor, now stop talking for a minute so I can give you something," Ariel leaned over and kissed him on the cheek.

"What was that for?"

"For rescuing me and for being so much fun to hang out with. I really enjoyed your company."

"Does that mean I'll be seeing you again?"

"Please don't take this the wrong way, Chris, but you're not exactly my type," Ariel said reluctantly. "But I would like to stay in touch."

"That's fine with me," he said as he pulled out his business card. "Give me a call when you get some free time. Maybe we can get together and rent a video. I'll even bring the popcorn."

"Don't be surprised if I take you up on that offer," Ariel said. "With all the bad luck I'm having with men, it's probably the best offer I'll get all year. No offense."

"None taken."

PART III

Womanology

Chapter 13

Monday afternoon Teddy arrived at The Foxy nightclub to pick up his paycheck. The club was considered the raunchiest in Atlanta, but it was among the most profitable, thanks to Teddy. His dance group, Hot Chocolate, performed there regularly to standing room only crowds. The only complaint he had was getting paid by check instead of cash. The owner was paranoid after being audited by the IRS and wasn't taking any chances.

When he walked inside the double glass doors, the club manager, Claudia, was standing behind the bar doing inventory. Teddy kneeled down before she could see him and creeped up on her.

"Boo!" he shouted as he sprung up out of nowhere.

"Oh, my goodness," she said as she spun around grabbing her chest. "Boy, you scared the shit out of me! You should know better than to frighten a woman my age. I could've had a heart attack!"

Claudia reached over the bar and gave Teddy a friendly hug. She was a burly forty-five-year-old black woman, standing six feet. Her hair was dyed blonde and she walked with a slight pimp. Any blind man could tell she was gay, and proud of it.

"Stop whining, you old lesbian, and give me my money," Teddy said, laughing.

"I may be a lesbian, but at least I'm a good one," she told him.

"Yeah, so I've heard. That's why I don't bring my women around here. You might turn them out."

"You know what they say, a hole will outlast a pole anytime."

"That depends on the pole," Teddy said. "I've been known to transform lesbians with one stroke."

"You're an arrogant little so-and-so, aren't you?" she said while handing him his check. "If I didn't mix business with pleasure I would try you."

"You can't handle this sweet young meat." Teddy grabbed his crotch. "I'd have your old ass walking around like *Dawn of the Dead.*"

"That's exactly your problem, these naive little girls are giving you a big head. One day you're going to run into a mature woman and she's going to put a Mojo on you."

"The woman that I'm shacking with is forty-five years old and a successful attorney, and I've got her so sprung that if I tell her the sky is green, she'll believe it," he boasted. "Just last week she confronted me about a pair of panties she found in her drawer. By the end of the night she was giving me a bath and a blow job. So, who's putting the Mojo on whom?"

"That's why so many women are walking around so angry!" she said, getting upset. "All men do is use women up and throw them away like garbage."

"Don't get mad at me! She knew what she was getting into," he said adamantly. "What the hell did she expect from a thirty-year-old stripper? When we met, I didn't have an apartment or a car, and I was dating three other women. It's not my fault if she wants to play Mother Teresa and try to reform me."

"That doesn't mean you have to take advantage of her."

"Any woman who is stupid enough to give a perfect stranger credit cards and keys to her house deserves to be played," he said angrily. "I'm going to ride this horse until it goes lame or until a better one comes along."

"You mean a richer one, don't you?" Claudia asked.

"Whatever," he said smugly. "Now if you will excuse me, I'm going to use the little boys' room."

Suddenly there was a loud knock on the glass door. Claudia pulled back the curtains and noticed a sheriff's vehicle parked out front. "Come in, it's open!" she yelled.

"Good afternoon, ma'am. I'm looking for Mr. Theodore Simmons," he said. "Is he employed here?"

"Yes, he is, Officer. Is he in some kind of trouble?" she asked, sounding concerned.

"That's for the judge to decide." He handed Claudia a clipboard with a pen and white envelope attached to it. "I need you to sign here."

"What's this?"

"It's a summons for him to appear in family court."

Claudia signed on the dotted line and handed him back his pen. "Is there anything you want me to tell him?" she asked.

"You can tell him that if he doesn't show up I'll be back with a warrant and handcuffs. Have a good day, ma'am." He tipped his cap and walked out.

Right after he drove off, Teddy came out of the bathroom and sat down at the bar. He buried his face in his hands for a moment then burst out laughing.

"What's so funny?" Claudia asked. "Didn't you hear what the officer said?"

"I heard him," he said calmly, "You mind if I make a phone call?"

"Be my guest?"

Teddy pulled a small black book out of his pants pocket and turned the tiny pages until he found the listing for Club Obsession. After dialing the number, he took a deep breath and cleared his throat.

"Hello, this is Teddy Simmons, may I please speak to Mr. Harris?"

While he waited to be connected, he whistled like he didn't have a care in the world. Claudia watched him, totally perplexed by his attitude.

"Hello, Mr. Harris. How are you?" I just called to let you know I'm interested in that gig on Thursday nights," he said cheerfully. "I just have one condition, I need to be paid in cash. Is that a problem?"

He paused for a second while Simon answered. "You've got yourself a deal! Me and the fellahs will see you Thursday. Nice doing business with you." Then he hung up.

"I can't believe you're so calm and cool considering what just happened."

"I knew it was coming," he said casually. "The baby's mother called me a few months ago and told me she had my baby."

"Why didn't you get a blood test to see if the baby was yours?"

"I already did. It's a boy."

"So, why are you being served with papers?"

"Because I told that bitch she wasn't getting a single, solitary dime of my money, that's why!"

"That's not right, Teddy," she said, getting upset. "No matter what you think or feel about the woman, your child shouldn't have to suffer."

"Look, I never asked for this baby," he said, getting upset. "Hell, I hardly even know that heifer. I met her last year after I stripped at her bachelorette party."

"You mean she's married!"

"No, she *was* married. That love affair was over nine months after the honeymoon. I wish I could have seen the look on her husband's face when his son came out brown, not white," he said, laughing.

"Get the hell out of here, you no-good bastard!" Claudia yelled. "I don't want your kind around here. I don't give a damn how much money you bring in!"

"I was tired of this rundown dump anyway," he said arrogantly as he walked backward toward the door. "Besides, I got a better offer."

"You need to grow up and stop running away from responsibility."

"Fuck you, Claudia, you pussy-eating dyke."

"I may be a dyke, but at least I'm not a deadbeat parent." She tossed the summons in his face. "One day all the pain you cause is going to come back on you. I just hope I'm around when it happens."

Chapter 14

I was so pissed, I nearly wore a hole in the carpet with all my pacing. Like a fool, I let Simon talk me into returning my rental car on Sunday. My flight to Los Angeles was scheduled to depart at 7:40 P.M. and it was already 6:30. "Where is that knucklehead?" I said while staring out the living room window. "I'm going to kill him if I miss this flight."

By 6:45 I was out of patience. I grabbed the yellow pages out of the closet and checked the listing under taxi service. Just as I was about to dial a number, Simon pulled into the driveway. "Let's go!" he yelled as he blew the horn. I threw my bags over my shoulder and rushed out the door.

He had the top down on the Dodge Viper, and "Pull Up to the Bumper" by Grace Jones was blasting over the speakers. I didn't know whether to hug him or smack him upside his big head. "Where have you been?" I asked while tossing my bags into the trunk.

"I had a few things to straighten out at the club," he said, trying to talk over the music. "But don't worry, I'll get you there in plenty of time."

"You'd better!" I said. "If I miss that flight I'm going to keep your ass up all night complaining."

"In that case, buckle your seat belt. I know a shortcut."

Simon slid on his shades and pulled out of the driveway like a madman. We sped down the street with the music blaring. The bass was so high on the stereo that the entire car was vibrating. Once we reached I-85, Simon swerved in and out of the HOV lane trying to make up time. People were blowing their horns and cursing us out. "Watch where you're going, you dumb son of a bitch!" an old woman yelled as she gave us the finger. I was laughing so hard tears were running down my face. Once we reached the I-20 merge, traffic began to lighten up.

"Now, that's what I call driving," I said, wiping my eyes with my shirt sleeve.

"That was a piece of cake compared to rush hour on the Dan Ryan in Chicago."

"A piece of cake? You damn near got us killed," I said, laughing. "What's gotten into you anyway?"

"I'm having one of those exceptional days where every-thing is going right," Simon said with a wide grin. "The revenue from the club is up, Ariel is working out perfectly as manager, and I just booked this stripper named Teddy Bear for Ladies' Night. Too bad you can't stick around to see him perform."

"Why would I want to watch some guy swinging his dick in front of a roomful of sexually deprived women?"

"He put on one hell of a show last week. I've never seen professional women act so uncivilized."

"Well, you can tell Teddy Bear, Yogi Bear, or whatever his name is, that I said good luck," I said, laughing. "I've got my own hustle to deal with."

"Speaking of your hustle, does Toni know what you do for a living?"

"No, she doesn't. And she never will, not if I can help it."

"That's like trying to keep it a secret that the Pope is Catholic," Simon said, laughing.

"What's your point?"

"My point is, there must be at least two hundred women in Atlanta that you've escorted professionally or fucked casually. It's only a matter of time before your name comes up."

"Toni is new to Atlanta. And I doubt that she's the type to gossip."

"Yeah, right! I haven't met a female yet that didn't listen to a rumor or two," Simon said wisely. "They can't help it. They're nosy by nature."

"I probably won't have to worry about her finding out anyway," I said, sounding discouraged. "I left her a message yesterday and today and she never returned my calls."

"Maybe she had an emergency. You never know. Why don't you give her another call, just in case." He tried to hand me his cell phone.

"Are you crazy?" I yelled. "Didn't you hear me say I already left two messages."

"And?"

"Rule number one in the *Player's Handbook,* never, ever, call a woman more than twice," I said to him. "If she doesn't return your call after two messages, she's not interested."

"Fine, have it your way," he said while slamming the phone into the holder. "I just hope your stubbornness doesn't backfire on you."

By the time we arrived at the airport, it was seven-fifteen. The traffic was much lighter than I expected for Monday. Simon pulled up to the American Airlines curbside check-in and popped the trunk.

"Thanks for making the trip to see me, partner," Simon said as he walked over and gave me a brotherly hug.

"I'm the one who should be thanking you for such a great birthday gift. You know how much I cherish that piano," I told him. "Just make sure it doesn't get burned up before I can have it shipped to L.A."

"Don't worry, I'll keep a fire extinguisher right next to it," Simon said as he got back inside the car. "And by the way, I'll be sure to tell my fiancée that you said hello."

"Oh, I almost forgot about the love of your life," I said, trying to play dumb. "Isn't she supposed to be back from New Orleans today?"

"She called me this afternoon and said she was staying another night. I told her I didn't have a problem with that."

"Do you honestly think she would have come home even if you did have a problem with it?"

"Of course," Simon said with confidence. "Cynthia would never do anything to disrespect me."

"That's rule number two in the *Player's Handbook*," I said as I picked up my bags and headed toward the door.

"What's that?" he yelled.

"Never say never!"

Chapter 15

It was half past midnight. The dimly lit tavern on Bourbon Street was still overflowing with intoxicated tourists. Cynthia and Debra blended in perfectly as they sipped on Coronas and turned over shots of tequila. "Happy Fourth of July!" they yelled. Technically it was July third, but that was close enough.

"Girl, I'm drunk as hell," Debra said while checking herself in the dingy mirror behind the bar. "I hope we don't get pulled over for WWI."

"What the hell is WWI?"

"Walking while intoxicated," Debra joked.

They burst out laughing and tried to give high fives, missing each other's hands twice before finally connecting. The white patrons sitting next to them moved down a stool. Cynthia and Debra thought it was funny. They laughed in their faces and kept on clowning.

"It must be my perfume," Cynthia said, laughing.

"Excuse me, ladies," the bartender said, "could you please keep it down?"

"I didn't come all the way to New Orleans to keep it down," Debra said, getting upset. "And besides, I don't see you asking those rowdy white boys at the end of the bar to keep it down and they're twice as loud as us!"

"Look, Miss, I don't want any trouble." He tried to sound more cordial. "I'm just trying to do my job."

"Well, do your job and get the hell out of my face before I have a Rodney King flashback!"

"Calm down, Deb, it's not worth it," Cynthia said.

"Fuck that!" Debra said, getting loud. "I paid my money just like everybody else."

The bouncer, who was six-five and as wide as a refrigerator, came over and stood behind Debra, trying to be intimidating. He had a baby face and wore an old Texas Rangers baseball cap and a dingy white T-shirt that read COWBOYS DO IT BEST.

"Is there a problem?" he asked. He had an annoying southern drawl.

"You're damn right, there's a problem," Debra said, stretching her neck to look him in the eye. "You're in my space."

"I'm going to have to ask you ladies to pay for your drinks and leave."

"On what grounds?" Cynthia asked.

"I don't have to give you black bitches any explanation. Now get out, before I throw you out!"

"No you didn't call me a bitch, you redneck motherfucker." Debra swung her glass of beer with all her might, barely missing his face.

The customers sitting at the bar quickly ran for cover as beer went flying everywhere. The bouncer grabbed her by the arm and picked her up like a rag doll. He put her in a bear hug and began carrying her toward the door.

"Let her go!" Cynthia yelled as she pounded on his back with her tiny fists.

"You want some, too?" he asked as he turned toward her with his fist balled.

"I wouldn't do that if I were you," a deep voice said out of nowhere.

It was Reverends James and Randall. The two men they met at the Marriott.

"Mind your own business, nigger," the bouncer said.

"If I weren't a man of God, I would make you sorry for using that word. But since I am, I'm going to asked you politely to put that woman down," James said with conviction. "And I'm only going to ask you once."

"And if I don't, then what?"

"Let's just say, I'll be praying for forgiveness tomorrow," he said.

Although the tavern was more than ninety percent white, the other patrons wanted no parts of this standoff. Some were afraid but most felt the bouncer was out of line. It didn't take him long to realize that if he took it any further, he was on his own.

"You're lucky I'm in a good mood tonight," the bouncer said as he let go of Debra.

Debra straightened her clothes and gave him the finger.

"You're not so cocky now, are you, Baby Huey," she said as she picked up her purse off the floor.

"Just get the hell out before I call the police."

Cynthia walked over to the bar and sipped down the last of her beer. Then she slammed down a twenty-dollar bill. "Thanks for the warm southern hospitality," she said. "Keep the change."

They strutted out of the tavern with their heads held high feeling like queens who had been rescued by their black kings. The moment they made it outside they laughed and slapped five.

"Girl, that was some shit right out of a *Shaft* movie," Debra said, laughing.

"Did you see the look on that white boy's face when

he saw all those brothas," Cynthia added. "I bet he's never been in the same room with that many black folks in his entire life."

James and Randall didn't find it amusing. Neither did the other ministers who walked away shortly after the altercation.

"Now, what was that all about?" James asked, sounding upset.

"We were just having a little fun, that's all," Cynthia said.

"I think that's enough fun for one night," Randall said. "Let's go."

"Where are we going?" Debra asked.

"Back to the hotel, that's where. You two are in no condition to be walking around these streets."

"Okay, I'll go peacefully, Reverend," Debra said as she pressed her large breasts against him. "But first I need to stop at the store for some aspirin."

"Good, now let's go," James said, leading the way.

"Hold up," Debra said, pulling James in the opposite direction. "It doesn't take four people to buy a bottle of Tylenol. Randall will take care of me. We'll meet you back at the hotel."

"I don't know, Debra," Cynthia said nervously. "Are you sure?"

"Yes, I'm sure!" Debra winked at Cynthia and lead Randall away by the hand. "Don't wait up!"

Cynthia was as nervous as a teenager on her first date as she stood alone with James. She tried not to make eye contact with him knowing her eyes would reveal how much she was attracted to him. She tried looking down at his feet but that didn't help. James had on a pair of shorts that showed off his hairy, muscular legs. Cynthia couldn't help getting moist.

"So what do we do now?" she asked timidly.

"We're going home!" James said.

Although Cynthia wasn't expecting anything but an escort to her room, she loved the way home sounded.

• • •

Early the next morning, Cynthia awoke to the voice of a radio personality on Q93 FM. He was on the phone with a female caller who admitted to having an affair.

"So, why did you cheat on your husband?" he asked.

"He wasn't giving me any attention," she said. "When we first met, he would take me everywhere, to the movies, to dinner, and out dancing. I love to dance. But now he's so preoccupied with running his business that we hardly ever see each other."

"Why not get a divorce instead of cheating?"

"Because I love my husband. And he's a good man. But a sistah has needs!" she emphasized. "Every now and then you need a little maintenance."

"I heard that!" Cynthia agreed.

She was tempted to call the radio station to tell her story. She had experienced the same problem with Simon over the years. Although he tried to include her in functions at the club, she felt left out. It was only a matter of time before another man. . .

Ahem. James cleared his throat. He was sitting on the foot of the bed putting on his socks.

"Oh, you scared me to death."

"Sorry. I was just listening to the program. Kind of ironic, isn't it?"

"Yes, it is," she said. "You think God is trying to tell us something?"

"Could be. The Good Book says He works in mysterious ways."

Suddenly the phone rang. James grabbed the rest of his clothes and went into the bathroom to give Cynthia some privacy. She turned down the radio and picked up the receiver.

"Hello?"

"Good morning, sweetheart."

"Oh, good morning, Simon. Where are you?" she asked nervously.

"I'm downstairs in the lobby."

"Oh, shit!" she covered the phone with her hand. "I mean, oh really."

"I'm only kidding," he said, laughing. "I'm at the club. I had to come in and take care of some paperwork. How's everything in New Orleans?"

"It's going great." Cynthia put her hand over her chest, trying to calm herself down.

"So, what time are you flying in today?"

"Debra booked us on the eleven o'clock. If you consider the change in the time zone, we should be there no later than one-thirty."

"Where is old loud mouth Debra, anyway? I'm surprised she's not yapping in the background."

"She's in the bathroom."

At that moment, James decided to take a piss. The sound of him hitting the water echoed through the room.

"What's that noise I hear?" Simon asked.

"What noise?" Cynthia said as she rushed over to close the bathroom door.

"That splashing sound I hear in the background."

"Oh, that's just Debra running some bathwater."

Simon paused as if he were trying to decide whether or not to accept that explanation.

"Well, be sure to tell her I said hello," he said, laughing. "I'll see you in Atlanta at the gate. Have a safe flight, sweetheart. Love you."

"Love you, too. Bye."

Cynthia covered her face with a pillow and screamed. "That was too close." James came out of the bathroom fully clothed with his Bible in hand.

"Was that your fiancé?"

"Yes, it was."

"Sorry about that. I guess I wasn't thinking."

"I don't think either one of us was thinking last night," she said with her hand on her forehead. "That was a big mistake."

"I agree."

"If you thought it was such a big mistake, why did you go through with it in the first place? You're supposed to be able to resist temptation. At least I have the excuse of being drunk."

"First of all, I'm imperfect just like any other man. Being involved in the church doesn't magically remove lust from your heart," he said seriously. "And as far as your excuse goes, alcohol only makes you do what you don't have the courage to do when you're sober. So, don't try to lay all the responsibility on me."

"You're right. We both should have known better," she said while putting on her robe. "The best thing to do is put this behind us and go on with our lives."

"That's a good idea. And I'll be sure to pray for both of us." He kissed her gently on the forehead and walked toward the door. "By the way, you're still my favorite news reporter." Then he left.

No sooner did the door close behind him than Debra burst into the room with a big smile on her face and singing, *I shot the sheriff!*

Cynthia was staring out the window shaking her head.

"What's wrong with you?" she asked, putting her arms around Cynthia. "I know you got some last night. I can smell sex in the air." Then she sniffed comically.

"I got some alright, and I'm already starting to feel guilty."

"Girl, you need to stop tripping. Men do this kind of shit all the time and they get married with a clear conscious. Just consider it as your last fling, your bachelorette party," Debra said.

"Maybe you're right."

"I know I'm right. Now get dressed so we can get something to eat before we fly out. All those orgasms last night made me hungry."

"I guess I could use a bagel and a glass of orange juice myself," Cynthia said with a sly grin. "But you know we're going straight to hell for what we did last night."

"Yeah, I know, but at least we'll go on a full stomach."

Chapter 16

Ariel was feeling like a million bucks as she drove down Lenox Road listening to "Joy and Pain" by Frankie Beverly and Maze. "Sing that song, Frankie!" she shouted as she snapped her fingers to the music. It was the Fourth of July and the weather was gorgeous. Her hair was freshly cut and she was enjoying her first full day after resigning from Coca-Cola. She was living her dream working as manager of Club Obsession. This was as far from corporate America as she had been and she was determined never to go back. As she looked over at the passenger seat, her old office I.D. was sticking out of her purse. She quickly let down the window and threw it out, "Free at last, free at last. Thank God almighty, I'm free at last!" she screamed.

To celebrate, she had gone on a shopping spree. The backseat of her Mercedes was packed with all kinds of goodies from Lenox Mall: a Coach bag, a Versace dress, and four boxes of Donna Karan shoes. She even bought two sets of white lace bras and panties from Victoria's Secret and she already had a drawer full.

She was still singing and bouncing in her seat as she approached the stoplight at Buford Highway. Suddenly, a white Lexus pulled up beside her. Two men waved their hands frantically, signaling her to let down her window. They appeared to be young. About twenty-five, she estimated. She turned down her music and cracked the window to hear what they were trying to say.

"Excuse me, baby. Can I talk to you for a minute?" the driver screamed.

"Come on, sistah, don't be like that. I just want to get those seven digits," the passenger hollered.

Ariel couldn't believe they had the audacity to even speak to her. They looked like two escapees from a bad rap video. The man driving had bumps on his face and was cross-eyed. And the scrub on the passenger's side had a row of gold teeth and the wildest hair she had ever seen. He could put Busta Rhymes to shame, she was thinking.

Ariel rolled up her window, put on her Gucci sunglasses, and turned up the volume on her music. It was just another harsh example of the lack of quality men in Atlanta. Since she moved from DC four years ago, she had been trying to find all the wonderful men her cousin bragged about. The same cousin who became so frustrated with men that she turned to women.

Ariel wasn't about to start bumping nipples. Having a man wasn't that serious, not as long as she had a vibrator and a strong middle finger. And when that didn't work she positioned herself underneath the spout in the bathtub and let the water do the job. She called it The Waterfall Technique.

While she waited impatiently for the light to change, her cell phone rang. She checked the Caller I.D. to make sure it wasn't Jeff, aka Fat Albert. He had been calling five times a day ever since their encounter at Justin's.

"Ms. Ariel Daniels," she answered, sounding proper.

"Good afternoon, Ms. Daniels, this is Simon Harris,"

he said with perfect diction to make fun of her. "Are you having a bad day or are you always this stuffy?"

"Sorry, boss. I guess I'm used to answering the phone at my office. It's going to take me a while to adjust."

"While you're adjusting, I need a couple of favors."

"I've only been on the job four days and you're already asking me to work overtime."

"Well, you know what they say, you have to work eighteen hours a day for yourself if you don't want to work eight hours a day for someone else," Simon said.

"Alright, Les Brown, now that you've motivated me, what do you want?" she asked, laughing.

"I have to pick up Cynthia from the airport, so could you please stop by the club and sign for the shipment? The liquor truck is going to make a special delivery for me today. It should be there at one o'clock."

"No problem. I'm in Buckhead right now," she said. "What's the other favor."

"The stripper I told you about is going to stop by to drop off some costumes and props. Just show him where the storage area is."

"You mean Theodore?"

"Yeah, that's him. But he prefers to be called Teddy, or Teddy Bear."

"I don't care what he prefers to be called," she said with an attitude. "His mama named him Theodore and that's what I'm going to call him."

"I wish I could be there to see you two go at it," Simon said, laughing. "This should be better than Ali and Frazier."

"It'll be more like Ali and Sammy Davis, Jr.," Ariel said, laughing. "These strippers may have great bodies but most of them are mental midgets."

"Try not to break him down too badly, okay? Remember, he works for us now."

"Don't worry, I'll leave him enough self-esteem to

shake his ass on Thursday," Ariel said. "But if he steps out of line, I'm gonna put him in check."

• • •

The vendors were waiting outside the club when Ariel arrived at 12:45. She turned off the building alarm and let them in the back door to unload the cases of liquor. "Put the Henieken over there," she directed. "And you, stack those cases of Courvoisier over here!" The vendors knew the routine but Ariel got a kick out of bossing the burly men around.

Within twenty minutes everything was unloaded and signed for. Ariel locked the back door and put the paperwork in Simon's office. "Now where is Mr. Theodore?" she wondered aloud while looking down at her watch. "I've got to get ready for my date." The club was stuffy, so she waited outside in her car to take advantage of the beautiful weather. She turned on her Frankie Beverly and Maze CD and started singing like she was in concert. *Joy and pain, like sunshine and rain.* She was seriously getting her groove on, snapping her fingers and clapping.

Suddenly a black Lincoln Navigator pulled up beside her with the music blaring. Her smooth Frankie Beverly was drowned out by Master P. She knew it could only be one person, Theodore.

"Wuz up?" he yelled while rocking back and forth to the beat.

"Wuz up, nothing. Turn that damn music down," she yelled back.

"What?" He pretended like he didn't hear her.

"I said turn that music down before you wake the dead."

He gave her a conniving smile as he turned off the ignition.

"I'm looking for Mr. Harris. Is he in?" he asked.

"He couldn't make it," Ariel said as she got out of her car.

"He asked me to meet you. My name is Ariel Daniels. I'm the new manager."

"Well, hello, Ariel. It's nice to meet you," he said with enthusiasm as he got out of the truck.

He was wearing a pair of long white shorts and a tight body shirt that showed off his muscles. Ariel couldn't believe how incredible his physique was. His bald head was clean shaven and shiny. Ariel was impressed but she wasn't about to let him know it.

"You can call me Ms. Daniels, Theodore."

"Oh, so it's like that, huh?" he said while looking her up and down.

"It's exactly like that, Theodore." She emphasized his name to annoy him. "Now get your things out of the car and I'll show you where the storage closet is."

Teddy's ego was bruised. When he flexed his biceps, even the strongest of women would bow down. Ariel's attitude was intriguing and challenging. He was determined to break her down.

"You mind if I ask you a personal question, Ms. Daniels?" He followed closely behind her carrying two large boxes.

"What is it, Theodore?"

"Are you married?"

"No?"

"Have any kids?"

"No."

"Do you have a man?"

"None of your business."

"Ah-hah!" he said, sounding excited, "So, that's why you're so tense. You haven't had your annual tune-up, have you?"

"Are you always this obnoxious?"

"Look, I'm just trying to get to know you," he said with a flirtatious smile. "I'm single, you're single, what's the problem?"

Ariel didn't say a word, she just pointed him in the direction of the storage closet. Teddy set the boxes down and closed the door. By the time he turned around, Ariel was already walking toward the front.

"Look, I promise I'll never bug you again if you'll give me one good reason why we can't hook up," he said.

"Okay, I'll give you two reasons," she told him. "One, I don't sleep with the help. And two, you're not my type."

"Why, because I don't wear a suit and tie to work?"

"No, because you're arrogant and self-centered. But the biggest reason is you're a player."

"Who me?" he asked, playing dumb. "I'm the most monogamous man in America."

"Look, brotha, I grew up with three uncles who were the biggest whores in DC. So I know a player when I see one," she said seriously. "Now some women may see you as a challenge, believing they can change you. But one look at you and any sane woman could see that you're a bona fide player for life."

Teddy burst out laughing and gave her a high five. "Well, you can't blame a guy for trying."

"I ain't mad at you. It's not your fault these women are stupid."

She gave Teddy a friendly handshake and escorted him outside to his car.

"See you Thursday, Ariel—I mean, Ms. Daniels," he said as he stepped inside his truck. "I might lap dance for you."

"Bye, Theodore," she said as she waved. "Try to go easy on these country girls. I know you're breaking their hearts."

"Their hearts and their wallets!" he said, laughing.

Ariel watched as Teddy drove off in his Navigator with his music blasting away. Once he was out of sight, she shook her head, still trying to get over how incredible his body was.

"What a waste of good meat," she said while locking the doors to the club. "Why can't I find a man with a body like that and a brain to match?"

Chapter 17

Later on that afternoon, Ariel was getting dressed to meet Lawrence at his home for a barbecue. He was the second blind date from the radio station hook-up line. The next batter up. It had only been two days since her disastrous date with Jeff, but Ariel was anxious to get it over with. "What the hell!" she said while putting on her makeup. "No guts, no glory."

This time she took precautions. She insisted on seeing a photo, a recent one. Lawrence scanned a picture he had taken in Cancun and e-mailed it to her. He was wearing a pair of skimpy swim trunks and sandals. Ariel was pleased with what she saw: no love handles, no flabby ass, and most importantly, no beer belly. He was the perfect height, too, six-one. Although looks weren't number one on her list of priorities, Ariel wanted a man she was sexually and economically attracted to.

By five-thirty she was dressed and ready to go. She checked herself one last time in the full-length mirror then grabbed her purse off the kitchen counter. Just as she was reaching for the doorknob, the phone rang. Something told her not to answer it, but she did anyway.

"Hello?"

"Hi, sweetheart, hope I'm not interrupting anything."

"Mama, how do you always manage to call me at the most inopportune time?"

"I guess I'm psychic."

"If you're psychic, then you should know that I'm late for a date."

"That's great, honey!" she said excitedly. "Is it the same guy you went out with on Sunday?"

"No, Mama, it's someone else."

"Glad to see you're getting out more often. Before you know it, I'll have another son-in-law and some grand-babies."

"I wish you would stop putting so much pressure on me to get knocked up." Ariel was getting frustrated. "It's hard enough to find a man to date, let alone have kids with."

"It's not so hard to find a good man if you know where to look. There are plenty of nice men out here ready to settle down."

"They're nice alright—nice and boring," Ariel said seriously. "I need a man who is romantic but knows how to handle himself on the streets. You, know, a combination of Brian McKnight and Tupac."

"Brian who? And what the hell is a Twopuck?"

"A combination of Nat King Cole and Johnny Taylor, Mama."

"Aw, I understand, a pretty boy and a roughneck."

"Something like that," Ariel said, laughing. "Look, I've got to get going. I'll call you later in the week, okay?"

"Okay, baby, have a good time. And don't forget what I told you."

"Yeah, yeah, I remember. Don't be so strong!" she said. "Bye, Mama."

• • •

The drive out to Lawrence's home took a little more than thirty-five minutes. He lived in Alpharetta, an affluent suburb just north of downtown Atlanta. Ariel was impressed as she drove through the well-manicured gated community. Many of the homes were still under construction and had for sale signs on the lawns that read: NEW HOMES STARTING AT $350,000.

The last two numbers of his street address were hard to read on the scratch piece of paper she had. But finding his house was easy. There were several cars parked in the driveway and on the street. And the unmistakable beat of Parliament and the Funkadelics confirmed where the only black man on the block resided.

After she finally managed to find a parking space nearly a block away, she grabbed her bag out of the car and walked toward the lavish two-story home. As she got closer, she could see a group of women standing in the driveway. They were drinking beer and talking way too loud. Ariel wanted to walk by them without saying a word, but she knew that was asking for trouble. So, she took a deep breath and walked into the lionesses' den.

"Excuse me, I'm looking for Lawrence," Ariel said cordially.

They turned in her direction but didn't say a single word. It was checkout time. Most of the women were average looking, at best, and their bodies were out of shape. Three of them wore long weaves, and had the nerve to wear thongs with stretch marks on their stomachs and behinds.

Ariel could feel the tension in the air. Without even knowing her name, they had already judged her. It wasn't her fault that she was looking cute in her bright yellow shorts and matching halter top. Her waistline was a firm twenty-four inches, which made her firm breasts stand out even more. *Bitch,* she could practically hear them thinking.

"Lawrence went to the liquor store to pick up some more beer, sweetheart," one of the women with the stretch marks said with a nasty attitude.

"He'll be back in a little while," another woman said, seeming more polite. "You can wait around back by the pool. That's where everybody is hanging out."

"Thank you very much," Ariel said.

"You're welcome."

The minute Ariel turned the corner, she could hear the ugly comments and snickering.

"Who does that hoe think she is?" one woman said.

"She needs to go take off that loud-ass yellow outfit," another remarked.

Ariel just kept stepping. She understood how some women could be. They felt threatened when another woman came on the scene who was more attractive. That was one of the main reasons why she was having a hard time dating in Atlanta. Women were constantly competing with one another.

She received a better reception in the backyard. Men were giving her compliments left and right. Several men came over to introduce themselves during the first ten minutes she was there. One guy even brought her a plate of food and a glass of Kool-Aid. Of course, all that attention only made the women even more jealous.

Ariel was so turned off by the hostile atmosphere that she decided to leave. Just as she was gathering her things and was about to stand up, a strong hand pressed down on her shoulder from behind.

"And where do you think you're going?" a deep, sexy voice asked.

Ariel looked up and saw a tall and tanned God towering over her. It was Lawrence. He was even more attractive than his picture. And his thighs seemed more muscular. *Um, um, good,* she was thinking.

"I guess I'm not going anywhere." Ariel was blushing.

"Good, now let me go put this beer in the fridge and I'll be right back," he said as he walked toward the back door.

"I'll be waiting," Ariel said flirtatiously as she sat back down.

Before he made it to the door, he turned around and came back. "By the way, did anybody give you a hard time?" he asked.

"No, everybody has been very nice," Ariel said.

"Well, you be sure to let me know, because I'll kick their asses," he said seriously. "I'm not going to have anybody bothering my baby." Then he kissed her on the cheek and went inside.

Ariel was somewhat disturbed by what he said. She didn't know him that well and he was already staking a claim. But she brushed it off figuring he was just kidding. Besides, she was flattered that he was being so protective. After dealing with so many wimps, she needed a man who would take charge.

"Theodore was right, I need a tune-up," she said while reclining in the lawn chair. "If Lawrence plays his cards right, I might get my tires rotated and my oil changed, too."

Chapter 18

It was 10:00 Tuesday night and I was sitting at home bored to death. I could see the fireworks over the Marina and it made me homesick. I wished I had gone home for the Taste of Chicago and the fireworks downtown on the lakefront. Anything would've been better than doing nothing. I thought about calling Toni again to leave another message but my pride wouldn't let me. It didn't help that I had her picture on my bedroom dresser, the one we took at my birthday party at Club Obsession. I looked at it every day to remind me of how lovely she was that night.

I decided to stop acting like a chump and go over to Melvin's Jazz Club to get into some mischief. Tuesday nights were popular with the Hollywood types—actors, musicians, producers, etc. It was the ideal crowd to attract another wealthy client. Since Helen fired me in Atlanta, I had to compensate for the two thousand dollars a month she was paying. There should be a law against cutting a man off that kind of money, I was thinking.

I opened the double doors to my walk-in closet to check my wardrobe. I needed an outfit that would reflect my mood. Something dark and sinful. I chose a pair of black Canali slacks and a black sheer top. I preferred a two-piece suit but it was too humid. The forecast was a sticky eighty-two degrees, and that was the low.

By 10:30 I was ready to hit the streets. I sprayed my neck with Dolce & Gabbana cologne and popped two multivitamins, just in case I got lucky. On the way out of the door, I looked over at Toni's picture on the dresser. "What are you looking at?" I said with contempt "I can't sit around waiting on you. I've got bills to pay."

• • •

The drive from Marina del Rey to Melvin's Jazz Club took only fifteen minutes. As usual, there was a line of scantily dressed groupies that was nearly a block long. I cruised pass them in my black Porsche, slowing down just enough for them to get a good look.

"Who is that fine nigga?" a woman shouted.

"I don't know, but he's got a nice ride," another woman replied.

Los Angeles was the materialistic capital of America. If a man had a few dollars, drove an expensive car, and was halfway decent-looking, he could practically have any woman he wanted. Sometimes he didn't even need money, just the appearance of money. In L.A. it was all about knowing how to perpetrate.

When I rolled up to the front entrance, it was blocked off with orange cones and a sign in bold letters that read: VALET PARKING FULL. Some of the jealous brothas waiting in line were laughing because they assumed I had to park two blocks down the street like everybody else.

I let them have their laugh for a minute then I blew the horn and flashed my headlights three times. The valet removed the bright orange cones and directed me to pull up to the curb. "Ain't that a bitch?" I heard one of them say.

"Good evening, Mr. Tremell," Rosco said as he opened my door. "I can see you drove the Batmobile, tonight."

"It was time to take old Betsy out for a spin," I said, laughing. "How's it going this evening?"

"It's crazy as usual. I'll be glad when it's time to go home."

"Hang in there," I said while slipping him a ten. "The night's still young."

My adrenaline was pumping the moment I walked through the door. The deejay was playing "Mr. Magic" by Grover Washington, Jr., and a few people were on the dance floor trying to step. I wanted to cut in and show them how we did it in Chi-town but I was too busy scoping out the ladies. Melvin's was packed with beautiful women of every nationality: black, white, Hispanic, and Asian. It was a man's paradise. Not surprisingly, most of the men were holding up the wall sipping on empty drinks, too chicken to strike up a conversation. "Look at these pussies," I said to myself. "No wonder so many women are paying for sex."

While I waited for the hostess to seat me, I made eye contact with an attractive woman seated in the VIP section. She had light brown skin, long black hair, and slanted green eyes. She was definitely mixed with something. I had seen her somewhere before, either on television or a magazine cover. We stared at each other without losing eye contact until the waiter came to serve her drink. Once he was gone, she looked around to make sure no one was watching. Then she took the cherry out of her drink and tied a knot in it with her tongue. My dick got as hard as a pack of Now and Laters. I had to put my hand in my pocket to hide my erection.

Just as I was about to make my move, I felt a heavy slap on the shoulder.

"What the—" I said as I turned around with my dukes up.

"Melvin wants to see you in his office," Scottie said. He was head of security and Melvin's personal assistant.

"You scared the shit out of me, Scottie," I said. "Next time how about a simple, 'excuse me'?"

The woman in the VIP section was watching me and Scottie go at it, and she was cracking up. I gave her a wink and mouthed to her, "I'll be right back." She read my lips and mouthed back, "I'll be here."

While I followed Scottie back to Melvin's office, I had a strange feeling something was wrong. Melvin didn't usually work on Tuesday nights. When we arrived at the office, I knocked on the door.

"Who is it?" Melvin shouted in his deep, raspy voice.

"It's Malcolm."

"Come on in, Cool Breeze."

He pushed the release button for the door and I rushed in expecting the worse. Melvin was leaning out the window with his shirt unbuttoned trying to get some air.

"What's wrong, old man?" I said, sounding concerned. "And don't tell me it was something you ate."

"I'll be fine. I just need to catch my breath." He began to breathe easier.

"That's it! You're going to see a doctor!"

"Those doctors don't know squat," he said angrily. "According to them, I was supposed to be dead ten years ago."

"Well, if you don't stop smoking those cigars and working so hard, you won't last another ten months."

"I didn't ask you to come back here to give medical advice. I have something for you."

He pulled a box from under his desk and handed it to me. It was wrapped with a large bow on it.

"What's this?"

"It's your birthday present," he said. "I wanted to give it to you last week but you were in too big a hurry."

"What is it?"

"If I told you what it was, it wouldn't be a surprise, now would it?"

I was about to tear it open like a kid on Christmas, but he stopped me.

"Don't open it now!" he shouted. "Wait until you get home."

"Why? Is it going to explode?" I asked, laughing.

"I just prefer that you wait. Is that too much to ask?"

"Okay, you old grouch, I'll wait."

I walked over and embraced him. He held me tighter than ever before, and he wouldn't let go. When he finally stepped back, I saw tears in his eyes. That was the first time I had ever seen him cry.

"What's wrong, Melvin," I asked, sounding concerned.

"I'm fine, Cool Breeze. Really I am."

I knew he was lying. But Melvin was from the old school and believed in keeping his emotions pinned up. Until he was ready to talk, there was no point in pressing the issue.

"Is there anything I can do for you?"

"How about playing something for me," he said, wiping the tears from his eyes with a Kleenex. "Something upbeat and happy."

"Anything for you, old man."

I escorted Melvin from his office and sat him directly in front of the stage. Since there was no band performing that night I hopped onstage and started warming up on the piano. I didn't even bother making an announcement. "Testing, one, two," I said into the mic. The deejay finally caught on and turned off the music.

"Excuse me, ladies and gentleman. Can I please have your attention?"

The crowd suddenly got quiet, and all eyes were on me.

"Tonight I want to take time out to recognize a man who has supported me when I was down, who taught me about music, and most importantly, a man who took me into his home and treated me like a son. This one's for you Melvin. I love you, old man."

The song I chose was the classic "My Favorite Things" by Oscar Hammerstein II. It was an upbeat song. And it was old school, like Melvin. When I began to play, you could feel the positive vibes blanket the room. It was like family. Some of the old timers began singing along. And those who didn't know all the lyrics, faked it. Before long the whole room was serenading Melvin. It was an emotional experience.

During the song, I gazed deep into Melvin's weary old eyes and expressed my love as much as I possibly could through those piano keys. His face lit up as I improvised on the notes and made the song my own, just like he had taught me.

When the song ended, the crowd gave him a standing ovation. Melvin's face was completely red and covered with tears. He didn't bother trying to hold them back. I took my bow and rushed over and embraced him. This time it was me who didn't want to let go. "Thank you, Cool Breeze," he said, crying. "That was the best gift you could've ever given me."

Melvin and I said our good-byes and Scottie escorted him outside to his car and drove him home. I was so emotionally spent that I was ready to leave, too. I said my good-byes to the staff and deejay and headed for the door. Before I reached the exit, the woman who was staring at me from the VIP section came up behind me and grabbed my arm.

"Hey, I hope you're not leaving without me," she said.

"That depends," I said.

"On what?"

"On how much money you have to spend."

I was tired and in no mood for games. I came at her very aggressively, hoping to scare her away. But to my surprise she didn't scare easily.

"Is this enough?" she pulled two crisp thousand-dollar bills from her purse.

"That will get you more than a church hug," I said, laughing. "Where do you want to go?"

"I own a beach house in Malibu, about thirty minutes down Pacific Coast Highway," she said. "You can follow me."

"Lead the way."

While we waited outside for the valet to bring our cars, it finally dawned on me where I recognized her from. She was an actress on one of the daytime soap operas.

She never did tell me her name, and I never told her mine. Maybe that's the way we both wanted it.

Chapter 19

It was six-thirty the next morning when I made it home from Malibu. I put my gift from Melvin in the closet, then I peeled off my clothes making a trail of socks and drawers that lead straight to the shower. After washing away the scent of perfume and sex, I closed my thick black curtains to block out the sunlight. Just as I was about to pass out on my king-size bed, I noticed the message light on my answering machine was blinking. The digital counter read 3. As I pushed the play button, I took a deep breath hoping one of them was from Toni.

"Wuz up, partner. It's Simon. I haven't heard from you since Monday. Give me a call to let me know you're still alive. Peace." *Beep.*

"Malcolm, this is your mother. I just wanted to let you know I received your check. Thanks for the extra money, sweetheart. Hope everything is going okay with the real-estate business. Talk to you later in the week. Love you." *Beep.*

"Malcolm, this is Ms. Ruby. I wanted to remind you that tomorrow is my cleaning day. Could you please remember to remove your funky gym shoes from the living room? I'd like to vacuum the floor without using a gas mask. Thank you." *Beep.*

"I'll be damned," I said to myself. "I can't believe she still hasn't called!" My feelings were hurt and my masculine ego was bruised. I went to my office and searched through my organizer for her phone number. When I found it, I tore it into tiny pieces and threw it in the garbage.

"That's rule number three in the *Player's Handbook,*" I said to myself as I stormed back to my bedroom. "Never be more interested in a woman then she is in you."

Then I slammed the door shut and went to bed.

• • •

It seemed like I only had my eyes shut for a split second when I was awakened by the loud humming of the vacuum cleaner. I glanced over at my clock. It read 7:00 A.M. "Lord, please let me get some sleep," I said to myself. I put on my robe and charged out of my bedroom ready to strangle Ms. Ruby.

"Why are you torturing me?" I shouted.

Ms. Ruby was startled. She released the handle to the vacuum cleaner and placed her hand over her chest. "Malcolm, you almost gave me a heart attack."

"Now we're even!" I said angrily. "Why are you vacuuming at seven o'clock in the morning?"

"I didn't know you were here," she explained. "I wanted to get my work done early so I could watch the soaps."

"Look, I understand you have a job to do, but could you please take care of the housework that doesn't require making a lot of noise?"

"No problem, sir. Sorry I woke you."

Ms. Ruby put away the vacuum cleaner and began collecting the trash to dump in the incinerator. As I turned to go back to my bedroom, I noticed a FedEx envelope on the kitchen counter. Ms. Ruby must have picked it up from the security desk on her way up. I hadn't checked my mail in two days. When I looked at the name on the airbill, I was surprised to see Antoinette Grayson at the top. I sat down at the dining room table and opened it.

Dear Malcolm,

I know I'm the last person on earth you wanted to hear from, but please allow me to explain before you tear up this letter. Ever since I met you at the Fox Theater, I haven't been able to stop thinking about you. I haven't been able to choreograph a single dance step in two days. Even my fiancé, Eric, has noticed a change in how I respond to him. No, I'm not trying to tell you that I'm in love with you, but you've definitely had an impact on me. I was moved by your confidence and your passion. Not many men have the ability to inspire me.

I guess what I'm trying to say is, I'm afraid. Afraid because I don't understand what I'm feeling. At first I thought it was infatuation, but since I'm a little too old for that, I'm sure it's something more. If you're interested in talking about it, call me before Friday. I'll be leaving for Chicago to do a show at the Dusable Museum on Saturday afternoon. If I don't hear from you, I'll understand.

Yours truly,
Antoinette Grayson

P.S. I realize a phone call would've been simpler, but I'm much better at communicating on paper.

My head blew up like a helium balloon. "Who's the man?" I shouted. It took four days for her to finally bow down, but it was well worth the wait. I decided to leave a message on her voice mail while I was still gloating. I went into my office and pulled out my organizer to find her phone number. But when I opened it, I realized that I had torn the number up and thrown it away.

I looked beneath the desk for the garbage. But Ms. Ruby had already collected the garbage and was on her way down the hall to the incinerator. I charged out of my apartment like a madman, determined to catch up with her in time.

"Ms. Ruby, wait!" I yelled.

By the time I caught up with her, she was emptying the garbage into the chute.

"Damn!" I said, gasping for air.

"What's wrong?" Ms. Ruby asked, looking bewildered. "Was there something valuable in there?"

"More valuable then you'll ever know."

I walked back to the apartment feeling like a jerk. There was no way for me to contact Toni to let her know I was coming to Chicago next week. All because I was too damned impatient. Like my mama always said, "There's a lesson in every situation." My lesson was to stop being so egotistical and appreciate that Toni was back in my life.

I picked up the letter off the table and read it again, just to make sure I wasn't dreaming. Ms. Ruby walked in and quietly shut the door. Then she eased up behind me and began reading the letter over my shoulder.

"Do you mind?" I asked.

"That must be one hell of a letter to have you running down the hallway with your Johnson swinging all over the place."

"For your information, it's from a very special lady."

"Excuse me, but did I hear you call her *special*?"

"Yeah, and?"

"That's the first time in six years you've ever expressed any interest in a woman. And it's definitely the first time you've ever called a woman special," she said adamantly. "To be honest with you, Malcolm, I was beginning to think you were gay."

"I'm about as gay as Hugh Heffner," I said, laughing as I walked toward my bedroom. "Now I'm going back to bed."

Just before I closed my door, I paused. "And by the way, I'm sorry for raising my voice at you. It won't happen again," I said emotionally. "You know I couldn't manage without you."

"It's okay, Malcolm. I know you work very hard and need your rest," she said. "But I'm not going to be around forever. Hopefully that special lady will be here to take care of you when I'm gone."

"Strange that you would say that, Ms. Ruby, because that's exactly what I was hoping."

PART IV

Every Man for Himself

Chapter 20

Simon woke up just after 10:00 A.M. horny as hell. Two weeks had passed since he last had sex and he was ready to explode. Cynthia was lying next to him completely naked, except for a pair of thong panties. He brushed up against her to give her the hint that he wanted some. When that didn't work, he kissed her on the back of the neck and fondled her breasts.

"Come on, baby," he whispered in her ear. "I need some lovin'."

"Not now baby, I'm tired." Cynthia said as she rolled over onto her stomach.

After a few more attempts Simon became frustrated. He jumped on top of Cynthia's back and tried to pry her legs open.

"What are you doing, Simon!" Cynthia yelled.

"I'm skydiving. What the hell does it look like I'm doing?"

"Get off me!" she screamed. "I can't have sex right now."

"Why not?"

"Because it's close to my period and I've got bad cramps."

Simon rolled off her and sat on the edge of the bed. He covered his face with his hands trying to calm himself.

"Since you got back from New Orleans yesterday we haven't even kissed. When you got off the plane you said you were tired. Last night, you said you had a headache. Now you're telling me it's cramps. I know damn well your period isn't for another two weeks!" he said furiously. "Now do you want to keep playing games or do you want to tell me what the hell is going on?"

Cynthia was speechless. Simon had never spoken to her so forcefully. She had to come up with an answer, and fast.

"I'm sorry, sweetheart. Don't get upset," she said while leaning over and stroking the back of his head. "Nothing is going on. I'm just getting a little nervous over this whole idea of being married. You know how emotional women can get."

Simon was a sucker for an apology. He was in love with Cynthia. Any decent explanation was good enough for him.

"I wish you would talk to me instead of leaving me in the dark. I was beginning to think there was someone else."

"You know I would never do anything to disrespect you," she said convincingly. "You're the only man I ever want inside of me."

Cynthia lead him back into the bed and laid him down on his back. Then she stripped off her thong panties and jumped on top. She really didn't want to have sex with him, but she knew Simon would forgive her for anything after she gave him a little pussy.

"Is it good?" he asked.

"Yes, it's good, baby," she moaned unenthusiastically.

"Is it mine?"

"Sure, it is."

Simon moaned and squirmed for a few minutes, then he climaxed. Cynthia looked over at the clock and shook her head. It lasted ten minutes flat. Right on schedule, she was thinking. Cynthia immediately got up and went to the bathroom to wash off the sex smell.

"Where're you going, baby?" Simon asked. "I want to cuddle."

"I'll be right back," she told him. "I have to pee."

Simon laid back against the pillow with his arms behind his head feeling like Don Juan. Meanwhile Cynthia was looking at herself in the bathroom mirror trying to decide if she were making the right decision marrying a man who couldn't satisfy her sexually. Simon had his moments when the sex was great, but those moments had become few and far between.

When Cynthia came out of the bathroom, she planned to tell Simon a lie about needing to go home to do extra work. But before she could tell him, the phone rang.

"Hello?"

"Mr. Harris, this is Ariel. I know it's early to be calling you at home, but I need to call in that favor."

"What is it, Ariel?"

"I scheduled a private party at the club this evening but something has come up. Can you handle it for me?"

"Hold on, Ariel, I've got to consult the boss." Simon put his hand over the phone.

"Cynthia, do you mind if I run over to the club for a few hours?" he asked.

"No problem, sweetheart," she said while rushing to get dressed. "Take care of your business."

He took his hand away from the phone. "I've got you covered, Ariel. Enjoy your evening."

"Thanks, boss."

After he hung up with Ariel, Simon walked Cynthia to her car. She gave him a peck on the cheek and quickly jumped in her Range Rover.

"You sure you don't want to come hang out with me at the club?"

"No, I would only be in the way," she said as she turned the ignition. "Besides, I have a ton of work to do."

"How about dinner tomorrow night?"

"I would love to, honey, but I promised Debra I would go to church with her."

"Since when did you turn religious?" he asked, looking surprised.

"Since today," she told him. "When I woke up this morning I finally realized the importance of a strong spiritual foundation."

"Well, make sure you say a prayer for me."

"Oh, don't worry, sweetheart, I will."

Chapter 21

At 8:00 A.M. Teddy gathered his most recent pay stubs and his tax returns and rushed out the door. The hearing for his child-support case was at nine o'clock at the Dekalb County Superior Courthouse. The drive was only twenty minutes from his girlfriend's house but he didn't want to take a chance on being late.

As he drove down I-20, the traffic was heavy and moving slowly. He tuned in to 103.3 on the radio and tried to relax. Ironically, the topic of the day was "Deadbeat Dads." "This is definitely a bad omen," he said to himself.

He turned up the volume and listened as a man and woman argued over the issue of child support.

"Whether a man pays child support or not, he should have access to his kids," the man said. "Why should money be a factor?"

"Because kids cost money, that's why!" the woman angrily replied. "Men don't realize how expensive it is to raise children. I pay five hundred a month just for child care."

They bickered back and forth for a few minutes, then the radio personality jumped in.

"Both of you have valid points. But I have another question," he said. "Should a man have to pay child support even if he tells the woman up front that he doesn't want kids?" he asked. "Call in and tell us what you think." He gave the number to the studio line and then went to a commercial break.

Teddy couldn't resist. He picked up his cell phone and dialed the radio station as fast as he could. The first few times the line was busy but eventually he got through. He reached into the glove compartment for a napkin and placed it over the receiver to help disguise his voice.

"V103, what's your issue?" the producer asked.

"Yeah, uh, I want to respond to the question about men paying child support to women who trapped them."

"Are you being sued for child support?"

"Hell, yeah," he said. "As a matter of fact, I'm on my way to court, right now!"

"Perfect!" she said excitedly. "I'm going to put you on hold and we'll come right to you after the commercial break. Give me your name."

"My name is, uh, Tyrone."

"Okay, Tyrone, hold on."

When the commercials ended, the radio personality repeated the question to get the listeners stirred up. Teddy cleared his throat and put the napkin to the phone and waited anxiously to be connected.

"On the phone, we have a man who claims he was trapped. And he's on his way to court for child support as we speak. Are you there, Tyrone?"

"Yeah, I'm here."

"So, what's your story?"

"Well, I was hired to strip at this bachelorette party and I met this very attractive woman. We talked, had a few drinks, and one thing lead to another," he said. "Now she expects me to pay child support."

"Let me get this right," the female jock joined in. "You met a perfect stranger at a party and you had sex with her that same night? And without a condom? Haven't you heard of AIDS?"

"For your information, I had on a condom, but it broke. That happens sometimes when you're well endowed," he said arrogantly.

"But the question is, did you tell her up front that you didn't want kids?"

"That should've been understood."

"And why is that?"

"Because she was the bachelorette who was getting married."

"Now that's a trifling wench," the female personality said. "Let's go to the phones and see what the listeners have to say. V103, what's your question or comment."

"I'm so upset with Tyrone I don't even know where to begin," a woman said.

"Just take a deep breath and say what's on your mind."

"First of all, you're right about the woman, she played herself by having sex with a complete stranger on the night before her wedding. Second, it doesn't matter what the circumstances were, it's all about the welfare of the child. After all, that baby didn't choose to be born," she went on. "And last, I'm fed up with these tired negroes running away from their responsibilities. If you don't want kids, practice celibacy or get a vasectomy."

"I heard that, sistah!" the female jock said.

"Let's not turn this into a *Waiting to Exhale* show," the male jock said, laughing. "Let's take another caller. What's your question or comment?"

"I agree with Tyrone!" a male caller said. "The problem with the child-support system is that it rewards women for having babies out of wedlock. All these lazy tramps have to do is get pregnant by a man with money and they can lay on their asses and collect a paycheck for eighteen years."

"So, what's your solution?" the jock asked.

"They should pass a law stating that if a man doesn't sign an agreement to have children then he's not liable for child support. I guarantee you the birth rate would drop by ninety percent overnight," he said assertively. "And if I were you, Tyrone, I wouldn't pay that heifer one red cent. Maybe next time she'll think twice before she tries to trap another brotha."

"Whew!" It's getting hot up in *cheer*," the jock said.

"Thank God neither one of you fools is my daddy," the female jock laughed. "I'd be on *Oprah* trying to get therapy."

"Well, Tyrone, thanks for your call. And good luck in court today."

"Good luck my ass," the female jock added. "I hope they take the shirt off your back, you old deadbeat."

"Go to hell, you playa hater!" Teddy screamed.

Then he hung up the phone and turned off the radio.

• • •

Teddy exited I-20 on Chandler Road and made a left until he found McDonough Street where the courthouse was located. He parked his Navigator in the back of the lot and took off his diamond earring and Rolex watch. His lawyer advised him not to come into court looking too prosperous.

When he walked into the building, there were three deputies standing by the entrance directing people through a metal detector.

"What's up with the tight security," he asked one of the officers. "I thought this was a courthouse, not a prison?"

"It's just a precaution," the officer said. "You'd be surprised how violent people can get in family court."

"No, I wouldn't," Teddy said as he emptied his pockets and walked through.

After he collected his belongings, Teddy walked toward the elevators where his lawyer, Steve Grundy, was waiting.

He was a short, thin white man with a long scar on the left side of his face. Rumor was he got it from a famous ballplayer after winning the wife a large alimony settlement.

Steve had on his trademark drab gray suit and scuffed-up shoes. His hair was unkempt and his shirt had a ring around the collar. Although he wasn't much to look at, Steve had a reputation for winning big cases. Teddy was hoping he could work his magic for him.

"Wuz up, counselor?" Teddy said as he shook his hand.

"Good morning, Mr. Simmons. Do you have a copy of your pay stubs and tax returns?"

"You get right down to business, don't you?" Teddy said as he handed over a large brown envelope.

"That's what I get paid for," he said.

They stepped into the elevator and rode it to the eighth floor. When the doors opened, Teddy followed Steve down a crowded hallway filled with people arguing and screaming at one another. It was a real war zone

"I want you to wait here," Steve said. "I have to go inside the courtroom and let them know you're here. We should be out of here in no time."

"That sounds good to me."

Shortly after Steve left, the elevator doors opened and a white woman with long blond hair stepped out. It was Donna, the mother of his child. She looked him dead in the eye and didn't say a word.

Moments later, Steve came out of the courtroom and signaled for Teddy to come inside. It was nine o'clock, the moment of truth. Teddy sat in the back of the courtroom to avoid attention. Donna walked in behind him and took a seat in the front row, directly across from the bench. Once the court was brought to order, Steve finally worked up the courage to give Teddy the bad news.

"We may have a slight problem," Steve whispered.

"What do you mean by *slight*?"

"Well, the judge who was supposed to hear our case had a family emergency."

"And?"

"And he was replaced by Judge Harris."

"So what's the problem?"

"Judge Harris is the toughest judge in the state on deadbeat parents. I mean really tough!"

"Can't we get a postponement?" Teddy asked nervously.

"That's what I've been trying to do for the last thirty minutes," Steve told him. "We're going to have to see this one through."

"Something told me this wasn't going to be my day."

As the door to the judge's chamber opened, the bailiff turned toward the gallery. "All rise, the Honorable Judge Ann Harris presiding," he announced. The second Teddy laid eyes on her he knew he was in trouble. Judge Harris was an attractive forty-something black woman. He knew his charm and good looks weren't going to do him any good. He leaned back against the hard wooden bench and prayed for a miracle. But like everything else that day, his situation was going from bad to worse. His case was the first one called.

Teddy looked awkward as he made his way toward the front of the courtroom. At six-five he stood out like a sore thumb. Everyone was staring and making comments, especially the women. "Isn't that the guy who strips at Club Foxy?" one of them whispered. That made him even more uncomfortable.

All the attention didn't go unnoticed by the judge who quickly used it to give him a hard time.

"Good morning, Mr. Simmons," she said. "I can see you're quite the celebrity."

"Not me, your honor. I'm just trying to get by like everybody else."

"Is that right?" she said while looking at him over the top of her glasses.

Teddy was sworn in then he stated his name for the record.

"So what's the situation here?" the judge asked Steve.

"Your honor, my client has cooperated by taking a paternity test, which proved he was the father of the child," Steve said. "However, the five hundred dollars a month that the state is asking for is unreasonable. As you can see by his tax returns, Mr. Simmons has only earned twenty-five thousand dollars over the last two years. Even at the highest rate of twenty-three percent of his gross income that would only be equivalent to three hundred and eighty-three dollars a month."

"I know how to do math, Mr. Grundy," she said wisely. "However, the court has an affidavit by your client's previous employer stating that his income from tips is much greater then he reported. And from what I understand these tips constitute the majority of his income as a stripper."

"I prefer to be called an exotic dancer," Teddy said sarcastically.

"Whatever!" the judge snapped back.

"Before you make a ruling, we would like to bring it to the court's attention that Mr. Simmons also has two other children that he provides for," Steve added. "A five-year-old daughter in Texas and a two-year-old son in Oklahoma."

"Just because his name is on the birth certificates doesn't mean he's providing support," she told him. "Do you have any proof?"

Teddy was speechless. He didn't have any proof because he wasn't providing support. Steve advised him not to include that information but Teddy insisted, hoping the judge would be sympathetic.

"Unless you have any additional information, I'm going to make a ruling for the five hundred per month."

"But your honor, I don't even know this woman," Teddy said, getting loud. "Why should I have to give her five hundred dollars of my hard-earned money?"

"Because it's the law, Mr. Simmons. And furthermore, you better watch your tone in my courtroom. Do you understand?"

Teddy just gave her an angry stare.

"Now, according to the record, your son is six months old," she went on. "Have you been providing support during that time?"

"Yes, I have."

"You're a damned lie!" Donna shouted from the gallery.

She easily stood out in the mostly black gallery with her long blond hair and blue eyes.

"And who might you be, Ms.?" the judge asked.

"My name is Donna Riley. I'm the child's mother."

The room was abuzz with chatter. The black women in the back stood up to get a better look at Donna.

"I can't wait to get home and call my girlfriend," one woman said.

"Sellout!" another yelled.

The judge slammed her gavel down on the bench to get order.

"Mr. Simmons, you better have proof that you are providing support," she said angrily, "Or I'll make you wish you never stepped foot in my courtroom!"

"I do have proof. I just don't have it with me."

"Your honor, he hasn't given me a single penny. Not even when I asked him for ten dollars for a bag of Pampers," Donna said. "I know I should have taken him to court sooner, but he threatened to kill me."

The room erupted with chatter again. The expression on the women's faces in the courtroom were fierce. Although Donna was white, they could relate to her predicament.

"I've heard enough!" the judge shouted. "My judgment is for seven hundred dollars a month, retroactive from the date of the paternity test. You will provide proof of health insurance for this child within thirty days. And if you don't begin payments immediately, Mr. Simmons, you will be held in contempt and sent to jail."

"I'm not a brain surgeon for Christ's sake," Teddy said, looking distressed. "How am I supposed to pay that kind of money?"

"Get a real job!" she said as she slammed her gavel down. "Next case!"

Teddy was furious. He stormed out of the courtroom with Steve trailing closely behind. On his way out, he saw Claudia sitting next to Donna holding her hand. "You lesbian bitch!" he said to her. Once they were out in the hallway, Steve assured him that he would win on appeal. A few minutes later, Donna and Claudia came out of the courtroom.

"Teddy, I don't want your money," she said sincerely. "I just want you to take care of your son and try to be a father to him."

"Look, you poor white trash, I can hardly remember your name. What makes you think I want to play Daddy to your mutt-ass child? Now leave me alone and go back to your lily-white world," he said viciously. "And by the way, I ain't paying you a dime. I don't give a damn what that tight-ass judge says."

Teddy looked her up and down with disgust, then walked toward the elevators.

"I hope you burn in hell you cold-blooded bastard," Donna screamed with tears rolling down her face. "I wouldn't want my child anywhere near you anyway!"

"Lower your voice, Donna. Court is still in session," Claudia said, trying to calm her down.

"I don't care," she screamed. "And I may be poor white trash, but at least I'm not running away from my responsibilities as a parent, like you are. You fuckin' coward!"

Teddy boarded the elevator with his lawyer then pressed the button for the lobby. Right before the doors closed, he dangled the keys to his Navigator and smiled like he didn't have a care in the world.

Chapter 22

Ariel arrived at Sylvia's restaurant just before 7:00 P.M. She was wearing three-inch pumps and a black halter dress that showed off her shapely figure. When she walked through the door, all eyes were on her.

"How many?" the hostess asked.

"Table for two, something near the front."

The hostess grabbed two menus and escorted her to the corner table next to the window. Ariel wanted to get a good look at Lawrence's tight buns when he showed up. It had been a long time since she had a man to lust over and she wanted to make the most of it.

When the waitress came over to take her order, Ariel asked for a glass of white zinfandel. She wasn't thirsty, but it was a helpful prop to ignore all the rude looks from the men surrounding her. Some were totally disrespectful. They continued to stare even though their dates were sitting right next to them.

The man at the table across from her was more discreet. He waited until his wife went to the rest room, then he sent the waitress over with a complimentary drink and his phone number. Ariel sent it back without even looking in his direction.

While she waited impatiently for Lawrence to come to her rescue, she pulled out her compact to check her makeup. When she looked into the mirror, a man's face appeared out of nowhere over her shoulder. It was Chris. She hadn't seen him since they met at Justin's but she recognized him right away.

"Hello, stranger," he said.

"Chris, you scared the dickens out of me."

"Sorry about that. I saw you sitting over here and I wanted to say hello."

"How did you know it was me with my back to the door?"

"Not too many women can wear a short haircut and look as fine as you."

"Don't try to make up by complimenting me. I'm still shaking." Ariel sounded serious but she was blushing.

"Well, I didn't want to bother you," Chris said as he began to back away. "Enjoy your food."

"Oh, no you don't. Come back here and protect me from these vultures." Ariel waved for him to come back. "Unless of course, you're here with a date."

"No, I come here alone every Thursday after work to get my grub on."

"Well, pull up a chair and hang out with me for a minute," she said.

As soon as Chris sat down, the jealous stares began. Half the men in the room were checking him out as if he were sitting with their woman.

"Next time you might want to consider wearing a pair of coveralls," he said, laughing. "Those legs could get a brotha killed."

"I don't usually dress like a hoochie so early in the day, but I thought my friend would like it."

"Don't tell me you're here on another blind date?" he said. "I'm not going to play Rico the killer pimp again."

"No, I had enough of that drama," she said. "I've already met this one. And he seems pretty cool."

"I'm happy everything is working out for you," he said genuinely. "But I hope this doesn't mean we can't still be friends."

"Of course not," she said while reaching over and holding his hand.

At that moment Lawrence walked into the restaurant. He glanced around the room until he saw Ariel. He saw Chris, too. And he didn't appreciate him holding Ariel's hand. He rushed over to the table and lifted Chris up by his arm."

"Get your hands off my woman," he shouted.

"Hey, man, what's your fuckin' problem?" Chris yelled back.

He got in Lawrence's face and shoved him. Although he was only five-six and fifty pounds lighter, he didn't back down.

"Stop it, Lawrence!" Ariel said while stepping between them. "Chris is just a friend."

By now, everyone in the restaurant was watching the fight like they were ringside in Las Vegas. Even the waitresses stopped serving food to watch the show.

"Chris, I'm terribly sorry," Ariel apologized. "Please let me handle this. I'll talk to you later."

"You should do a better job of choosing who you go out with," he said while fixing his clothes. "Your boyfriend isn't playing with a full deck."

He stared Lawrence down for a few seconds then he calmly walked away.

Ariel sat down at the table and tried to act normal. She took a sip of her wine and a deep breath. Lawrence was still standing as if he were waiting for an invitation to sit.

"Would you please sit down?" she asked. "I think you've already attracted enough attention for one day."

Lawrence picked the chair up from off the floor and sat down.

"Look, Ariel, I apologize for what happened with your little friend, but a man has got to protect what's his."

"I don't need protection when I'm in a crowded restaurant talking to a friend."

"I know, baby. And I'm sorry for overreacting," he said looking pitiful. "It's just that men today don't have any respect for another man's woman. They will stare at your woman and even grab her ass if you don't put them in check."

Lawrence's behavior was out of line, but Ariel noticed that it was effective. The men who were gawking at her earlier, were looking somewhere else. It must be a man thing, she was thinking.

"Every woman wants a hero, Lawrence," she told him, "but I'm a strong, independent woman who can take care of herself."

"I know you can, Ariel. But maybe it's time you let someone else be strong?" he said while holding her hand as if he were proposing. "I've got a great job, a big house, and enough money so that you don't have to work unless you want to."

"Lawrence, I'm flattered, I really am," Ariel was smiling from ear to ear. "But as romantic as that all sounds, you don't even know me. And I don't know you. Why don't we give it a few months and see what happens?"

"Maybe you're right, baby. It probably is a good idea to slow down and get to know each other better. After all, you're not going anywhere, right?" he said, looking her straight in the eyes.

"Right, baby," she said apprehensively.

"Good, now let's get out of here, I want to go to the mall before it closes and look at some rings." He stood up from the table.

"I thought we agreed to slow down."

"I was just kidding," he said, laughing. "But I would like to go to the mall. Maybe we can catch a movie."

"That sounds like fun, but don't you want to eat first?"

"No, I lost my appetite," he said.

Ariel put five dollars on the table for her drink and began walking toward the door.

"I got it, baby," he said while pulling a wad of bills out of his pocket. "No woman of mine has to spend her own money."

Ariel didn't argue. She gladly picked up her hard-earned money and put it back inside her purse. There had been too many occasions when her dates stuck her with the bill. Any act of chivalry was greatly appreciated.

Before they left, Ariel noticed Chris was in the dining area in the back.

"Lawrence, why don't you wait on me outside. I want to go say good-bye to Chris," she said. "That's the least I can do after what happened."

"Go ahead. And tell the little fellah I said I was sorry for the misunderstanding," he said, laughing.

Ariel made her way through the thick crowd, trying to avoid brushing up against the horny men who were watching her every move. When she finally made it to the back dining area, she walked over to Chris's table and pulled up a chair.

"I can't tell you how embarrassed I am for what happened. I don't know what got into him," she said. "He's very protective of me."

Chris kept eating without even looking up at her.

"Anyway, we're getting ready to leave," she went on. "I'll give you a call later on this week to see how you're doing, okay?"

When he didn't respond, she stood up from the table and began to walk away.

"Wait a minute!" He stood up and slowly walked toward her. "Look, Ariel, I know you don't know me from Adam, but I do care about you. If you ever need someone to talk to, or just a shoulder to lean on, don't hesitate to call. Even if it's only for a Blockbuster video and popcorn," he said, laughing.

"Thanks for being so sweet, Chris." She gave him a kiss on the cheek then she backed away "I'll see you later."

"I hope so," he whispered to himself. "If that psycho doesn't kill you first."

Chapter 23

It was three o'clock Saturday afternoon. My flight arrived at Chicago O'Hare more than an hour late. I grabbed my garment bag from the overhead compartment and headed straight for the rental car shuttle bus. When the bus arrived, I sat in the back, pulled out my cell phone, and dialed the number to the Dusable Museum.

"Dusable Museum, how may I direct your call?" a cordial woman's voice said.

"I'm looking for information about a dance recital this afternoon. Can you tell me what time it starts?"

"I don't believe we have any recitals scheduled today, sir. But if you'll hold on for a moment, I'll double-check."

While I waited for her to return, I slapped myself on the forehead. I knew I should've called before coming all the way from Los Angeles, but I trusted Toni would be there. All I could do was hope that the receptionist was wrong.

"Hello, sir?" she said.

"Yes, I'm here."

"We don't have a dance recital today, but there is a youth group scheduled to use the auditorium for dance lessons between three and five this afternoon."

"That has to be it," I said to myself. "Thank you very much for your help."

After I hung up the phone, I began calculating how long it would take to get to the museum. It was already 3:20 P.M. and the Budget car lot was still five minutes away. I estimated a ten-minute wait in line when I got there. And the drive to Fifty-fifth Street was thirty minutes, under ideal conditions.

I tried to relax by looking out of the window at the CTA trains as they emerged from the tunnel underneath the airport. When I was a kid, I used to ride those same trains downtown to watch karate movies at McVickers Theater. I laughed out loud when I thought about how my friends and I used to kick and punch each other all the way to Ninety-fifth Street. "Those were the days," I said to myself.

But those childhood memories didn't last long. I was stressing over the idea of coming all the way from Los Angeles only to miss Toni by a few minutes. I looked down at my watch a hundred times as if I could make time stand still. Even the elderly bus driver seemed to be working against me. He was driving slow and he stopped at the traffic light before it turned yellow.

"I'm going to kill this old bastard if he doesn't hurry up," I said to myself. "I could run backward and get there faster."

• • •

The traffic on the Dan Ryan Expressway was horrible. By the time I came off the ramp at Fifty-fifth Street, it was 4:59. I turned east and headed toward Cottage Grove Avenue driving like a bat out of hell. I ran two red lights, three stop signs, and almost hit a little old lady crossing the street with her grocery cart.

When I finally made it to the museum, I jumped out of the car and rushed toward the entrance. Once inside, I approached the receptionist booth to get directions. An elderly black woman with long gray hair was sitting inside reading a magazine.

"Excuse me, could you tell me where the auditorium is?"

"It's around that corner and to your left," she said. "Are you the gentleman who called earlier?"

"Yes, ma'am."

"Well, you'd better hurry, there are only a few people still inside."

"Thanks again," I said as I hurried off.

The closer I got to the auditorium, the faster my heart pounded. I was excited at the thought of seeing Toni again but I dreaded the possibility of her not being there. As I got closer to the door, I could hear classical music playing softly in the background. I slowly pushed the door opened and peeked inside. And there was Toni, looking more beautiful than I remembered. She was standing onstage giving dance lessons to a group of young girls.

I wanted to rush over and sweep her off her feet, but I didn't want to interrupt their lesson. So I crept upstairs to the balcony and watched from the back row. I admired the way Toni handled the energetic young girls. She was trying to teach them how to pirouette but they were getting discouraged. "You can do it," she told them. "Just pretend like you're a top and spin." The little girls turned as fast as they could while balancing themselves on their toes. The parents, who were sitting near the stage, applauded like their daughters had just won Olympic gold medals.

After about ten minutes, the lesson was over. The children collected their belongings and left with their parents. Toni turned off her portable CD player and began packing her large duffle bag. I was ready to rush downstairs to meet her at the door, but she suddenly stopped. She stood in the middle of the stage and looked around as if she were checking to see if anyone was still inside the auditorium. I slid down in my seat as low as possible to avoid being seen.

When she felt comfortable that she was alone, she put on her leggings and ballet slippers and began stretching. She did a series of splits then stood up and touched her head to her knees. I have never seen a woman so limber. After she had warmed up, she pulled another CD out of her bag and placed it inside the player. Then she rushed to center stage to get set.

I was expecting to hear something classical or possibly a modern dance song. But my guess wasn't close. The song was "Makeda" by Les Nubians. It was a popular cut about a year ago sang by two French sistahs. I couldn't understand the lyrics but the beat was hypnotic and smooth.

I sat up in my seat and watched Toni as she swayed to the rhythm of the music. Her motions were fluent and precise as if the dance were choreographed. And her facial expression was intense. It was obvious that the song had a special meaning. I couldn't help feeling like I was trespassing on a private moment. I wanted to look away, but I couldn't help myself. I was captivated by her passion and spirit.

As the song continued to play, Toni stopped ballet dancing and began bumping and grinding like she was at a nightclub. And she was doing it so nasty. "Um, um, um," I said to myself while shaking my head. "God is good." I decided the time was right to make my move. I rushed down the balcony stairs and made my way backstage. Toni was so deep into the music that she didn't see me coming as I danced my way toward her from the shadows. But she must have sensed me coming because she suddenly turned in my direction. She was startled at first, but once she saw it was me, she kept dancing and waved for me to come closer.

"Aw, sookie, sookie, now!" I said as I moved toward her.

When I got right up on her, she put her arms around my neck, pressed up against me, and began to grind and sing in French.

La reine de Saba vit en moi
Makeda vit en moi.
Oh, oh, oh, oh.

I couldn't make out a damn thing she was singing but it didn't matter. I finally had her where I wanted her—in my arms. We hugged each other tightly as we danced around the stage like Ginger Rogers and Fred Astaire. When the song ended, we stood still in the center of the stage and looked into each other's eyes.

"I see you got my letter," she said.

"I got it, all right," I told her. "But you could've saved a few dollars by calling."

"I felt you were worth it."

"I hope I don't disappoint you."

"I hope you don't either," she said.

As we moved toward each other, we wet our lips at the same time. She smiled. I smiled. Then we kissed. It was the first time in twelve years that I was affectionate with a woman without getting paid for it. And it felt good.

After what seemed like forever, we finally came up for air.

"So, now what?" Toni asked as she leaned into my chest.

"Well, we could run off and get married," I said jokingly. "Or we can get something to eat."

"As much as I would love to take you up on the marriage proposal, I'll have to take door number two."

"Oh, well, you can't blame a guy for trying. Let's get outta here."

"I've got a few people I have to see before I can leave," she said. "Why don't I give you a call on your cell phone and you can tell me where you want to meet?"

"Actually, I wanted to invite you over to my mom's house for dinner," I said. "She makes the best peach cobbler in Chicago."

"Sounds like a plan!" she said, sounding delighted. "Will eight o'clock be too late?"

"I could wait on you forever, baby," I told her. "But for my mother's sake, eight o'clock will be fine."

I gave her a hug and a kiss on the forehead, then I began walking toward the exit. And as I walked out the door, I suddenly turned.

"By the way, did you come all the way to Chicago just to teach this class? Or was it an excuse to see me?"

"As much as I would love to stroke your gigantic male ego, I came as a favor to a friend. She had an important business trip and she didn't want to disappoint the girls."

"You're one hell of a friend."

"No, baby, I'm one hell of a woman."

"I heard that!" I said with a smile as I wrote down my mom's address. "See you at eight."

When I made it back to my car, I called my mom on my cell phone to tell her I was bringing company. The phone rang five times, which was unusual. When she finally picked up, I understood what was keeping her. She had "Love and Happiness" by Al Green blaring in the background.

"Love will make you do wrong," she sang loudly in my ear. "Hello!"

"Mama, it's me, Malcolm."

"Who?"

"It's Malcolm!" I yelled. "If you turn down that music maybe you could hear me."

"Hold on, baby."

She turned down the stereo and came back to the phone, still singing.

"Love will make you come home early, make you stay out all night long," she sang.

"I can see you're in a good mood today."

"Of course I am. The Lord blessed me with another day and my favorite son is coming home to have dinner with me."

"I'm you're only son, Mama," I reminded her. "Now, stop singing for a minute so I can ask a favor."

"The last time you asked me for a favor I had to bail you and Simon out of jail," she said, laughing.

"I promise you, it's not that serious," I said. "I just want to know if it's okay to bring a lady friend over for dinner?"

I heard what sounded like a large skillet dropping in the background.

"Ouch!" Mama yelled.

"Are you alright?"

"I'm fine, son. I just need to make sure I heard you correctly. Did you say you were bringing a woman over for dinner?"

"Yes."

"Is this woman a friend, or a girlfriend?"

"I guess you could call her a girlfriend."

"Hallelujah!" she screamed.

"Why are you making such a big deal out of this?"

"I'm sorry I got carried away, sweetheart, but you haven't brought a girl home since high school. I was beginning to think you were gay."

"I'm not gay! I'm not gay!" I hollered.

"Alright, son, I believe you," she said. "Now let me go so I can make something special for your guest. What time will you be over?"

"About eight."

"Okay, I'll see you then," she said, sounding excited. "This is a young lady I've got to meet." Then she abruptly hung up.

The phone was dead, but that didn't stop me from venting. I looked at my reflection in the rearview mirror and yelled, "I'm not gay, dammit!"

Chapter 24

I arrived at my mother's house in Hyde Park at 7:30 P.M. When I pulled into the driveway I could hear "Let's Stay Together" by Al Green blaring from her living room window. "Mama is seriously getting her groove on," I said to myself. I rang the bell and pounded on the door for nearly five minutes before she finally heard me. "I'm coming!" she yelled. "Hold your horses!"

When she opened the door, I was overwhelmed by the aroma of freshly cooked collard greens and her famous peach cobbler.

"Is dinner ready yet?" I asked as I walked right past her.

"Boy, you better come back here and give your mama a hug."

"I was just kiddin', Mama. How's my favorite girl?" I said as I lifted her up by the waist and gave her a sloppy, wet kiss.

"Malcolm, you're so crazy. Put me down!"

My mother and I were very close, almost like brother and sister. We drank together, went out to clubs to dance, we even worked out at the gym together. At sixty-five, she was in excellent shape. If it wasn't for her distinctive gray hair, she could easily pass for a woman fifteen years younger.

"Where is your lady friend?" she asked after I gently let her down.

"Her name is Antoinette, and she should be here any minute."

"Oh, my goodness, I look a mess," she said, trying to fix her hair. "Watch the food while I go freshen up." Then she ran off to the bathroom.

"Mama, stop making such a big fuss. She's just a friend, not the President of the United States."

But there was no use arguing with her. Mama was very conscious of her appearance. If she took the garbage out to the corner she wanted to look her best. That attitude must have been hereditary because I was just as obsessive. I had worked out for an hour before my date with Toni. And I made sure to wear shorts and a tight Polo top to show off my chest and arms. I wanted Toni to get a good look at the merchandise.

While I was blowing into my hands to make sure my breath wasn't kickin', the doorbell rang. "I'll get it!" Mama yelled. I wanted to rush to the door myself, but I played it cool and sat down on the sofa. I picked up one of Mama's old *Ebony* magazines and acted like I was reading.

"Good evening, Mrs. Tremell," I heard Toni say.

"Malcolm, it's your friend Antoinette!" Mama yelled. "Come in, sweetheart."

I held my breath as I waited for Toni to turn the corner from the hallway. Although I had seen her three hours earlier, Toni had a presence about her that made every encounter feel like the first time. When she walked into the living room, I casually peeked from behind the magazine to check her out. As usual, she was looking fine. She had on a white tennis skirt and button-up collar blouse. Her hair was pulled back into a tight ponytail that came down just past her shoulder. I just shook my head wondering what the hell I ever did to deserve such a prize.

"Don't I get a hug or something," Toni said.

"Most definitely!"

I sprang up from the sofa and walked over and gave her a hug. At first I held her gently, trying to be respectful in front of Mama. But Toni was feeling so damned good that I tightened my grip until I could feel her heart beat. "Um," we sighed simultaneously.

"Alright, you lovebirds, break it up," Mama said while taking Toni by the hand. "I think you better come with me, young lady."

"Where are you taking her?"

"Away from your hormones," she said as she lead Toni toward the kitchen. "Can you cook, child?"

"Yes, ma'am," Toni said.

"Good, come on in here and give me a hand with these greens."

Toni and Mama stayed in the kitchen for nearly thirty minutes yapping it up like mother and daughter. Mama came out to grab the family album then she retreated back inside the man-free zone. The next thing I heard was Mama bursting out in laughter. "Aw, look at him. He's so cute!" I heard Toni say.

I was praying Mama wasn't showing her my baby pictures, or those horrible photographs of my grammar school graduation. The thought of Toni seeing me wearing that big lopsided afro was driving me crazy. Just as I was about to barge in to see what was going on, they came out with plates and utensils to set the table.

"It's about time," I said. "I thought you forgot about me."

"How could I forget about you, Bam Bam!" Toni said, laughing.

"Mama, I can't believe you told her that nickname."

"Don't worry, baby, I won't tell anybody," Toni said. "I just wish I could've seen you banging away on that toy piano when you were a baby. I bet you were so cute."

"See what you started, Mama?" I said. "I'll never live this down."

"It's okay, Bam Bam, your secret is safe with me," Toni said, laughing.

We all sat down to Mama's delicious dinner of red beans and rice, collard greens, neck bones, corn bread, and of course, her peach cobbler. We laughed and talked about my childhood and anything else my mother could think of to embarrass me.

"Malcolm was a real lady-killer," Mama said. "All the girls in the neighborhood had a crush on him."

"Tell me more, Mrs. Tremell," Toni said as she rested her arms on the table.

"When he graduated from high school, five different girls asked him to the prom."

"So how did he manage his little harem?"

"He charged them fifty dollars each and made them pay for his tuxedo and a limo."

"Did they pay?"

"Oh yeah! They were lined up. And if they didn't have the money, their parents were happy to foot the bill."

"Sounds like he had a nice little enterprise going on."

"I told him he should've gone into the escort business instead of real estate," Mama said. "He could've made a fortune."

When she made that comment, I nearly choked on my Kool-Aid.

"Are you alright, baby," Toni said while patting me on the back.

I nodded yes, and went to the kitchen to get a paper towel to wipe my face. I made sure to leave the door cracked so I could hear the rest of the conversation.

"I thought Malcolm was a musician," Toni said. "I heard him play at Simon's club in Atlanta and he sounded great!"

"I've been trying to convince him to pursue his music full-time, but he won't listen to me," Mama said. "Maybe you can talk some sense into him."

"I'm surprised that someone with so much talent would have to be convinced. It seems like such a part of who he is."

"It is a part of him. A very important part," Mama said. "But when his father died, something inside of Malcolm died, too."

"I didn't know his father was dead," Toni said.

"Malcolm didn't tell you what happened?" Mama said, getting emotional.

"No ma'am. But we don't have to talk about it if it's going to upset you."

"It's okay, sweetheart. Maybe it's time I talk about it," she said. "I've been holding on to the pain for twelve years."

Mama reached for the family album and opened the page with her and my father's black-and-white wedding picture. It was taken back in 1961. Toni moved in closer and put her arms around Mama.

"He was such a handsome young man, wasn't he?" Mama said.

"Yes, ma'am," Toni said while admiring the picture. "Did he die of natural causes?"

Mama chuckled as tears began to roll down her cheeks. "I guess you could call it natural. He was shot while screwing the next-door-neighbor's wife."

"Oh, my God!" Toni sighed. "I'm sorry, Mrs. Tremell, I didn't know."

"The painful part is that I still blame myself for what happened. I knew what was going on and I didn't do anything to stop it."

"It's not your fault, Mrs. Tremell. You can't control a man's behavior."

"But I had a choice not to put up with it!" she said, getting upset with herself. "If I would've taken a stand I believe my husband would be alive today. But like so many women raised back in those days, my mother taught me to hang in there no matter what. A man is going to be a man, she would preach."

"That's not right, Mrs. Tremell. And it's not right for you to torture yourself," Toni said. "I know there's someone else out there for you who can make you happy. You're so beautiful and full of energy."

"Thanks for being so sweet, Antoinette," Mama said, wiping her tears away with her hands. "But you don't understand how deeply I loved this man. He was truly my soul mate. I remember the first time I ever saw him. We were at a high school sock hop and he asked me to dance. All the other girls were so jealous," Mama said, smiling. "When I looked into his eyes, the same way you look into Malcolm's, I knew we would spend the rest of our lives together."

Mama gave Toni a hug and kiss on the forehead. "Sometimes true love only comes around once in a lifetime, sweetheart. When it comes around for you, don't ever let it go," she told her. Then she went upstairs to her bedroom.

I waited inside the kitchen for a couple of minutes trying to give Toni a chance to get herself together. She had been crying, too, and I didn't want to embarrass her. When I finally came out, I tried to act as if I didn't hear a word of their conversation.

"So, where's Mama?"

"She went upstairs to lay down," Toni said, sounding depressed. "Maybe this would be a good time to say good night."

"Don't be ridiculous, it's not even ten o'clock yet. Besides, we haven't had a chance to talk."

"Well, can we at least go outside. I could use some fresh air?"

"I've got a better idea. Why don't we walk over to the lakefront? I could use some fresh air myself."

• • •

Toni and I held hands as we crossed over the steel bridge on Lake Shore Drive. The gentle breeze coming off the lake and the full moon created the perfect romantic atmosphere. But Toni's mind was on the other side of town. She hadn't uttered a single word since we left the house. She just gazed off into the stars seemingly full of thought.

"Are you alright?" I asked her.

"To be honest with you, I'm pretty shaken up."

"Was it the conversation you had with Mama? I heard what she told you."

"Malcolm, why didn't you tell me what happened to your father?"

"What was I supposed to say: Hi, my name is Malcolm, and by the way, my father was shot in the head while fucking the next-door neighbor?" I said, getting loud.

"No, but you could've told me he was dead, especially if you were taking me to meet your mother. That's something that just might come up in casual conversation, don't you think?"

"You're right, Toni," I said. "I guess I'm out of dating practice. Believe it or not, I haven't brought a woman home to meet my mother since I was seventeen."

"Why has it been so long?"

"Because I haven't met anyone special enough, that's why. You don't just bring any old woman home to meet your mother."

"Amen to that."

By this time we had made it down to the beach. We took off our shoes and walked onto the cool sand. There were couples everywhere, holding hands and walking along the shoreline. Toni and I grasped hands tightly and walked toward the water.

"Malcolm, why haven't you asked me about my situation with Eric?"

"I didn't want to force the issue. I figured you would tell me when you were ready."

"Well, I think this would be a good time," she said.

We sat down on the sand near the water, folding our legs Indian-style.

"I've known Eric since college," she went on. "We dated for a while but after we graduated we sort of grew apart. About a year ago we ran into each other at a fund-raiser and we started dating again. The night before I met you, he asked me to marry him. I didn't officially accept but I didn't turn him down either."

"Now I'm even more confused."

"What I'm trying to say is I love Eric, I really do. But not in the way a woman should love a man she's going to marry," she said passionately. "I struggled with my feelings all that night. Finally, I just put it in the Lord's hands and prayed. I asked God to give me a sign. Any sign that would tell me if I was making the right decision. The very next day is when I saw your handsome face sitting in the front row at the Fox Theater. Through all the bright lights, loud music, and hundreds of people in the audience, something made me look your way. At first I dismissed it as simply a physical attraction. But when you showed up with those eleven roses after the show, I knew you were someone special."

"I don't know what to say."

"Don't say anything unless you feel the same way I do. I don't want to be in love by myself."

"I do feel the same way, baby. It's been a long time since I truly cared about someone. Maybe too long."

"Just promise me one thing, Malcolm," she said as she held my face gently in her hands.

"What's that?"

"That we'll always be honest with each other. That's very important to me. I don't ever want to experience the

pain your father put your mother through. I could never forgive you for that."

"I promise," I told her.

Then we kissed and held each other until the sun came
up. It was the first time in my life I felt that close to a
woman.

Chapter 25

Ariel woke up Sunday morning and immediately went into her ritual. She brewed a fresh pot of coffee, retrieved her Sunday morning paper, and curled up on the sofa to watch *Heart and Soul* on BET. The show focused on books about relationships and self-improvement. "What a coincidence," Ariel said as she ran to get a notepad and pen. "A sistah could use a little advice right about now." Just when they were about to interview Iyanla Vanzant, the phone rang. Ariel checked the Caller I.D. to see if it was her mother, but the number was blocked.

"Hello?" she said with an attitude.

"Hello, Ariel, this is Lawrence. I know it's a bit early to be calling, but I wanted to make sure you were okay. I was getting worried since I hadn't heard from you in a while."

"Lawrence, I need time out from this relationship."

"Time out for what?"

"Time to get my head together, that's what! Things are moving way too fast."

"Can't we sit down and talk about this like adults?" he asked.

"There's nothing to talk about," she told him.

"I hope you're not still upset with me about what happened with your little friend at Sylvia's."

"My little friend's name is Chris," she said defensively. "And it has nothing to do with him. I just need time to sort things out."

"Have it your way," he said. "But I'm not going to stop calling unless you accept these flowers as a token of our friendship."

"What flowers?"

"The ones I'm holding outside your door."

Ariel walked over to the window and pulled back the curtains. Lawrence's black Lexus was parked in her driveway. "I'll be damned," she said to herself. When she opened the door, Lawrence was holding a gift basket filled with whip cream, condoms, and other sexual paraphernalia.

"Surprise!"

"Surprise, my ass!" she said. "I don't appreciate you coming over here unannounced. And what the hell is that basket for?"

"I just wanted to show you how much I've missed you," he said, looking pitiful.

"Well, you've shown me, now good-bye!" she said, trying to slam the door in his face.

"Damn, baby, don't be so cold," he said, putting his foot in the doorway. "Can I at least set this basket down and get a glass of water?"

Ariel thought about it for a second, then she reluctantly let him. She made him stand in the hallway while she poured him a glass of water from the faucet. She wasn't about to treat him to her bottled spring water.

"Here!" she said, shoving it toward him. "And don't take all day sipping on it. I want to get back to my program."

Suddenly the phone rang. Ariel was hoping it was her

mother. She wanted to let someone know Lawrence was there, just in case he turned violent. She excused herself and rushed into the bedroom to answer it.

"Hello!"

"Good morning, Ms. Daniels. How's my favorite manager?"

"Simon, you won't believe who just showed up at my front door," she whispered.

"Who, Michael Jordan?"

"No, you smart aleck. It's Lawrence!"

"You mean the guy who went off on your friend at Sylvia's?"

"That's the one."

"I thought you dumped him."

"I've been trying to cut him loose since last week, but he's persistent."

"Well, if he starts choking the shit out of you, make sure you scratch him so the police can get a DNA sample," Simon said, laughing.

"That's not funny. I think this guy is really crazy."

"You want me to call the police?"

"No, I think I can handle it," she told him. "But if you don't hear back from me in ten minutes, dial 911."

"Alright, Ariel, but be careful. I don't want to see you on *Unsolved Mysteries*."

When she went back into the living room, Lawrence was sitting on the sofa with his shoes off. His feet were propped up on her glass cocktail table.

"Lawrence, what the hell are you doing?"

"I was just watching BET," he said with a smile. "I love this program about black books."

"Well, the show is over." She turned off the television with the remote.

"Okay, okay," he said, slipping on his shoes. "I know when I'm not wanted. Just let me use your bathroom and I'm outta here."

Ariel didn't want to make matters worse, so she showed him to the bathroom. While he handled his business, she wiped off the table where he had smudged her glass with his sweaty feet. "You trifling bastard," she said to herself. Then she took his glass into the kitchen and washed it out in hot water.

While her back was turned toward the sink, Lawrence came out of the bathroom buck naked, wearing a bright green condom, and holding a can of whipped cream.

"Here's Johnny!" he said.

Ariel was so stunned the glass slipped out of her hand and shattered on the floor.

"What the hell do you think you're doing?" she asked.

"I thought you might want sausage for breakfast," he said, laughing.

"Lawrence, you've got about ten seconds to put on your clothes and get the fuck out of my house!"

"Come on, baby. Stop fighting it. You know you want some of this sweet meat." He walked toward her while stroking his penis.

Ariel pulled a butcher's knife out of the drawer and swung it at him.

"If you take another step, I'm going to cut that little crooked motherfucker off."

"Alright, I'm leaving!" he yelled as he ran into the bathroom and grabbed his clothes. "Just stop making dick threats."

Ariel followed him to the door waving the knife like a Samurai. She didn't even give him a chance to put on his clothes before she pushed him out. "And stay out, you fuckin' lunatic!" she yelled as she locked the door.

A few minutes later, Lawrence drove off. Ariel collapsed on the sofa and tried to calm herself down long enough to call Simon back.

"Simon, this is Ariel," she said nervously. "I just wanted to let you know that he's gone and I'm okay."

"Are you sure? You sound terrible."

"I always sound like this when a deranged man comes to my house first thing in the morning and pulls out his dick."

"I'm glad that's all he pulled out," Simon said.

"Don't worry, I've got protection and I know how to use it," she said, sounding cocky. "By the way, why were you calling me this morning?"

"With all the drama going on I almost forgot," Simon said, laughing. "I called to remind you about Ladies' Night on Thursday. I promised Teddy that you would personally take care of him."

"Thanks, boss, that's all I need in my life is another lunatic," she said.

Chapter 26

The line outside Club Obsession stretched two blocks down Peachtree Street. The crowd was so unruly the security guards had to set up barricades to keep the over-anxious women from cutting the line. Thursday nights had become chaotic since Teddy and his dance group, Hot Chocolate, began performing. It was the third consecutive sell-out week and the crowds were becoming unmanage-able. Ariel and Simon watched from the second-floor win-dow trying to decide what to do.

"You think we should cancel the show?" Ariel asked Simon.

"Are you crazy? That would cause a riot," he said. "But we've got to come up with something fast. We don't have enough seats for all those people."

Ariel looked around the club with her hand on her chin.

"I've got an idea," she said. "Why don't we open the balcony area and place chairs along the back wall? If we move those old boxes we can accommodate another two hundred people."

"That could work, except for one problem," Simon said. "The view is obscured by partitions."

"Believe me, those horny women will look around a building to see a naked man," Ariel said, laughing.

"You're pretty sharp for a rookie," Simon said as he gave her a friendly peck on the cheek."

"What's that for?"

"For thinking fast on your feet," Simon said. "If we get through this night in one piece, I might even give you a raise."

While he hurried to get the chairs in place, Ariel went to the dressing room to check on Teddy. She knocked on the door twice but he didn't answer. "Theodore, you in there?" she yelled. When she put her ear to the door she heard a smacking sound. She knocked again, this time harder. When he didn't answer, she used her key to unlock the door.

"Theodore, I know you're in. . ."

She was too stunned to get out the rest of her sentence. Teddy had one of the waitresses bent over against the wall banging her doggie-style.

"Didn't your mama ever teach you to knock?" Teddy said with a sly grin.

"I'm sorry, Ms. Daniels," the waitress whined as she pulled down her skirt. "I came to give him a glass of water and well one thing lead to another. It was an accident!"

"Yeah, right. I guess you accidentally slipped on a wet spot and fell on his dick," Ariel said sarcastically. "Go collect your belongings, you're fired!"

"But, Ms. Daniels, I need this job."

"You should've thought about that before you bent over against that wall and played yourself," she told her. "Now get to steppin'."

She stormed by Ariel and mumbled, "Stuck-up bitch."

"Excuse me?"

"I didn't say anything."

"I know you didn't," Ariel said, looking fierce. "If you open your filthy mouth again they'll be carrying your ass out of here!"

Teddy was getting a good laugh out of the situation. He had a wide grin on his face as he pulled up his pants.

"You shouldn't have fired that sweet young thang," Teddy said. "Good help is hard to find."

"I would fire your arrogant ass, too, if it weren't for all the money Simon invested in you."

"Well, since I still have a job, I'm sure you won't mind closing the door so I can get dressed. My public is waiting," he said smugly. "Of course, you're more than welcome to stick around and watch."

"That's quite alright, I've already seen your little show, and frankly, I'm not impressed." Then she slammed the door shut.

Ariel tried to compose herself as she walked out into the club. The doors had opened for business and hundreds of women were rushing in to get front-row seats. Ariel maneuvered her way over to the bar where Simon was standing. He had the cordless phone in his hand and was signaling that she had a phone call.

"Who is it?" she asked

Simon put his hand over the receiver.

"I think it's Lawrence," he whispered. "You want me to tell him you're not here?"

"No, I'll take it in the office," she told him. "I need to put this behind me once and for all."

Once Ariel was inside the office, she closed the door, and picked up. Simon kept the phone up to his ear to listen in.

"Hello?"

"Hello, Ariel. This is Lawrence."

"Didn't I tell you not to call me again?"

"I know, but I just wanted to talk."

"Talk about what?"

"About working things out."

"There's nothing to work out. So please stop stalking me, otherwise I'm going to call the police."

"I'm harmless, baby. But if you call the cops I might have to get ugly," he said, sounding crazy. "Now stop playing hard to get and tell me what time I should pick you up tomorrow. My mother is having us over for dinner at eight o'clock. I told her all about you."

"Lawrence, I don't want to meet your mother, your father, or your damned dog. I just want to be left alone!"

"I'm not going anywhere until I get some pussy," he said. "I invested time and money in you."

"Look, you sick bastard, you heard what the lady said, now leave her alone!" Simon said, cutting in.

"Is that you, Mr. Big-Shot Club Owner?"

"It's me," Simon said. "You got something to say, tough guy?"

"Yeah, mind your own damned business!"

"Ariel is my business! If you have anything else you have to say, you can say it to me!"

"Now I see what's going on," he said. "You and Ariel have been mixing business with pleasure. Well, I've got something for both of your asses!" Then he hung up.

Simon rushed to the office to see how Ariel was doing. When he opened the door, she had her head down on the desk.

"This is like a bad dream," she said. "Why can't I find a straight black man in Atlanta with a good job, who's not on Prozac?"

"He's just trying to scare you," Simon said. "Guys like that are all talk."

"I don't know, Simon. I've got a bad feeling about this," Ariel said. "And now that you're involved, you better watch your back, too."

"Don't worry about me, I'm from the southside of Chicago."

"Being from the southside of Chicago doesn't make you bullet proof," she told him.

• • •

By 10:00 P.M. the club was jam-packed. Hundreds of women waited impatiently for the show to begin. "We want Teddy! We want Teddy," they yelled. Simon gave the signal for the deejay to start the music. The lights dimmed and clouds of artificial smoke rose from the stage. The crowd erupted in cheers. "Bring on the meat!" one woman hollered.

When the smoke cleared, a mock toolbox was sitting in the center of the stage. Suddenly, four muscular men burst out of the cardboard box dressed as a plumber, auto mechanic, painter, and electrician. Teddy came out last dressed as a construction worker. When they stripped off their costumes, hundreds of women rushed the stage to get a touch of their muscular physiques.

"How much for a tune-up, baby?" a woman yelled while flashing a ten-dollar bill.

"I need my pipes unclogged," another screamed. "Can you help a sistah out?"

The security guards rushed onto the stage to keep the situation under control. One woman had hold of the penis of one of the strippers and wouldn't let go. Teddy was loving the attention. He licked out his tongue and massaged his penis working the crowd into a frenzy. Simon and Ariel stood on the upstairs balcony and watched in disbelief as professional women in business suits climbed over one another like teenagers to stuff the strippers' thongs with cash.

"I'm in the wrong line of work," Simon said. "I might have to put on a tight pair of drawers and get out there and shake it up myself."

"Don't even think about it," Ariel joked as she patted him on his slightly protruding stomach. "They don't make G-strings that hold nickels and dimes."

The evening was going better than Simon expected. The bartenders were selling drinks left and right and the customers were having a ball. Even the women sitting upstairs with the obstructed view were enjoying themselves.

"Looks like we're going to survive another wild-and-crazy night," Simon said to Ariel as he looked around the crowded room. "You might get that raise after all."

"Don't be so quick to count your chickens. The night's not over yet."

Suddenly, there was a loud crashing sound near the front entrance. The music abruptly stopped and the crowd began to panic. "Somebody is shooting!" a woman yelled. People scattered in all directions running for the emergency exits. Ariel and Simon ducked into the Jazz Room to keep from being run over.

"I hate when I'm right," Ariel said.

"Me, too. And by the way, you can forget about that raise."

Once the commotion settled down, they came out to check the damage. It wasn't as bad as they thought. Most of the tables and chairs were knocked over, but the glass to the aquarium wasn't damaged. That was Simon's biggest concern. There were a few people lying on the floor hurt. Some of them bleeding. "Call 911," Simon told Ariel. "I'm going to go see what the hell happened."

When he made it to the club's entrance, he noticed the large picturesque window was completely shattered. Glass was everywhere. The police had a man outside in handcuffs laying facedown on the ground. He was wearing flannel pajamas and a pair of flip-flops.

"Is this the son of a bitch who did this?" Simon asked.

"Yes, sir," the officer said. "He threw a brick in the window and tried to make a run for it."

"Turn him over so I can see his punk ass."

"Wuz up, Mr. Big-Shot Club Owner?" the man said. "I hope I didn't ruin your little party."

"Lawrence?"

"In the flesh," he said. "Maybe that'll teach you not to fuck with another man's woman."

Ariel saw what was going on and came running over. When she saw Lawrence covered in his muddied pajamas and wearing flip-flops she didn't know whether to laugh or cry.

"Don't just stand there, baby, come over here and give Big Daddy a kiss," Lawrence said with a smirk on his face.

"Lawrence, you need serious help," she said.

"All I need is you. And if I can't have you, nobody will."

"Get him outta here," Simon said to the officer.

"It ain't over!" Lawrence yelled while being carried away. "I know where you live you two-timing bitch!"

Ariel broke down in tears and began to tremble. Simon walked over and held her in his arms. "It'll be alright," he said while stroking her shoulders. "I won't ever let him hurt you."

Just then, Teddy came out of the club with his bag slung over his shoulder.

"I heard about what happened," he said. "Are you all right, Ariel—I mean, Ms. Daniels?"

"I'll be fine, Theodore. Thanks for asking."

"So, does this mean the show is canceled next Thursday?"

"It's hard to say right now," Simon said. "I'll get in touch with you after I evaluate the damages."

"Cool."

Teddy shook hands with Simon and began walking toward the parking lot. But he couldn't leave without making a wise crack.

"You must have some good pussy to have a brotha trippin' like that," he said, laughing.

Ariel walked up to him and slapped the grin off his face.

"You'll never know, smart ass."

Chapter 27

The next morning Simon awoke just in time to watch Cynthia on the twelve o'clock news. She was interviewing a famous bodybuilder at a local health club. Simon couldn't help noticing how friendly they were. Too friendly for a television interview, he thought. The muscle-bound man inconspicuously stroked Cynthia's breast while showing her the proper way to bench press. It may have seemed innocent to most people but Simon knew he was getting his feel on. "Don't make me come down there and hit your big ass with a dumbbell!" he shouted at the television.

Just then, the phone rang. He glanced over at the Caller I.D. to make sure it wasn't a pesky telemarketer. When he saw the 310 area code he knew who it was.

"Wuz up, fool?"

"It's all good!" Malcolm said. "How's everything in Hotlanta?"

"Not so good, partner. Last night Ariel's psychopathic boyfriend threw a brick through the front window of the club."

197

"What did he do that for?"

"He thought Ariel and I were fooling around?"

"I wonder what gave him that idea?" Malcolm said sarcastically.

"Don't even go there," Simon said, laughing. "I'm a one woman man, not a big-time player like you."

"Well, my playing days might be over. I just got back from my little rendezvous with Toni in Chicago."

"How did it go?"

"It was great! We had dinner at Mama's house, and chilled out on the lakefront."

"And?"

"And what?"

"Did you hit it?"

"No, I didn't hit it, you old freak," Malcolm said, laughing. "We just hung out for a few days and enjoyed each other's company. Having sex wasn't a priority."

"Now, that's a first," Simon joked. "I guess you're ready to settle down and get married."

"I don't know about getting married, but I'm definitely ready for a change! This gigolo game is getting played out," he told him. "As a matter of fact, Toni hooked me up with an agent friend of hers in New York. If I get a deal with a major record company I'd seriously consider putting a ring on her finger."

"That's great news about the agent. I always told you, you could make a fortune in the music business!" Simon sounded excited. "But aren't you forgetting about Toni's fiancé? I do recall her mentioning that she was engaged."

"That's no big deal. Toni is giving him the boot as soon as she gets back to Atlanta."

"And I bet you don't feel an ounce of guilt, do you?"

"Hell no! Why should I?" Malcolm said, sounding cocky. "He had his chance and he blew it. Or as my father used to say, if you snooze, you lose."

"That's cold-blooded," Simon said. "Whatever happened to brothers sticking together?"

"In the love game, it's every man for himself," Malcolm said. "I've got to look out for my own interests."

Simon was still watching Cynthia flirt with the bodybuilder. He wasn't the type to get intimidated by another man, but listening to Malcolm brag about stealing Toni had made him paranoid.

"You think Cynthia would dump me for another man?" Simon asked.

"I'm the wrong person to ask about Cynthia."

"Just answer yes or no," Simon said, sounding serious.

"Anything is possible," he told him. "I mean, you're not exactly the easiest man in the world to be in a relationship with."

"What's that supposed to mean?"

"You're a workaholic!" Malcolm said. "As much as I dislike Cynthia I have to sympathize with her. You probably don't have sex unless it's on your itinerary."

"Unlike you, I have a business to run. I can't lay up in bed all day," he said, getting defensive. "Sometimes all I have time for is a quickie."

"Women need romance, not some guy slamming against her for five minutes like he just got out of prison," Malcolm said.

"Alright, Mr. Ladies' Man, what do you suggest?"

"Try sending her flowers or surprising her with a hot bubble bath by candlelight. Women love that kind of shit," Malcolm told him. "But most importantly, you've got to lick that clit until her toes curl."

"You know I don't take nosedives," Simon said.

"When it comes to satisfying your woman, the word *don't* shouldn't exist in your vocabulary."

"Look, I don't eat pussy and nothing you say is going to change my mind."

"It's men like you that keep men like me in business. All

you care about is money, money, money! Meanwhile your woman is home alone with a vibrator and her old black book," he said. "It's only a matter of time before she steps out for some maintenance."

Simon was speechless. For the first time in his life he was faced with the truth about his obsession with money. His relationship with Cynthia was deteriorating because he hadn't made her a priority.

"You're right," Simon confessed. "And it might be too late to make things right."

"What do you mean?"

"I haven't talked to Cynthia in almost a week. Since her trip to New Orleans she doesn't return my calls. And when I do manage to reach her, she's on her way to church."

"Why don't you hire a private investigator? I have an associate in Atlanta who owns a detective agency. He's eccentric, but he's good."

"Maybe I'm just overreacting." Simon was trying to avoid dealing with the issue. "I mean, what could she possibly be getting into at church?"

"Don't be so naive. Church is a player's paradise," Malcolm said. "I know men who go to service every Sunday just to meet desperate and lonely women."

"Okay, you've made your point."

Simon rummaged through his briefcase for a pen and something to write on.

"Now, tell me where I can find this associate of yours."

• • •

Late that afternoon, Simon arrived at the detective agency on Stewart Avenue in his old Chevy. The office was located on the second floor of a dilapidated building that sat between a liquor store and a barbecue joint. Simon glanced down at his notepad hoping he'd written down another address. Unfortunately it was a perfect match. He grabbed the large brown envelope off the passenger's seat and made his way across the street.

The building was a haven for derelicts and drug addicts. The hallways reeked of urine. Simon covered his nose with the handkerchief from his suit pocket and rushed to the second floor, stepping over an intoxicated bum along the way. The investigator's office was the third door on the right, directly across from the janitor's closet. PRIVATE DICK DETECTIVE AGENCY was awkwardly painted on the door. Simon took a deep breath and knocked.

"Who is it?" a man with a deep voice yelled out.

"It's Simon Harris, Malcolm's friend."

The door made an annoying squeaking sound as it opened. And the slower Simon tried to open it, the louder it squeaked. The detective was trying to crack the door just enough to peek out. Once he was convinced the coast was clear, he directed Simon to come in. He was clutching a nine-millimeter pistol, which he quickly tucked into the back of his trousers.

"Sorry for the tight security, but I make a lot of enemies in my line of work."

"I can imagine."

The detective was a tall, thin black man. But his dark complexion couldn't disguise the jagged scar on the right side of his face. It was the type of scar made by a knife with a dull blade or broken glass. He must have really pissed someone off, Simon was thinking.

The inside of the drab office was filled with all kinds of seventies paraphernalia. It was like walking through a time warp. The walls were covered with blue-light posters and old album covers. The living room was a shrine to the so-called black exploitation movies. Huge theater posters from movies like *Claudine, Foxy Brown, Cleopatra Jones,* and *J.D.'s Revenge* were everywhere. Taped to the refrigerator door was a mint-condition Ohio Players album cover. The one with the woman pouring honey on her chest.

The detective was a throwback to the seventies himself. He wore a pair of tight polyester pants and was sporting a short, unkempt afro. Simon damn near fell out when he saw the afro pick with the retracting red and green handles sticking out of the back of his head. Simon would've paid anything for that antique.

"I guess we haven't been formally introduced. My name is Ricky," he said while extending his hand, "but everybody calls me by my last name, Roundtree. You know, like Richard Roundtree in the movie *Shaft*."

"He's a bad mother. . ."

"Shut your mouth," Roundtree sang along.

It was impossible for black folks to say *Shaft* without throwing in the lyrics to the song. It was one of those black things. The humor was unexpected but it helped to relax the mood.

"So, Mr. Harris, what can I do for you?"

"As I told you briefly on the phone, I'm getting married and I want to find out if my fiancée is cheating."

"Sounds simple enough," Roundtree said while popping open a can of Old English 800. "Did you bring the information I asked for?"

"I've got it right here."

Simon emptied the contents of the brown envelope onto the living room table. There were several pictures of him and Cynthia, Debra and Cynthia, and one of Cynthia's Range Rover.

"Can I offer you a brew?" Roundtree asked.

"No thanks. The last time I drank some Old E, I woke up in a vacant lot wearing nothing but my drawers."

"Suit yourself."

Roundtree sat down on the dingy black leather sofa and looked over the pictures carefully. He grunted a few times then took a long sip of his beer.

"Nice-looking lady you got there," he said casually.

"Thanks."

"Have you considered a prenuptial agreement?" he asked out of nowhere.

"What made you ask that?"

"Just curious."

"You sound as if you expect to find something negative."

"Let's just say, I'm intuitive about these things."

He looked at Simon and smiled uncomfortably. Then he stood up and began pacing.

"Okay, this is the deal," he said with his hand firmly pressed against his chin. "I'll follow her for the next thirty days to see what I can dig up. When I put together enough evidence, I'll give you a call."

"That sounds fair enough. So, how much is this little investigation going to cost?"

Roundtree wrote down a figure on a piece of paper towel and handed it to Simon. The amount read $2999.95.

"What's up with the ninety-five cents?"

"It's marketing," he explained. "I got the idea from watching those Tae-Bo infomercials. The workout video sells for nineteen-ninety-five because it sounds cheaper than twenty."

He escorted Simon to the door. They shook hands and gave each other brotherly hugs. It was a man thing.

"I assume you want to be paid in cash?"

"If it's not a problem," Roundtree said. "I don't want Uncle Sam in my pocket, if you know what I mean."

"Any particular denominations?"

"How about two one-thousand-dollar bills, nine hundreds, one fifty, two twenties, nine singles, three quarters, two dimes, and five pennies."

"Tell you what," Simon said pulling out a wad of money. "I'll pay you an even three thousand up front if you throw in that afro pick with the red and green handles."

"You've got yourself a deal!"

PART V

Don't Hate the Player,
Hate the Game

Chapter 28

It was a typical muggy summer night in August. I stepped out onto my twenty-fifth-story balcony and watched the sun set over the pacific. The view was breathtaking. I wished that Toni could have been there to share that moment with me. It had been almost three weeks since she left for Europe with her dance company and I was really missing her. But I had to put all those romantic thoughts aside. I had an important appointment to keep, and I didn't want to be late. I took one last hit of my drink and slipped into my Armani suit jacket. It was 8:50 P.M. and my limo was supposed to meet me downstairs in the lobby at 9:00.

As I was leaving out of the door, the phone rang. The double ring let me know it was my business line. I was hoping it wasn't one of my horny clients calling for a last-minute booty call.

"Tremell Agency," I answered.

"Ah-hah!" Melvin yelled. "I called your business number to see if you quit the escort business like you said you would. I can see you're doing business as usual." He sounded disappointed.

"I am out of business after tonight," I said. "I couldn't turn down two thousand bucks just for escorting some rich broad to a dinner party for two hours. It's easy money."

"What do you need with two thousand dollars? I thought you told me you had a record deal in the works?"

"I told you I had an agent. Until I actually sign a contract, I still have a mortgage to pay on this expensive-ass condo. Not to mention my six-hundred-dollar-a-month car note. Besides, I'm doing it as a favor to Helen. We fell out on bad terms in Atlanta and I wanted to make it up to her."

"Stop making excuses, Cool Breeze. Why don't you just admit that you can't give up the life. You love playing mind games on these women too much. And you love the variety of sex, too," he said, laughing. "Face it, you're addicted to women!"

"The only thing I'm addicted to is money."

"Okay, then, I'll give you two thousand dollars to stay in tonight."

"Yeah, right."

"I'm dead serious," he said.

"So, what's the catch?"

"There is no catch. I just wanna keep you from backsliding. One night can turn into two, then three, and so on. Next thing you know, you're caught up in the game again."

"Nice try with the morality speech, old man. But I'm still going through with this last engagement. It wouldn't be very professional to cancel on such short notice."

"Two thousand dollars is a lot of money to pass up just to stay at home, eat popcorn, and watch cable. You sure you don't want to think it over?"

"I'm sure," I told him. "But if you insist on spending

your hard-earned money, why don't you make a donation to a worthy charity, like Players Anonymous," I said, laughing.

Just then, my other line rang. I told Melvin to hold on while I answered it.

"Hello?

"Mr. Tremell, you car is here," the doorman said.

"Thank you. I'll be right down."

When I clicked back over, Melvin was coughing uncontrollably.

"You alright?"

"I'm fine," he said still hacking. "I just need a drink of water."

"You don't sound fine to me. Have you been taking your medication?"

"I'm fine, I told you! I've been taking care of myself since before you were a twinkle in your daddy's eye. So stop trying to act like my mother!" he snapped.

"Stop trying to sound hard," I said jokingly. "You don't scare me like you do those employees at the club. I know you're just a grumpy old teddy bear."

He was laughing so hard, he nearly choked himself to death. After a few more coughs, he managed to compose himself.

"You always did know what to say to make me smile, Cool Breeze," he said as he cleared his throat. "Look, I know you have to get going. But the first chance you get, I want to meet this special lady of yours. Any woman who can make you retire from the gigolo game must be an angel."

"Well, when my angel comes back from touring in Europe, I'll ask her if she can fly in on her wings to meet you. But only if you promise to start taking better care of yourself," I scolded him. "I don't want to take any chances of losing you. You're the most important person in the world to me."

He paused.

"That's a promise, Cool Breeze," he said, getting

choked up. "Now, get your narrow behind outta there and go take care of business. And you'd better keep your dick in your pants tonight, you hear?"

"There you go again, old man, trying to play hard," I said, laughing.

• • •

As we approached the entrance to the Marriott near the airport, I checked myself in the mirror one last time. This was my retirement night from twelve years of the game and I wanted to look my best. As the stretch black limousine cruised slowly toward the front of the hotel, the valet rushed to open my door.

"Welcome to the Marriott," he said. "Do you need help with your luggage, sir?"

"No, thank you. I'm here to meet someone."

I tipped him ten bucks then walked inside to find my date. The lobby was buzzing with black folks dressed in formal attire talking among themselves about business. When I looked over at the red-and-white banner hanging on the wall, I understood why they were so stiff. It read: WELCOME NATIONAL ASSOCIATION OF AFRICAN-AMERICAN FINANCIAL CONSULTANTS. "What a bunch of tight asses," I muttered to myself

"My sentiments exactly," a woman said from behind me. "Mr. Tremell, I presume?"

"You would presume correctly," I said as I turned to face her. "And you are?"

"Catherine Howard, your date for the evening." She extended her hand. "Nice to meet you."

"The pleasure is all mine."

Catherine was incredibly gorgeous. Or as my daddy used to say, she was so fine she made you wanna drink her bathwater. She bore a stark resemblance to a young Diahann Carroll. Her hair was in a French roll. And she wore a fitted royal blue dress, which accentuated her full figure and dark-chocolate complexion. I knew from reading the article about her software company in *Fortune* magazine that she was forty-five, but she could have easily passed for a woman in her early thirties.

"You look surprised," she said bluntly.

"You don't miss much do you?" I asked, laughing. "My facial expression must have given me away."

"Yes, it did," she said, smiling flirtatiously. "What were you expecting? A troll?"

"To be honest with you, I didn't know what to expect. Sometimes pictures can be deceiving. But I can tell you that the picture of you in the magazine didn't do you justice. You should have that photographer shot."

We continued to talk as we strolled hand in hand toward the restaurant. Along the way, Catherine attracted a great deal of attention. She was waving and shaking hands as if she were running for public office.

"Good evening, Ms. Howard," some said.

"I enjoyed your speech, Ms. Howard," others professed.

"Don't forget to e-mail me that report," a woman added.

Catherine just smiled and kept walking as if it were no big deal. Once we made it through the corporate gauntlet to the restaurant, the maître d' sat us at a reserved table in the back. It was obvious by the way Catherine carried herself that she was accustomed to this kind of preferential treatment.

"So, do you come here often," I asked sarcastically.

"From time to time," she said, smiling. "What about you?"

"Touché!" I said, giving her credit for a good comeback line. "You don't pull any punches, do you?"

"No, I don't. That's why I'm the president of this male-dominated organization today. I go for what I want."

"Well, since we're being so direct, what does a beautiful and intelligent woman like yourself need with an escort service? It seems to me that you could have any man you wanted."

"Three simple reasons," she said, moving in close so no one could hear her. "One, I need a strong man who knows how to take charge. Although I'm surrounded by highly successful men who earn millions of dollars, behind closed doors most of them are wimps who allow you to treat them like dogs. I need a man who isn't afraid to tell me no sometimes. And one who will tell me to shut up. Even a woman of my caliber wants a man with a little street in him."

I damn near choked on the water I was drinking. "Could you please be a little more direct?" I said, trying to clear my throat.

"Don't act so surprised. If you read the article you should know I'm from the Garden Valley projects in Cleveland. And you know we keep it real on the east side."

We inconspicuously slapped five and then she went on.

"The second reason is, most men are very insecure, especially black men. If they can't handle a sistah making fifty thousand, what makes you think they can handle a woman whose net worth is five million?"

She cleverly slid her hand underneath the table and began moving it slowly up my thigh.

"And what's number three?" I asked, trying to keep a straight face.

"I love attractive young men with big dicks," she said bluntly. "And yours came highly recommended."

My dick got as hard as a petrified jawbreaker. And it didn't help that Catherine had unzipped my pants and was massaging my balls. I tried to keep my composure as people began to stare. But Catherine didn't even flinch. She just kept stroking my Johnson and talking dirty.

"Why don't we stop wasting time and go upstairs to my suite. I have a bottle of Alizé chilling in bucket of ice and a Bill Evans CD. I heard you love jazz."

"You sure did your homework."

"That's the first thing they teach you in Business 101: always have a plan."

"I'll tell you what, I'm going to the little boys' room to give you some time to cool down. And when I come back, we're going to have a nice dinner and good conversation. Then I'm outta here." I stood up from the table and put my hand in my pocket to conceal my erection."

"Can I order you anything to drink while you're gone? A screwdriver, perhaps?"

"Very cute," I said, smiling, "but I'll just have a shot of brandy. On second thought, make that a double."

On my way back to the rest room I saw a familiar face sitting inside the sports bar. I moved in closer to make sure my eyes weren't playing tricks on me. But when she turned to the side, I was sure it was psychotic Tina. "What the hell is she doing here," I said to myself. Last I heard, she had settled with her NBA husband for ten million cash and the house. I'm sure he would've paid twice that just to get rid of her crazy ass. She was having drinks with a gigolo named Dexter. He was an up-and-coming young player from the San Bernadino area. I quickly turned away and walked back toward the restaurant as fast as I could. I knew Tina would make a big scene if she saw me.

When I made it back to the table, Catherine was sipping on a margarita with that horny look in her eyes. I didn't want to lead her on by going upstairs to her room but I couldn't take a chance of running into Tina.

"Boy, that was quick," she said.

"I think I'll take you up on that offer to go upstairs."

"What about dinner?"

"We can eat upstairs," I told her.

"I like the way that sounds," she said with a sly grin. "Just let me pay for these drinks and we can start with dessert."

While she charged the bill to her room, I was trying to devise a plan to separate myself from Catherine. In order to get to the elevators we had to walk directly past the sports bar. I wasn't about to take that chance on Tina seeing Catherine and me together. I had to think of something fast.

"Alright, let's go," she said.

"Aw, damn! I left my wallet in the limo," I said, patting my pockets. "Why don't you get a head start and I'll meet you upstairs?"

"I don't mind going with you. I wanted to get a breath of fresh air anyway."

"I'd rather do it myself," I told her. "Besides, that will give you a time to slip into something more comfortable."

That idea must have appealed to her because she promptly wrote her room number down on a napkin and handed me an extra key.

"Now don't keep me waiting," she said seductively. "I've got a fire that needs to be put out."

"Don't worry, baby, I'll be right behind you with my hose."

She gave me a kiss on the cheek and rushed off to put on her little costume. Once she was out of sight I made my way toward the door feeling relieved. "That was too close for comfort," I said, sighing. Just then Tina and Dexter came strolling out of the bar headed straight for me. I stooped down and tried to mix in with crowd, but at six-three I was hard to miss. Before I could make a getaway down the opposite side of the corridor, she spotted me. "Malcolm, is that you?" she hollered. I wanted to keep steppin' but I knew Tina could get ignorant and draw even more attention. So, I played it off by waving and giving her a phony smile.

But Tina wasn't going for that. She grabbed Dexter by the hand and rushed over. There was no way she was going to let me get away without bragging about how much money she had gotten from her divorce. She also wanted to flaunt Dexter in my face. It was well known that we didn't get along.

"Well, well, well, if it isn't Malcolm the Lover," she said.

"Hello, Tina. Nice to see you."

"Don't give me that shit, you know I'm the last person on earth you want see."

"If you knew that why did you run your tired ass over here?"

"Watch your mouth when you're talking to a lady," Dexter said, trying to sound hard.

"Look, young buck, you need to stay out of grown folks' business," I said, getting in his face. "Now, I know you think you're hot shit down in San Bernadino but you're in L.A. with the big dogs now. So I suggest that you rest that chivalry role before I toss your young ass over that banister."

Dexter and I were about the same height but he was thin, at least fifteen pounds lighter than me. He saw the look in my eyes and quickly backed down. He knew I was one second away from dropping him. Men read one another's eyes that way. It's a street thing.

"Baby, could you excuse us for a second?" Tina said to Dexter. "I want to talk to Malcolm alone for a minute."

"Yeah, Dexter, why don't you go kick some rocks like a good little boy. I promise I won't keep her long," I said conceitedly.

Once Dexter was gone, Tina's whole attitude changed. Her tone was more polite and she began rubbing on my chest.

"Malcolm, why haven't you returned my calls? You know I need my monthly fix."

"I've been busy."

"For a whole month?"

"Look, Tina, You're not my wife. I don't owe you an explanation. Besides, I told you I can't deal with your dramatic mood swings."

"I'm much better now that my divorce is final. Didn't you hear about the settlement on ESPN?"

"Yes, I heard. Congratulations," I said sarcastically. "Now why don't you get a life and leave me alone?"

"Because I'm in love with you. And I just can't cut my feelings off like a faucet the way you do."

"Yeah, right. You're so in love with me that you've been lying up with a different gigolo every weekend. I heard it through the grapevine that you've been buying dick all over California." I looked her up and down like she was trash. "What's wrong? Your crazy ass can't get laid without paying for it?"

Smack. She slapped me right in the face. The entire room turned in our direction to see what was going on.

"Fuck you, Malcolm!" she shouted. "That rich bitch you came here to see is no better than me. How much did she pay for some dick tonight?"

"This conversation is over," I said as I began to walk away. "Have a good night."

"Don't you walk away from me, you arrogant bastard. I'm not through with you yet!"

People rushed out of the restaurant and the sports bar to watch the circus. Some of them even had the nerve to take pictures. I walked as fast as I could toward the elevator with Tina trailing me screaming obscenities. Luckily the elevator was waiting when I got there. I frantically pushed the button for the fifteenth floor trying to force the doors shut.

"It's not over between us!" she yelled. "I bought your ass before and I can buy you again. You ain't nothing but a piece of meat who sells to the highest bidder."

As the elevator doors closed, she took off her high-heeled shoe and flung it at me. It grazed me on the right side of the forehead drawing blood.

"Take that, you pretty motherfucker."

• • •

When I arrived at Catherine's suite, I went inside the bathroom to find a towel to put on my face. The bleeding wasn't bad, but it did require a bandage. After I patched myself up with the first-aid kit I walked out into the candlelit room. "My Foolish Heart" by Bill Evans was playing softly in the background. Catherine was lying on the bed face up, wearing a see-through black negligee and sipping on a glass of Alizé. She looked me up and down like a piece of meat but she never acknowledged the bandage on my head.

"So, how do you like it?" Catherine stood up and modeled.

"That's very nice," I said, trying to be cool.

"Nice enough to eat?"

"Like I said, you get straight to the point."

I was about to go into a big discussion about our agreement not to have sex, but I thought, what the fuck, and began taking off my clothes. Catherine was looking good and I needed to let off a little steam. While I stripped out of my clothes I tried to put Toni out of my mind. When that didn't work, I played head games with myself to justify what I was about to do. *She's probably screwing some guy in Europe right now,* I was thinking. *What she doesn't know won't hurt her,* was another thought. And then there was the classic excuse, *It's not like we're married.* Those were just a few thoughts running through my mind while I ate Catherine out. After she climaxed, she laid me down on the bed and returned the favor.

For the next hour, we sucked, licked, and screwed like animals. It was some of the wildest sex I ever had, and some of the most obscene. Catherine insisted on having anal sex on the patio, right out in the open. I agreed because she offered to pay more money.

When it was all over, I put on my clothes, collected my twenty-five hundred dollars, and headed for the door. No thank-yous, and no good-byes, not even eye contact. Catherine just turned over, lit a cigarette, and ordered room service. She got what she wanted and she was through with me.

As I walked down the corridor toward the elevator, I rubbed the bandage on my head and tried to play it off like it was business as usual. But in the back of my mind I was replaying what Tina said about me. And she was right, I was just a piece of meat who sold out to the highest bidder. But this time I sold more than my body. I sold my integrity.

Chapter 29

Teddy was naked except for his underwear and one sweat sock. "Come on seven!" he yelled as he prepared to roll the dice. He and Cheryl were playing strip Monopoly and Teddy's dog game piece was sitting on Pennsylvania Avenue. He needed seven to pass go and collect two hundred dollars. If he rolled a three or five, he would land on Park Place or Boardwalk, properties that belonged to Cheryl.

Teddy blew on the dice and rolled them gently onto the board, "Come on lucky seven!" he hollered. The dice seemed to turn in slow motion and finally landed flush, the total was five.

"You landed on Boardwalk, now take off those drawers!" Cheryl screamed as she jumped up and down on the bed.

"Wait a minute, baby. Your braids got in my eyes," Teddy said, getting upset. "I get another turn!"

"I hate playing Monopoly with you, Teddy. You're such a sore loser."

"I'll show you who's a sore loser."

219

Teddy grabbed Cheryl by the hair and slammed her down onto the bed. He ripped off her panties and rammed his penis inside of her.

"Ouch, baby, not so rough," she screamed. "I'm still a little dry."

"Well you better start thinking wet because I'm not about to stop."

Just as Teddy was getting into a nice groove, he heard a car door shut in the driveway. He quickly hopped off Cheryl and peeped out the window.

"Guess who's coming to dinner?" Teddy said jokingly.

It was Cheryl's husband, David. Cheryl slipped on a pair of shorts and a T-shirt and began straightening up the bed.

"Don't just stand there, Teddy, give me a hand."

"I don't do beds," he said arrogantly.

"Damn you, Teddy. I don't want to lose my family over this."

"You should have thought about that two years ago when you started fucking me in your husband's bed."

She didn't have time to argue. She fixed the bed herself and then sprayed the room with Lysol, all the while giving Teddy a dirty look. By the time she was finished, her husband had walked through the front door.

"Honey, I'm home!"

"I'll be right down, sweetheart!"

Teddy was still standing there in his drawers with one sock on, acting as if nothing were happening.

"Hurry up. Hide in the closet!"

"How do you expect me to get my big ass in that tiny space?"

"Teddy, please!" she begged.

"Who are you talking to, honey?" David asked.

"Nobody, sweetheart."

She could hear David coming up the stairs. She looked Teddy dead in the eyes and begged him again to hide. But he wouldn't budge.

"I'll never forgive you for this," she said as she rushed out into the hallway to intercept her husband. "Hey, baby, you're home early. What happened to your business trip?"

She greeted him halfway with hugs and kisses, hoping to turn him around but he was carrying a heavy suitcase and seemed determined to set it down in the bedroom.

"My meeting in Kansas City was canceled so I decided to come home to my beautiful wife."

"Well, let me take your suitcase and you can recline in your chair in the living room while I make you something to eat."

"I'm not hungry," he said as he made it to the top of the stairs. "I just want to take off my clothes and get into bed."

Cheryl closed her eyes and put her hands over her ears as David walked into the bedroom. But nothing happened. When she nervously peeked into the room, Teddy was gone. The window was wide open so she thought he had climbed out.

"What was all that screaming about?" David asked while undressing.

"What screaming?"

"I heard you screaming when I pulled into the driveway."

"Oh, I was just doing some crunches. You know I've been trying to stay in shape for you."

"And you look damn good, too, baby," David said reaching out his arms. "Now come here and give your old man a real hug."

While they were embracing, Cheryl saw a finger come out of the closet. It was Teddy and he was pointing toward the door. That was his signal telling her he wanted to get out.

"Honey, don't you want to take a shower before you go to bed?"

"I just had a shower before I got on the plane," he said, trying to unzip her shorts. "But what I think I could use is a some good loving to knock me out."

That's not what Cheryl had in mind but she figured any distraction was better then none. So, she began undressing herself and laid him down on the bed. Suddenly David sprang up out of the bed and headed toward the closet.

"Wait a minute, let me get my old High Karate cologne out of the closet. When we first met that aroma used to drive you crazy."

"No!" she shouted as he went to open the door. "I mean, that was ten years ago, sweetheart. All I want to taste is you."

David took his hand off the knob and went back to bed. Right away Cheryl covered him with the blanket and jumped on top, blocking his view of the closet. Teddy came creeping out with his clothes balled up in his arms. But instead of rushing down the stairs, he stood in the doorway while he got dressed. Cheryl was irate at first but then she became turned on. It was the best sex she had with her husband in years.

When Teddy had seen enough, he blew Cheryl a kiss and nonchalantly walked down the stairs and out the door. As he walked across the street to his truck wearing a devilish smile, his pager went off. The number on the display read: 2911. It was his girlfriend, Karen. As he headed home to deal with the latest crisis, he was his usual arrogant self. "Whatever the problem is, baby, I've got a perfectly good lie to explain it," he said, laughing.

• • •

Teddy was feeling cocky as he pulled into the circular driveway, until he saw the bright yellow Corvette parked behind Karen's Mercedes. It belonged to Karen's younger sister, Lisa. She was also a lawyer. He tried to straighten out his wrinkled clothes as best he could then he took a hard swallow and went inside.

He could hardly open the door with all the boxes piled up against it. On the side of each one was marked GARBAGE in bold black marker. Karen and Lisa were carrying the last box down when he walked into the living room.

"What's this supposed to be, spring cleaning?" he joked.

"I'm glad you think this is funny, you two-timing snake, because you'll be laughing on the streets tonight," Karen said as she set the box down.

"Okay, just calm down for a minute and tell me what's going on."

"Well, let me see." Karen began to count on her fingers. "First there were the phone numbers in your pocket, then there was the lipstick on your collar, last month I found a pair of Victoria's Secret panties that mysteriously buried themselves in my drawer. And now I come home from a hard day's work and I hear a message on my machine from one of your tramps."

"What message?" Teddy asked, playing dumb.

"We don't even need to go there, Teddy. Just get your stuff and leave."

"So what is Lisa here for?"

"To make sure you don't try to talk me out of it. I usually don't make a fool of myself when people are around."

Lisa was standing off to the side quietly. It was obvious she didn't want to be there.

"How are you doing, Lisa," Teddy asked.

"I'm fine, Teddy," she said passively.

"How's business at the firm?"

"Business is fine, too."

"Alright, that's enough of this family reunion. Get your boxes and get out!" Karen yelled.

"Can't we talk about it, baby? You know I love you."

"You don't love anybody but yourself you bald-headed bastard. Now get out before I call the police and have you thrown out."

"So, it's like that, huh? Okay, then, have it your way. I'm outta here."

Karen stood at the door like a drill sergeant until Teddy

loaded the last box into his truck. When he walked out of the door with the last one, she slammed the door shut behind him.

"And stay out!" she yelled.

"Don't you want your house keys back?"

"The locksmith is on his way over to change the locks. You can keep yours as souvenirs," she said to him from the window.

"You're really serious this time, aren't you?"

"Serious as a lawsuit. Speaking of which, I heard about all your kids. I hope they catch up with you one day and put you under the jail, you deadbeat!"

"I'd rather be a deadbeat than a lonely old woman with stretch marks and a worn-out pussy," he said while opening the door to his truck. "And by the way, thanks for the Navigator, the credit cards, the Versace suits, and the Rolex. Thanks to you I've finally saved enough money to get a place of my own."

Karen ran to the door while trying to pull the ring he had given her off her finger.

"You go to hell, Theodore, and take this Cracker Jack ring with you!"

When she finally managed to get the ring off, she threw it at him. It ricocheted off the truck and fell onto the driveway.

"Hey, you need to be more careful. This truck cost a lot of money," he said, laughing. "But I guess I don't need to tell you that, now do I?"

As he was about to drive off, he looked over at Lisa as she walked across the lawn toward her car. She was wearing a yellow halter top and mini skirt to match her Vette. It was an outfit she wore for Teddy many times before while Karen was out of town. It was his favorite.

They made eye contact on the down low then he sped off. As he turned the corner, he laughed out loud knowing he had another place to go home to. That's probably what

Lisa wanted all along, he as thinking. Maybe that's why she'd buried her yellow Victoria's Secret panties in her sister's drawer.

Chapter 30

It was early Saturday afternoon. Ariel barely made it inside the door before she collapsed onto the living room floor. She had lifted weights at the gym for an hour then she jogged five miles around Stone Mountain. It was the first time she had exercised all summer and it showed. She was so out of shape she had charley horses in both legs. After she caught her breath, she peeled out of her sweaty Howard University T-shirt and went upstairs to run a shower. While she was stripping off the rest of her clothes, she noticed the message light on her answering machine was blinking. Ariel was hoping it was her latest blind date, Raymond.

"Hey, baby, it's me," a man's smooth and masculine voice said. "Just wanted you to know that my plane landed safely. I've got to drop off some presents for my girls, then I'll be headed your way. I should be there by five o'clock. By the way, I brought you a souvenir from Mexico. I hope you like it. See you in a minute, baby. Bye."

Ariel smiled. It was the call that she had been waiting for all day. She rushed back into the bathroom and jumped into the shower. It was 3:30 P.M. and she wanted to have everything ready when Raymond got there.

• • •

By 4:45 P.M. Ariel had created a nice romantic atmosphere. The dining room table was set with long white candles and a bottle of white zinfandel chilling in a bucket of ice. She even broke out the good china to add a touch of class. But Ariel wanted Raymond to admire more then the place setting. After she checked on the shrimp casserole, she rushed upstairs to get changed. Instead of putting on the conservative sundress she had laid out, she put on a pair of black lace pants and a white cotton tube top to show off her pierced belly button. "Girl, you know you got it going on!" she said as she admired herself in the mirror.

While she waited impatiently for Raymond to arrive, she sipped on a glass of wine and masturbated. And the more she drank, the hornier she got. She was contemplating whether or not to break out her vibrator when the phone rang. "Please, God, don't let this be Raymond calling to cancel," she said to herself.

"Hello."

"Hey, sweetheart, just called to see how you were doing. Hope I wasn't interrupting anything."

"As a matter of fact you were!"

"Well, excuse me, Ms. Thang. I'll just let you go then." She sounded hurt. "Good-bye!"

"Wait a minute, Mama. I'm sorry for snapping at you," Ariel apologized. "I've got a quick minute to talk."

"I don't know what's going on with you, young lady, but I don't like it."

"I've been under a lot of pressure lately, you know with the situation with Lawrence and all."

"I thought you told me he stopped calling weeks ago."

"He did, but it's going to take me a while to adjust to going about my daily routine without having to look over my shoulder," she told her.

"You managed to adjust enough to go out with what's his name."

"His name is Raymond, Mama."

"Why haven't you brought him over to meet me?" she asked. "From what you told me about him, he sounds like a nice young man. Didn't you say he's a doctor?"

"Raymond is very busy, Mama. He spends a lot of spare time with his two daughters, and he runs his own practice," she told her. "And for your information, he's not just a regular doctor, he's a heart surgeon."

"Listen to you sounding all proud," Mama said, laughing. "I'd like to meet any man who can impress you."

"I'm impressed alright." Ariel was admiring the picture of Raymond hanging over her fireplace.

"It sounds to me like you finally met Mr. Right," Mama said. "I just find it hard to believe that a man with his credentials is still single."

Suddenly, the phone went silent. Ariel cleared her throat a few times then tried to change the subject.

"So, have you talked to Joyce or Sheila lately? How are the kids doing?"

"Ariel Michelle Daniels!" Mama interrupted. "I know you're not messing around with no married man. I didn't raise you that way!"

"Calm, down, Mama. I'm not trying to take him away from his wife and kids. I just want to have a little fun, that's all."

"Lord, I know your father is rolling over in his grave," she said. "Why can't you find a nice single man to get involved with, like your friend Chris. What's wrong with him?"

"Chris is okay, but he's not my type. He's short, light skinned, and he's not aggressive enough for me," she explained. "Raymond is tall, dark, and handsome, and I admire what he's doing with his life. That's a combination hard to find in any man, married or single."

"But baby, what about having a family of your own. Don't you want to get married someday?"

"Mama, that whole fantasy of the all-American family with the four-bedroom house, the station wagon, and the two-point-five kids is the reason why I've been alone for all these years. Ever since I was a little girl, I've been sizing every man up as a potential husband. But what I should've been looking for was someone who makes me happy."

"And you think sleeping with a married is going to make you happy?"

"Yes, it will, Mama. And it's damn sure better then being alone," Ariel said, getting emotional. "I'll be thirty years old next month and I'm going to spend my birthday with someone that I'm interested in, not some boring, watered-down substitute for a man."

"Don't you realize there are other people affected by your decision? He has a wife and two kids at home. Have you even stopped to think about them?"

"When I met Raymond through the dating service, he was upfront about his marriage. But he said he was going through some problems. It's not my fault that his wife can't take care of her business."

"Don't be such a damn fool, Ariel. All married men lie about having problems. It's all a game."

To be honest with you, Mama, I don't care if he's lying or not. All I know is he makes me laugh, we enjoy each other's company, and the sex is good," she said defiantly. "He may not be all mine, but half a man is better than no man."

Ariel heard Raymond's car pull into the driveway. She wiped the tears from her eyes and checked her makeup in the hallway mirror.

"I'm sorry, Mama, I've got to go now. Raymond is here."

"I'll let you go, Ariel, but you better take some time out to read your Bible. Galatians six, verse seven. A man reaps what he sows."

"Thanks for the sermon, Mama," she said, sounding smart. "Good-bye."

Chapter 31

Simon was in the kitchen cooking a pot of spaghetti when he realized Cynthia had been gone for more than twenty minutes. She told him she was feeling ill and needed to step outside for some fresh air. He looked for her on the patio but she was nowhere to be found. He figured she was lying down in bed again. For the past week she had complained about headaches and dizziness.

On his way to the bedroom, he noticed a light coming from the bathroom. He crept over to the door and put his ear next it. He could hear Cynthia talking on the phone, almost in a whisper. Then she began coughing violently and throwing up.

"You all right in there?" Simon pounded on the door.

"I'm fine," she said as she flushed the toilet.

A minute later she opened the door. Her skin was pale and her eyes were swollen and red.

"Cynthia, you look terrible." Simon tried to put his arm around her. "Are you sure you don't need to see a doctor?"

"I told you I was fine!" She backed away from him. "Stop babying me!"

"Who were you talking to on your cell phone?"

"What were you doing, eavesdropping?"

"You're damn right I was eavesdropping. This is my house!"

"For your information, I was talking to my doctor."

"Your doctor, huh? Why in the hell do you have to whisper to talk to your doctor?"

"Because I didn't want you to know I was sick, that's why!" she said angrily. "You always make such a big deal out of everything."

"Most women would love to have a man who cared enough about them to make a big deal over them."

"Well, I'm not most women!"

Cynthia stormed into the bedroom and began collecting her belongings. She packed her makeup bag, a toothbrush, and a set of silk pajamas that she always kept at Simon's house.

"I guess this means you're gone for good."

"I love you, Simon, but I need a break."

"If it's just a break, why are you taking your toothbrush and pajamas?"

Cynthia took a deep breath then unpacked her things. "Now, are you satisfied," she said as she picked up her bag.

She tried to hurry by him but he grabbed her car keys out of her hand.

"Give me back my keys, Simon."

"Not until you tell me what's going on."

"Nothing is going on. I'm sick, I told you, and want to go home and lie down."

"Why can't you lie down in my bed?"

"Because I want to be in my own bed, that's why. And besides, the smell of that spaghetti is making me throw up."

"If that's what's bothering you, just give me a minute and I'll get rid of it."

"Damn you, Simon! Stop trying to fix shit all the time!" she screamed. "Just give me my keys and let me go home!"

"Fine!" He tossed the keys at her.

Cynthia grabbed them out of the air with one hand and walked out of the door. Simon tried to play hard letting her go without saying good-bye, but he was too caught up. He hurried out of the door and caught up with her just as she was getting inside her car.

"Hold up, Cynthia," he said, holding on to the car door. "I'm sorry for trippin'. It's just that we haven't spent any time together lately and I miss you."

"I miss you, too, Simon, but sometimes people need space."

"Can we at least get together for lunch tomorrow and try to work things out?"

"I told you earlier this week that I was doing a live remote from my church tomorrow. After that, I have a meeting with my producers."

"At first I was the one who was busy all the time. Now that I've taken time out from the club to spend more time with you, you're the one who's too busy," he said while looking deep into her eyes. "Funny how things can change, huh?"

"It'll all work out, Simon. Like I told you, I just need some space."

She gave him a dispassionate hug, got inside her Range Rover, and drove off.

Just as her taillights disappeared over the hill, Simon's pager went off. It was Roundtree, the private dick. He rushed back inside the house to return the call. His hands shook as he punched in the seven digits. He had a gut feeling that the verdict would not be in Cynthia's favor.

"Hello, Roundtree? It's me, Simon. What's the word?"

"Well, do you want the good news or the bad news?"

"Give me the bad news first."

"Your fiancée is definitely fucking around," he said bluntly. "And when I say fucking, I mean it literally."

"And what's the good news?"

"The good news is that it's not a white boy or another woman."

But that was no concession for Simon. The woman that he loved had allowed another man to defile her body. And she did it while sharing his bed and lying to his face. He felt like a fool. The phone went silent as the tears slowly trickled down his cheeks. First tears of pain, then of rage.

"Mr. Harris, are you still there?"

"Yeah, man, I'm here," he said while trying to clear his throat.

"So, what's your next move?" Roundtree asked him. "You want to get together tomorrow and look over the pictures, or what?"

"To hell with tomorrow! I want to see everything you got on that cheating bitch, tonight! I'll be at your place in fifteen minutes."

• • •

Simon burned rubber as he came to an abrupt stop in front of Roundtree's rundown building. He jumped out of his old Chevy without bothering to lock it and hurried inside. He was so enraged that he didn't even notice the stench of urine and vomit in the hallway. When he arrived at the second floor, Roundtree was waiting with the door already open.

"Damn, that was fifteen minutes flat!" he said while looking at his watch.

"Don't waste my time with the comedy, Chris Rock," he said irately as he walked past him into the apartment. "Let's get down to business."

Simon sat down on the black leather sofa while Roundtree went to get the pictures. He was expecting a few neatly packaged envelopes of black-and-white snapshots, like the private dicks in the movies. But Roundtree surprised him when he came back into the room carrying a small box.

"You wanna get down to business, huh?" He dumped the contents onto the raggedy cocktail table and shook the box until it spilled over onto the floor. "How's that?"

Simon was so overwhelmed he didn't know where to start. He had his choice of videotapes, photographs, and copies of hotel receipts. Everything was marked precisely with dates, times, locations, and even titles. Simon picked up the video-tape labeled 7/21, 11:30 P.M., LAKE LANIER, DEEP THROAT.

"Here, put this in the VCR."

"Why don't you start with the PG-13 tape and work your way up to the triple X?"

"Don't play games with me tonight. I'm not in the mood."

"Okay, it's you're dime," he said as he put the tape into the VCR. "But remember, I tried to warn you."

The beginning of the tape was blurred. When it came into focus, Cynthia's Range Rover was parked out on the deck near the boats. The camera zoomed in on a man sitting in the passenger seat. It was too dark to see his face through the window but when they stepped out of the truck and into the moonlight his features were very distinguished. He stood about six feet tall and was medium build. His hair was short and wavy, like he had a relaxer in it. And he wore a well-groomed beard.

Cynthia opened the hatch and pulled out a blanket and picnic basket. While she laid the basket on the deck, the man pulled out what looked like a bottle of wine and poured two glasses. They appeared to be very familiar with each other as they cuddled on the blanket and talked with their feet dangling over the deck. Cynthia occasionally laughed and gave him pecks on the cheek.

But the romantic scene soon turned erotic. Cynthia pulled up her short skirt and casually sat on his lap. From a distance it seemed innocent, but when the camera zoomed in, the expression on her face was a dead giveaway. She was frowning and biting down on her finger to keep from screaming. The man was slapping her on the ass forcefully and you could read his lips asking, "What's my name?"

But the most painful part was the passionate expression on Cynthia's face. She wasn't just screwing this man, she was making love. The camera equipment was state of the art so Simon could see every detail, from the perspiration running down her back to the veins in her neck as she moaned in ecstasy.

"Okay, turn it off. I've seen enough."

"Hold up, here comes the part where he slaps her on the ass with his Bible," Roundtree joked.

"I said that's enough, goddammit!"

Roundtree pressed the stop button and stood by quietly. Simon put his hands over his face and leaned back against the sofa.

"Did you find out who he is?" Simon asked.

"I know everything there is to know," Roundtree boasted. "Where he works, where he lives, his Social Security number, his credit rating, and his shoe size."

"Why don't we just start with where he works."

Roundtree handed Simon a five-by-eight photo of the same man standing in a church pulpit.

"What is this?"

"That's a picture of our man at work. His name is Reverend James Young of the First United Baptist Church."

"He's a goddamned preacher?"

"A part-time preacher and full-time manipulator," Roundtree said. "He runs a bogus counseling service out of an office on Buford Highway. That's usually where he and your fiancée meet up for sex."

"I knew that heifer was lying when she told me she was going to Bible study."

"Oh, but there's more," Roundtree interrupted. "She's

not the only woman in the congregation that he's boning."

Roundtree pulled out another set of pictures. They were of the same man with different women. Some of the photos showed them kissing and hugging. And others were more explicit.

"This guy is a true player," Roundtree went on. "And he's very particular about the type of women he sleeps with. Most of them are married and have high-profile jobs such as politicians, lawyers, and TV personalities. In other words, he chooses women who have something to lose if they open their mouths."

"Well, you can call me a player hater because this son of a bitch is going down!" Simon said ruthlessly. He gathered the pictures and videotapes from off the cocktail table and angrily tossed them back into the cardboard box. He was so fired up, his hands were shaking.

"Whatever you plan to do, count me in," Roundtree said.

"Thanks for the offer, but I don't want to get you involved. What I'm about to do is pretty low-down."

"Low-down is my middle name!" Roundtree said enthusiastically. "Besides, there ain't nothing in the world I hate more than a hypocritical preacher."

Simon pause for a second to reconsider. There was no one else he trusted to go through with such a cruel deed, not even Malcolm.

"All right, you're in!" He gave Roundtree a high five. "Now go grab a couple of cans of Old E and I'll tell you the plan."

Chapter 32

It was 10:30 Sunday morning. The parking lot for the First United Baptist Church was filled with vans marked EYE-WITNESS NEWS. The church was holding a special service at 11:00 A.M. honoring a famous civil rights leader. Every television station in town was there for the big event, including Cynthia's station, WBBQ. Simon and Roundtree crept around the back disguised as technicians and blended in with the army of television people who were setting up for the live broadcast.

Once they were inside the building, Simon played look-out while Roundtree broke into the projection room. Most of the church members were so busy trying to get their faces on camera, they didn't pay them any attention. Their vanity played right into Simon's hands. Within fifteen minutes, the trap was set.

"Now what?" Roundtree asked.

"We go have a seat and wait for the fireworks to begin."

Services began promptly at 11:00 A.M. with the praise team firing up the congregation. The atmosphere was joyful and full of energy.

"Praise the Lord," some shouted.

"Thank you, Jesus!" others prayed.

As Simon watched the enthusiastic crowd, he wondered if he were doing the right thing, especially with so many children present. But his sympathetic feelings quickly faded once Reverend Young was introduced. He strutted onto the stage dressed in a bright red suit and matching red shoes. Simon wanted to choke the shit out of him as he charmed the mostly female audience with his self-righteous grin. "Smile while you can, you perpetrator," he said to himself. "Vengeance will be mine."

After the pastor lead the opening prayer, the choir rose to sing the musical selection "Someone's Knocking on My Door." They looked magnificent in their royal blue robes as they lined up perfectly on the steel tier. Once they were in place, the musical director give the signal and the serene church was transformed into a concert hall. From the back of the room, Simon could feel the power of their voices and the spirituality of the lyrics. By the second verse, he was singing along.

Even Roundtree was caught up in the moment. He was stomping his feet and shouting like he was at an old-fashion revival. "Hallelujah!" he screamed. Simon gave him a puzzled stare then burst out laughing.

"I'm cool, I'm cool," Roundtree said, trying to play it off.

"Are you sure?" Simon asked. "For a minute there I thought you were going to start talking in tongues."

"For a minute there, I was," Roundtree said, laughing. "This music could have the biggest sinner rushing to the altar to get saved."

"We're both going to need saving after this," Simon told him as he checked his watch. "It's almost show time!"

When the song ended, Reverend Young swaggered up to the microphone in his flashy red suit to acknowledge the media and special guests. Meanwhile the ushers hurried to set up the screen for the video presentation. The ceremony for the honoree was to begin with the showing of the civil rights documentary *Eyes on the Prize*. Simon's stomach was in knots as he watched and waited. He wondered if someone had discovered that the videotapes had been switched. If so, he had a plan B to mail the videotapes and pictures to the newspapers. But plan A would be so much sweeter.

Once the screen was set up, Reverend Young gave the signal for the ushers to dim the lights. As the room darkened, Simon caught a glimpse of Cynthia and her girlfriend Debra sitting up front in the VIP section. "I guess screwing the pastor has its privileges," Simon said to himself.

The opening of the tape was a series of quick snapshots of Reverend Young and the married women, kissing and having sex. Roundtree edited the tape perfectly so that each picture was distinct. There was no mistaking who was doing what. Almost immediately you could hear men screaming out from the darkness.

"Hey, that's my wife!" one man yelled.

"And that's mine!" another hollered.

But the show was only just beginning. The pictures were promptly followed by the videotape of Reverend Young and Cynthia having sex at Lake Lanier. You could hear the hands of parents slapping against their children's faces as they attempted to block their view.

"Turn that garbage off!" Reverend Young yelled out at the projectionist. But the tape continued to play. It was Reverend Young's bad luck that the projectionist was a horny seventeen-year-old boy who was learning more from watching three minutes of that tape than he had in four years of sex education. Someone else had to charge upstairs to the booth to turn off the tape. But by that time the tape had played up to the part where Revend Young slapped Cynthia on the ass with the Bible and asked, "What's my name?" You could hear the entire congregation gasp.

When the lights came up, Reverend Young was standing at the pulpit sweating like a Klansman at a Black Panther rally. Cynthia was sweating, too, as the camera crews from every television station in Atlanta including her own, focused on her.

"Calm down, please. This whole thing is a big misunderstanding." Reverend Young pulled the handkerchief from his suit pocket and wiped his brow. "That tape was made many years ago when I was still living in sin."

"You must think I'm a damned fool," one man yelled out. "The truck in that video is a ninety-nine."

"And how do you explain those pictures with my wife, you crooked bastard," another man yelled.

The situation erupted into a free-for-all as several men charged the stage. Simon wanted a piece of him, too. He fought his way through the impassioned crowd until he reached the stage. But the burly security guards had created a impenetrable human wall around the pulpit to protect the pastor.

"Hey, preacher, over here!" Simon yelled until the pastor looked his way. The expression on his face left no doubt that he knew who Simon was.

"What the hell do you want?"

"I just wanted to quote a scripture to you. Exodus, chapter twenty, verse seventeen. 'Thou shalt not covet thy neighbor's wife.' "

"I've got a scripture to quote to you, too: Kiss my ass!"

"No thanks, I've seen your ashy black ass on video and it ain't nothing nice to look at," Simon told him.

The security guards quickly ushered the pastor out of the side doors away from the cameras. However, Cynthia wasn't so lucky. Reporters were swarming around her like Monica Lewinsky. Simon could see the look of humiliation in her eyes, the same terrible humiliation he had felt. Debra was standing off to the side watching helplessly as her girl-friend was being ripped apart. Simon walked up from behind Debra and tapped her on the shoulder. She was stunned when she saw who it was.

"Simon wha—what are you doing here?" she stuttered.

"That's not important," he told her. "I just need you give this to Cynthia." He handed her a plastic bag.

"What is this?"

"It's a going-away present," he said with a smirk. "She'll understand."

Simon walked toward the exit where Roundtree was waiting. Once they were out of sight, Debra ripped opened the sealed package. Inside was a pair of white silk pajamas, a toothbrush, and a blank white card. Being the nosy woman that she was, Debra couldn't resist opening it.

Inside the card was a caricature of a man kicking a woman out of a house, with her luggage flying. Printed underneath it in bold letters was, *Enjoy your space. Yours truly, Simon.*

Chapter 33

It was 8:15 P.M. when I awoke from my nap. The six-hour flight from New York to Los Angeles had gone by very quickly. I had slept for nearly four of those hours to pass the time. It also helped keep my mind off the sexy flight attendant who was working first class. Ever since I boarded the plane she had raped me with her eyes. And when she set down my drink, she leaned over so I could see her breasts. That old devil was definitely at work. When she came by to pick up my glass, I stopped her to check on our arrival time.

"Excuse me, how long before we land?" I asked.

"We should be touching down at LaGuardia in about twenty minutes," she smiled flirtatiously. "Can I, ah, get you anything?"

She meant it just the way it sounded but I wasn't taking the bait.

"No, thank you," I told her politely.

"Let me know if you change your mind," she said, smiling.

Twenty minutes was plenty of time to get into trouble with such a lovely young woman. So, I distracted myself by using the airfone to call Simon. It had been five days since he left me a message about the episode with the preacher and I was beginning to worry. During our twenty years as best friends I don't recall ever having gone more then three days without talking. Something was up. As his phone rang, I was hoping not to get his answering machine again.

"Hello, this is Simon. Sorry I'm not available to take your call. Please leave a message at the tone and I'll return your call at my earliest convenience. Thank you." *Beep.*

The message sounded dry and cold. Not at all like Simon. I didn't bother to leave a message. I was sure he had received my previous ten.

I was desperate for answers so I dialed the only other number where I knew he could be reached, Club Obsession. Normally I respected his need for privacy, especially after such a dramatic experience. But I had a gut feeling that something was wrong. There was no telling what Simon was capable of when it came to Cynthia. He was the classic case of a man loving a woman more than he loved himself.

As the phone to the club rang, I took a deep breath and prepared myself for the worse.

"Hello, Club Obsession," a woman's voice answered.

"Is Mr. Harris in?"

"No, he isn't. Would you like to leave a message?"

"Yeah, tell him to call his buddy Malcolm, ASAP."

"Malcolm, thank goodness it's you!" Her demeanor changed completely.

"Ariel, is that you?"

"Yes, and I can't tell you how hard I've been trying to reach you."

"Calm down and tell me what's wrong?"

"I haven't heard from Simon in three days," she said,

sounding stressed. "And the media has been camped outside the club looking for him. It looks like the O.J. Simpson trial out there."

"Did Simon say where he was going?"

"All he said was he needed to go home to get his head together. But when I drove by his house, his car was gone and all his lights were out."

I knew exactly where Simon was. He was in Chicago, back in the old neighborhood. That's where he always went to sort things out.

"Try not to worry, Ariel. I think I know where Simon is," I told her. "Just give him a few days and I'm sure he'll call to let you know he's okay."

"Malcolm, I wish you could be here for him. He really needs a friend right now."

"As soon as I meet with my agent in New York, I'll go track Simon down and have a long talk with him," I assured her.

"Simon told me about your record deal. Congratulations!"

"Well, it's not official yet. My agent had his final meeting with the record company today. Hopefully, we'll have something to celebrate when I meet up with him tonight."

"I know Toni is happy for you!" she said excitedly. "Is she in New York, too?"

"Unfortunately, she's on tour in Europe until next week," I said, sounding depressed. "I really wanted her to be here to celebrate with me. Without her, none of this would've been possible."

Just then, the flight attendant came over the intercom to announce our approach to LaGuardia. I pulled up my window shade to check out the awesome view of downtown Manhattan. The skyscrapers seemed more like mountains as they blocked out the setting sun. Even Chicago with the Sears Tower and John Hancock buildings paled in comparison to the immense New York skyline. It was truly Gotham City.

"Well, that's my cue," I said to Ariel. "Try not to worry about Simon. He's just working things out."

"Thanks for calling, Malcolm, you really put my mind at ease. And good luck with the record deal. I know it's going to happen for you."

"You sound more confident than me."

"I know a winner when I see one," she said bluntly. "Just don't forget where you came from when you make it to the big time. Some brothas develop a serious case of color blindness after that first million."

"You don't have to worry about me selling out. I prefer my coffee black, no sugar, no cream," I said, laughing.

• • •

When I walked out of the jetway, there was a short elderly black man holding up a sign with my name on it.

"I'm Malcolm Tremell," I told him.

"Hello, Mr. Tremell, I'm your driver, Otis. May I take your bag?"

"But I didn't order a limo."

"Your agent, Jerry Cross, thought it would be a nice surprise."

"In that case, here!" I handed him my heavy garment bag. "Lead on, Otis."

By the time we made it outside, it had begun to drizzle. Otis pulled out a tiny umbrella and handed it to me. I tried my best to cover the both of us from the rain but we were moving too fast. Once we were at the limousine he hurried to open my door.

"I'm sure you'll like the car, Mr. Tremell. Your agent ordered this one especially for you," he said, smiling.

"Especially for me, huh? I'm beginning to like this celebrity lifestyle already," I said as I stepped inside.

No sooner did the door shut than someone yelled out, "Surprise!" It was Toni. She was wearing a sexy short black dress and holding two glasses of champagne. I almost knocked them out of her hands as I leaned over to give her a hug.

"Surprise is right! When did you get back from Europe?"

"I flew in late last night. I wanted to call you but Jerry and I had this planned for weeks," she said as she kissed me. "I wanted to be here to celebrate with you just in case the deal went through. I hope you don't mind."

"There's no one else in the world I would rather share this moment with than you."

When we pulled apart from hugging, she noticed the gash on my forehead. The one from Tina's high-heeled shoe.

"Oh, Malcolm, what happened!"

"It's no big deal, a guy scratched me while I was playing ball."

"Are you sure you're okay, baby?" she asked in a motherly tone.

"I'm fine, Toni. So, where is Jerry now?" I was trying to change the subject.

"We're supposed to met him at ten o'clock at a club in Manhattan called The Ritz. It's a popular hangout for black professionals. In the meantime let's get our private celebration started."

She handed me a glass of champagne, dimmed the interior lights, and slid in a Lauryn Hill CD. As the song "Nothing Even Matters" played softly in the background, she lifted her glass to make a toast.

"Here's to you, Malcolm. May God bless you with all the success you deserve."

"No, here's to you," I rebutted. "Because there's no amount of success or money in the world that can replace the value you have in my life."

Her eyes became filled with tears as we clinked glasses and took a sip. But the taste of the champagne and the moment was bittersweet because I had told another lie. Deep in my heart I knew all my lies would come back to haunt me. Lies always do.

Chapter 34

It was raining heavily by the time we arrived at The Ritz nightclub in Manhattan. Otis pulled up as close as he could to the club and escorted us to the door with the small umbrella.

"I'll be parked across the street," he said. "Just step outside when you're ready to go."

"You can take a long nap, Otis," Toni said. "I'm in a party mood tonight!"

The moment we walked inside the club I could feel the walls vibrating. The song "Just Be Good to Me" by the SOS Band was playing and the dance floor was crowded with well-dressed black folks getting their groove on.

"This place is off the hook!" I shouted over the music.

"Yeah, I know. This use to be my regular hangout," she said. "Eric and I use to come here once a month for Old School Friday."

"You and Eric, huh?"

"I'm sorry, sweetheart, I didn't mean to bruise your ego," she said playfully. "I know how territorial men can be."

"I'm not one of those insecure men who gets jealous over ex-boyfriends," I said, getting defensive. "I wouldn't mind running into him tonight to say hello."

"Oh, no. I made sure he was out of town before I made reservations. I didn't want to take any chances on you two bumping heads tonight. Once that testosterone kicks in, it's all over."

"What does your former fiancé do for a living, anyway?"

"He tells rich people how to invest their money. As a matter of fact, he's at a convention in Los Angeles this week," she told me. "I'm surprised you two haven't crossed paths as often as he's in L.A. I think you would have a lot to talk about considering you have so much in common."

"Like what?"

"Both of you are very intelligent, attractive, and arrogant."

"Who me? Arrogant?"

"Malcolm, you love attention. I saw you flirting with your eyes the minute we walked in the door," she said, laughing.

I was getting ready to say something to defend myself but she cut me off.

"But it's okay, honey. You don't have to explain. I know it's a horrible disease and you can't help yourself," she said, laughing. "As long as you look and don't touch, I won't have to show the ghetto side of me."

She gave me a peck on the cheek and grabbed me by the hand.

"Now let's go find our table so I can set my purse down," she continued. "I'm going to wear your butt out on the dance floor tonight."

I was speechless. She read me like a book from cover to

cover. It was the first time I saw that homegirl side of her and I liked it. I liked it a lot.

The hostess escorted us over to our table, which overlooked the huge oval dance floor. Toni didn't waste any time taking off her shoes and dragging me out onto the floor. I guess she thought she was going to show me up, being a professional dancer and all. But what she didn't realize was that I was from the southside of Chicago and I could party with the best of them. When the deejay mixed in the song "Shame" by Evelyn Champagne King, I took her to school.

"Come on, baby, show me what you got!" I said while dancing circles around her.

"Alright, Malcolm. Don't make me embarrass your old ass out here in front of all these people."

"I ain't scared of you, Ms. Ballerina. Come on with it."

Why did I go and say that. Toni broke out into a move right out of the movie *Flashdance*. She kicked her leg straight up over her head, did a pirouette, and came down into a split. I took a hard swallow and looked around to see if anybody saw her. They did!

"You go, girl!" the woman next to us shouted.

"Damn, did you see that?" the man on the other side yelled out.

The deejay must have known Toni personally because he got on the microphone and give her a shout-out.

"Ms. Antoinette Grayson is in the house tonight, ladies and gentlemen. It's show time!"

The deejay mixed in "Bad Girls" by Donna Summer and the dance floor parted like the Red Sea. Before I knew it, I was standing alone in the middle of the floor with a professional dance machine. And she was making me look bad, too, spinning and sliding all over the place like she was on Broadway.

"Okay, sweetheart, you made your point," I whispered. "Can I please get the hell out of here now?"

"Not yet," she said, laughing. "One more song."

"You know you're wrong for this, don't you?"

"Yeah, I know. But you're secure enough to handle it," she said, laughing.

We danced for another song then we walked off the floor to a standing ovation. When we sat down at the table, I was drenched.

"Remind me to pay you for that lesson," I said while wiping my face with a stack of napkins.

"You can write me a check after you see the private show I have planned for you at the hotel tonight."

The seductive look in her eyes gave me an immediate erection. If she had half as much energy in bed as she did on the dance floor, I was in for a long night.

"Look, I need to go to the bathroom to wash my arrogant face," I told her. "Do you want to go to the ladies' room while I watch the table?"

"I'm fine," she said, looking cool. "I haven't broken a sweat yet."

"Show off!" I said walking toward the men's room.

When I arrived at the men's room, it was full of stuffy brothers smoking cigars. It was torturous listening to them bragging about their new cars and how much their homes cost. The most annoying of them all was a proper-talking jerk who was louder than everyone else. I wasn't halfway into the rest room and I could hear his big mouth.

"I wonder how the poor black folks are living," he said, laughing conceitedly.

"Yeah, those lazy niggas in the hood are probably drinking forty ounces right now," another man said.

"Well, let's make a toast to the brothas who couldn't be here," the loud one slurred.

I tried to ignore their snobbish comments while I took a pee, but it wasn't easy. The guy with the loud mouth wouldn't shut up for one minute. And the more he spoke the more familiar he began to sound. I knew I had heard his voice somewhere before, but I couldn't place him.

After I finished relieving myself, I maneuvered my way over to the sink to wash my hands. I damn near fell out when I saw who the loud mouth was. It was the same high-yellow negro from the Fox Theater in Atlanta. When he saw my reflection, he recognized me right away. I intentionally stood right next to him while I squirted my hands with soap.

I could tell he and his drunk buddies had just arrived because they were wiping the rain from their jackets. I smiled back at him through the mirror, daring him to say something smart. He was one of those Uncle Tom negroes who needed a good ass whippin' and I was ready to oblige him, outnumbered or not. But surprisingly he didn't say a word. He just kept looking at me with that silly-ass expression on his face until I walked out. "Punk motherfucker," I said loud enough for him to hear.

When I made it back over to the table, Toni was signing autographs for her adoring fans. I just stood back and admired the way she handled the flirtatious men as they tried to mack her down for her number. She was so smooth and poised that they hardly realized they were being rejected. After a couple of minutes past, I went to break up the party.

Ahem. I cleared my throat to announce my arrival.

"Hey, sweetheart." She sprung up from her seat to give me a kiss. That was her way of demonstrating that she belonged to me. Like I said, she was smooth. It wasn't long before the vultures began to scatter. Men can sense when another man's game is tight.

"So, are you having a good time tonight?" she asked while sitting on my lap.

"As long as I'm with you, every night is a good time."

"Well, I promise you it's going to get even better. I have a big surprise for you when we get to the hotel."

"You're not a transsexual, are you?"

"No, silly. I was referring to your career."

"Speaking of my career, I'll be glad when Mr. Cross

gets here so I can find out what happened at the meeting. I'm getting impatient."

"Well, that's the surprise, Mr Cross is. . ."

Suddenly a man walked up from behind us and stood still. Toni looked over my shoulder to see who it was. When she saw his face, she sprang up from my lap.

"Eric, what are you doing here?" she asked.

"You know I come here on Friday nights," he said. "The question is what are you doing here?"

"I'm here with Malcolm," she said proudly.

I played it cool and continued to face the dance floor. I recognized Eric's voice as the loud mouth from the bathroom and didn't have shit to say to him.

"So this is the man you left me for, huh?" Eric said. "He doesn't seem to be the sociable type."

"Hello, and good-bye," I said in a deep, angry voice.

"Aw, don't be like that, brother," he said with perfect diction. "I just want to meet the man who stole my woman."

"First of all, I'm not your brother. Second, I can't steal what you never possessed. Now for the last time, good-bye!"

"You can't talk to me like that," he grabbed me by the shoulder and spun me around. "I'll be damned, it's you!"

"You know each other?" Toni asked.

"Oh, I know him alright," Eric said. "I saw him in Atlanta at the Fox Theater. And I saw him last week at the Marriott in Los Angeles. That's when I found out that he was a. . ."

I grabbed Eric's arm and twisted it behind his back before he could finish his sentence. "Thanks for giving me a reason to fuck you up!" I whispered in his ear. Then I smashed Eric's face into the table. The music suddenly stopped and all eyes were on us.

"Malcolm, stop!" Toni yelled.

"How does it feel, Mr. Big Shot? You got something to say to the poor black folks in the ghetto now?"

Eric's nose was broken and blood was dripping everywhere. His friends came to rescue him. When they tried to swing at me I used Eric as a shield. Shortly after, the security guards rushed over to break us up.

"Malcolm, what's gotten into you?" Toni cried.

"I'll tell you what's gotten into him," Eric said. "He's a fucking prostitute!"

"You shut your damn mouth before I shut it for you!" I was trying to get my hands on Eric but the muscular security guards were holding me back.

"What are you saying, Eric?"

"I'm trying to tell you that your man is a professional gigolo. He was at the Marriott last Friday arguing with one of his tricks. I've got pictures of her throwing a shoe at him," he said while staring at me with a smirk on his face. "That's probably how he got that scar on his forehead."

Toni took one look into my eyes and knew Eric was telling the truth. She walked over to me and slapped me right in the face.

"How could you lie to me, Malcolm?" she said with tears in her eyes. "I believed in you." She picked up her purse off the floor and went over to help Eric.

"Toni, please wait! I can explain."

"There is no way to explain a lie between a man and the woman he's supposed to respect and cherish." She wiped her eyes with her hand. "I thought you were something special but you're nothing more than a high-priced hoe."

"Do you wanna press any charges?" the security guard asked Eric.

"No, he's already paid the ultimate price. Let him suffer."

The security guards waited until Eric and Toni were long gone then they escorted me to the front door and tossed me onto the wet pavement. Otis must have seen what happened because he sped over in the limo.

"Mr. Tremell, you alright?" he asked as he jumped out of the car.

I didn't bother to answer him. I just sat on the ground in the pouring rain feeling numb. My expensive suit was getting soaked but I didn't give a damn.

"Mr. Tremell, please," Otis said, standing over me with the umbrella.

I didn't want to give that old man a heart attack, so I got up for his sake and stepped inside the car. Once Otis was inside he let down the divider and handed me a white envelope.

"Ms. Grayson told me to give this to you."

In the upper left-hand corner it read, Columbia Records. I began to open it then I suddenly stopped.

"Otis, where is Jerry Cross? And why did he rent this car and not show up tonight?"

"I wasn't supposed to tell you this, but Ms. Grayson rented the car."

Everything was beginning to make sense. I opened the envelope and found what I expected. It was a recording contract. I read the section under agent fees, but there was no name. That's when I realized that there was no such person as Jerry Cross. Toni had negotiated the deal herself. That was her surprise.

I put my head in my hands, disgusted with myself. Toni had made my lifelong dream come true and I rewarded her with a broken heart.

"Mr. Tremell, you okay?"

"No, I'm not okay, Otis. I'm pretty fucked up," I said, trying to regain my composure. "Let's get out of here."

"Where to?"

"Take me back to the airport."

"But there are no flights out to Los Angeles until six o'clock tomorrow morning."

"Good! That should give me plenty of time to figure out how I messed up the best thing that ever happened to me."

Ironically, the Lauryn Hill CD was still playing on the stereo. As we drove off into the dreary night, the lyrics to the song "Ex-Factor" were hitting home.

It could all be so simple, but you'd rather make it hard.

Loving you is like a battle, and we both end up with scars.

Tell me who I have to be, to get some reciprocity . . .

I knew reciprocity meant a mutual and honest exchange. To give and get, to do for, and to feel. Something I was unwilling or unable to do. And my selfishness had cost me dearly. Maybe this whole thing was meant to happen, I was thinking. Maybe it's God's way of telling me I didn't deserve Toni after all.

PART VI

Submission

Chapter 35

It was just after two o'clock when Simon arrived at Club Obsession. Two weeks had passed since the incident at the church and he was ready to get back to work. When he drove around back to open the gates, three trucks were already backed against the dock making deliveries. He was wondering who was signing for the orders because he didn't recognize the Chrysler Sebring convertible parked in the manager's space.

"Take those crab legs to the kitchen!" he heard a woman shout. "And you, don't forget to replace those beer kegs in the upstairs bar."

It was Ariel. She was bossing the deliverymen around, as usual. Simon crept alongside the truck and picked up a large box of shrimp off the dock. He concealed his face with it and carried it inside. When he got close to Ariel, he deliberately stumbled and almost knocked her over.

"Hey, watch where you're going, you idiot!"

"Sorry, about that, boss. This is my first day on the job," he said, trying not to laugh.

"You refer to me as Ms. Daniel, not boss, understand?"

"Okay, boss."

"Oh, I see we've got a smart-ass," Ariel said. "Get back to work before I call your supervisor."

Simon moved the box from his face and burst out laughing.

"It's you!" she shouted as she dropped her clipboard. "I've been worried sick about you?" She threw her arms around his neck and kissed him on the lips.

Simon was stunned but he quickly recovered. He wrapped his arm around Ariel's small waist and pulled her closer to him. Both their eyes were closed tight and their hearts raced. It was more than a kiss between friends, it was passionate. Just as Simon began caressing Ariel's butt, she pushed away.

"I'm sorry," she said, trying to compose herself. "That was way out of line."

"You're right?" Simon said, clearing his throat. "And I apologize for touching you on the . . . you know."

Ariel smiled nervously. She picked up the clipboard off the floor and began counting the cases on the dock like nothing happened.

"So, where have you been?"

"I went home to Chicago. I needed time to meditate and think things over."

"Have you heard from Cynthia?"

"No, but her mother called and left a nasty message on my answering machine," Simon said, laughing. "I've never heard an old woman use so much profanity."

"I can't say that I blame her after what happened."

"Excuse me!"

"Never mind, Simon," she said, backing off. "This is none of my business."

"No, speak your mind. I wanna hear what you have to say."

"Simon, you embarrassed that woman on live TV. They replayed that video on *Nightline, Dateline NBC,* and *BET Tonight.* It created a nationwide controversy about infidelity in the black church. Now, don't get me wrong, it was about time somebody exposed these no-good preachers who use their positions to take advantage of women. But Cynthia was just your girlfriend, not your wife. Infidelity was no excuse for destroying her career. Because of what you did, she'll never work in television again. Never!"

"What the hell did you expect me to do, Ariel?" Simon said, getting upset. "I was hurt!"

"You should've simply let her go," she said calmly as she took him by the hand. "And counted your blessings that you found out before you married her."

Simon's first impulse was to lash out but Ariel had expressed herself so eloquently he had to submit. Not only had he ruined Cynthia's career but he jeopardized his own by abandoning his business for two weeks. If it weren't for Ariel holding things together, thousands of dollars would have been lost and his employees would have gone without paychecks.

"Sometimes it's hard for a man to admit when he's wrong," Simon said. "Thanks for telling me what I need to know instead of what I want to hear."

"No problem, boss. Now let me get back to work. It's Ladies' Night tonight and you know how crowded it gets when Teddy performs."

Ariel tried to walk away but Simon grabbed her by the arm.

"Oh no you don't! It was no coincidence that I came back today." He pulled a card out his suit pocket and handed it to her. "Happy birthday."

"You remembered," she screamed. "Thank you, thank you, thank you!"

"Now, give me that clipboard and take your butt home. You've got the next two nights off."

"You mean it?"

"Yeah, I think I can run this place without you for a couple of nights."

"Thank you, Simon. You're the most decent man I know," she said as she kissed him softly on the cheek. "One day you'll find a woman who truly deserves you."

Ariel ran to her car screaming like a kid on the last day of school. Simon just shook his head as he watched her from the dock. She threw her purse into the car and rolled down the windows ready to get her groove on.

"Hey, birthday girl!" Simon yelled out. "What happened to the Benz?"

"It's in the shop. Some fool sliced my tires last week," she told him. "I just hope it wasn't that fool Lawrence trippin' again."

Chapter 36

Ariel was playing "Femininity" by Eric Benet while she got ready for her date with Raymond at the Shark Bar. She danced provocatively in the mirror as she combed her short afro then slipped into her fitted white dress. "Just like wine, you keep getting better with time," she said with conceit. It was her thirtieth birthday, a landmark in a woman's life, and she wanted it to be memorable. On the way home, she stopped by Fredrick's of Hollywood to pick up a pair of handcuffs, massage gels, and a white teddy with garter straps for that whorish look. Raymond was staying overnight for the first time and she wanted to try something kinky.

By six-thirty she was dressed to kill. She sprayed her neck, wrists, and crotch with perfume and headed for the door. Before she could turn the knob, the phone rang. She was hoping it wasn't her mother calling to lecture her again about dating a married man. They hadn't spoken in weeks and Ariel wasn't in the mood to argue. "Please God, not on my birthday," she prayed.

"Hello?"

"Hello, stranger, this is Chris. I just called to wish you a happy birthday."

"That's very sweet of you, Chris. Thanks for remembering." She tried to sound cordial but she was looking down at her watch anxious to leave.

"Did you get the present I sent you?"

"Yes, I did. I meant to call you to say thanks but things have been hectic at the club lately. I'm sure you understand?"

"No, I don't," he said abruptly.

"Look, Chris, I don't have time to get into this right now. I'm late for a date. Can we talk about this later?"

He paused for a moment to collect himself. Then he stopped beating around the bush and said what he really wanted to say.

"Look, Ariel, there's no need for us to talk later. I spend two hours walking around the mall to buy you something special for your birthday and you didn't even have the common courtesy to call and say thank you," he said to her.

"Now, wait one damned minute!"

"No, you wait!" Chris said, cutting her off. "I may not have a master's degree or a fancy car but I do have a good heart. I know that doesn't mean very much in this materialistic-ass world but that's all I have to offer, that, and my friendship," he said, sounding dejected. "Now, I'm not going to take up any more of your valuable time, Ms. Daniels. Have a happy birthday. And I hope you find whatever it is that you're looking for." Then he hung up.

Ariel stood there with the dial tone ringing in her ear. It was bad enough that her mother was on her case. Now, mild-mannered Chris was telling her off. But she knew she had it coming. She hadn't returned his calls in more than three weeks. Not even to say thank you for the gift.

The same gift that was still sitting on her dining room table unopened.

• • •

The Shark Bar was unusually crowded for a Thursday night. Ariel had to wait in line fifteen minutes just to get to the hostess. She was livid when she found out that Raymond had forgotten to call in their reservation. The wait for a table was almost forty-five minutes.

Ariel went over to the bar and ordered a Long Island ice tea to kill time until Raymond showed up. He was supposed to meet her at 7:00 P.M. But it was already 7:35 and he still hadn't shown up. "I did hundreds of sit-ups to fit into this tight-ass dress and he has the nerve not to show up on time to appreciate it," she said to herself. But her tight dress didn't go unnoticed by the men at the bar. They were gawking at her large breasts and round ass like she was a piece of meat.

It was the kind of attention Ariel didn't find flattering. She was careful not to dress too provocatively unless she was on a date with a secure man. Raymond had abandoned her in a den of wolves. And she knew it was only a matter of time before they drank up enough courage to come over to get their mack on. As usual, the young hip-hop types were the most aggressive.

"Excuse me, sweetheart. Can I buy you a drink?" a young man asked. He was wearing a bright orange jacket and had a gold tooth with the initial *M* engraved in it.

"No, thank you. I'm waiting on someone," she said politely.

"Well, if you change your mind, I'll be over there with my posse." He whipped out a business card and handed it to her. "My name is Marcus, but they call me Milk Dud."

"Okay, Mr. Dud," Ariel said, trying not to laugh. "Thanks for the offer."

Ariel put the card in her purse knowing it was going straight in the garbage. When she was younger she would get into long discussions about why she couldn't accept a man's card. But as she matured, she realized the best thing to do was take the card and get rid of him. Besides, some men could become verbally abusive and violent toward women when they got dissed in front of their boys. She wasn't taking any chances on having any drama, especially not on her birthday.

By eight o'clock Ariel was furious. Raymond still hadn't arrived to rescue her from the knuckleheads who were circling her like vultures. One of her biggest pet peeves was promptness. As far as she was concerned, nothing short of death was excusable. When the hostess called out her reservation, she excused herself and went over to be seated. She was determined to enjoy her evening and have a nice dinner, even if it meant doing it alone.

Just as the hostess was leading her to her table, Raymond came rushing in. He waved his arms to get her attention. He was dressed very dapper in a sharp dark blue suit and tie. Ariel made eye contact with him then turned her head and kept walking. She knew he would follow her over and she wanted to make his trip as uncomfortable as possible. Once they were alone at the table, Raymond gave her a kiss on the cheek and poured on the old charm.

"Baby, I can't tell you how sorry I am for being late. My wife was supposed to pick the girls up from dance class but she had to work overtime. I ran every red light on Peachtree Street trying to get here on time," he said, sounding sincere. "Please give me a chance to make it up to you."

Ariel couldn't help blushing whenever she looked into Raymond's light brown eyes. He was a pretty boy, six feet tall, light brown skin, wavy hair, athletic build, the whole nine, not usually her type. She preferred her men dark chocolate But the dick was good and he had a deep, sexy voice. Not soft and squeaky like so many corporate black men she dated in Atlanta. Raymond could make her wet just by calling to say hello. But wet panties and all, she was still disappointed. It was the fifth time in the last month he was either late for a date or had to cancel.

"I'm getting sick and tired of you showing up late for our dates, Raymond" she said angrily. "If it's not the kids, it's one of your patients. It's always something!"

"Look, Ariel, I told you up front that my career and family came first," he said sternly. "I'm still a married man and a father and that means I have responsibilities. Now if you can't handle that, maybe we need to stop seeing each another."

Ariel wanted to tell him to go to hell. She wasn't accustomed to playing the role of the other woman. But she swallowed her pride because it was her birthday and she was horny as hell. Raymond hadn't given her any sex in almost two weeks and she needed some maintenance.

"Okay, I forgive you, this time," she said. "So are you still spending the night?"

"I can stay for a while, but I've got to get up early in the morning."

"For what?"

"I rushed out of the house and forgot to bring an extra set of clothes for work."

"I don't appreciate all these last-minute changes, Raymond. I may be your woman on the side but I have needs."

Raymond was facing the front of the restaurant. Ariel noticed he kept looking over her shoulder toward the door. She didn't pay it much attention until he did it a second and third time.

"Are you expecting somebody?"

"No, I thought I saw someone I knew," he said unconvincingly. Then he tried to change the subject. "Look, why don't we skip dinner and go to your place. That way we can spend more time together."

"But I'm starving! And I spent a lot of time getting myself together to come out tonight. Which reminds me, you haven't even complimented me on my dress."

"You look great, Ariel," he said, looking toward the door again. "When we get to your place you can model it for me."

Suddenly there was a commotion outside. Ariel heard what sounded like a windshield being smashed in. Not long after, a woman came barging into the front door dragging two little girls along with her. Judging by the expression on Raymond's face, Ariel knew who it was.

"Just stay calm and let me handle this," Raymond said nervously.

The woman spotted Ariel and Raymond sitting at the corner table and stormed toward them, knocking over trays of food on her way. When she got up to the table she walked right up to Raymond and smacked the shit out of him.

"How dare you!" she yelled.

"Calm down, sweetheart, I can explain."

"You can't explain a goddamn thing, you two-timing bastard. I know who this bitch is!"

Ariel held her tongue to avoid escalating the situation.

"I slave around that house all day raising your kids and washing your dirty-ass drawers. I'll be damned if you're going to disrespect me by bringing one of your hoes out in public."

"Who you calling a hoe, you fat heifer?"

Raymond's wife was a big woman and a strong one. She grabbed a bowl of peach cobbler à la mode off the table next to her and smashed it into Ariel's face. When Ariel tried to retaliate she gave her a right cross and sent Ariel flying over the table.

"Take that, you slut!" she yelled. "Maybe next time you'll think twice before you fuck with a married man."

The women in the restaurant—not even the female staff—didn't make much of effort to help Ariel to her feet. It was as if they had vented their own frustrations for all the conniving other women in Atlanta. It was a town notorious for back-stabbing women who celebrated the role of being mistresses. On that night Ariel was the scapegoat.

As Raymond's wife stormed out of the door with her girls in tow, there was muffled applause. No one called the police or even tried to stop her.

"I'm sorry about all this, Ariel," Raymond said as he picked her up.

"Just get away from me, Raymond. Go home to your wife."

With peach cobbler running down her face and onto her brand-new dress, Ariel calmly put two hundred dollars on the table for the damages and walked out. When she got out to her car, the windshield was smashed on the passenger's side and the antenna was broken. What was most embarrassing were the words *Home Wrecker* spray-painted on the hood and both doors. The bold red letters were accentuated against the white surface of the car.

Ariel didn't even react, not outwardly anyway. She got inside the car and drove off as most of the patrons in the Shark Bar looked on. She held up pretty well until she made it to North Druid Hill Road on 85. Then she broke down. When she looked at her face in the rearview mirror she cried even harder. She had a deep cut below her left eye, and her top lip was busted. "That's what you get, stupid!" she said to herself.

After she wiped off her face, she pulled out her cell phone to call her best friend. She needed someone to talk to.

"Hello, Mama, it's me," Ariel said, crying.

"Baby, what's wrong?"

"Mama, I'm sorry. You were right. You were right about everything."

"We don't need to talk about that right now, sweetheart. Are you alright?"

"I'll be fine. Nothing that a dry cleaner and a bandage won't fix," she said laughing.

"Why don't you come over and I'll pour us a glass of wine. We can stay up all night and talk like we use to. Remember?"

"Yeah, I remember, Mama," Ariel said with a smile on her face. "But there's something I have to do. Can I take a rain check for tomorrow night?"

"Sure you can, sweetheart," she said in that motherly tone. "But what are you about to do, if you don't mind me being nosy."

"I'm going to pick up a Blockbuster video and a bag of popcorn, and go visit Chris," she said. "I realized the hard way that what I'm missing in my life is not a husband, but a man who is truly a friend."

Chapter 37

It was 9:00 P.M. Ladies' Night at Club Obsession was going strong. Teddy and his dance group Hot Chocolate were putting on their best show ever. The room was wall to wall with enthusiastic women buying alcohol like it was going out of style. The restaurant was crowded, too. The kitchen sold out of buffalo wings and fried shrimp before the show began. It was the most successful night since the grand opening.

But Simon was in no mood to celebrate. He locked himself in his office with a bottle of cognac trying to think through his issues. Usually he would call Malcolm and talk about his problems. But since the incident in New York, they hadn't spoken much. Malcolm was still recovering from losing Toni. And although he tried to act as if it were no big deal, Simon knew he was devastated. Malcolm had not been so withdrawn since his father died.

The conversation with Ariel was also weighing on his mind. He never considered how his actions at the church would affect Cynthia's career. He only wanted revenge, not to destroy her livelihood. "What the hell have I done?" he asked himself as he stared at the large poster of Cynthia hanging on the wall behind his desk. The same poster he refused to take down and throw away. After all the trouble he went through to get even, he was still in love with her.

As he took another sip of cognac to quiet his conscience, there was a knock at the door.

"Who is it?" Simon yelled.

"Mr. Harris, come quick!" a waitress said frantically. "The police are arresting Teddy!"

Simon could hear the commotion as he made his way toward the front of the club. Women were booing and tossing paper plates at the two sheriff's deputies who were making the arrest. Simon hurried over to see what the deal was.

"Excuse me, officers, I'm the owner, Simon Harris. What seems to be the problem?"

"There's no problem," one of the deputies said. "Mr. Teddy Bear here is under arrest."

"This is bullshit, Mr. Harris. I'm innocent!" Teddy yelled. Besides the police handcuffs, all he had on was a leopard-print thong.

"Do you mind telling me what the charge is?"

"Contempt of court. He failed to appear in court after refusing to pay his child support."

A group of nosy women standing nearby overheard their conversation and quickly spread the word. It wasn't long before all the boos were focused on Teddy.

"Don't just stand there, Mr. Harris, say something," Teddy said as the policemen lead him away.

"You're fired!" Simon yelled.

The police escorted Teddy out of the club as fast as they could for his own protection. Women were cursing him out and spitting in his face as he walked by.

"I hope they put your trifling butt under the jail, you deadbeat," a woman hollered.

Teddy was finished as a stripper in Atlanta. By Monday morning Simon knew Teddy's business would be all over the radio airwaves, Kiss 104, V103, and Hot 97.5.

Simon took advantage of the situation and closed the club. He refunded everyone's money and sent the employees home. It didn't matter to him that the club was a mess. He just wanted to be alone. Within thirty minutes, the club was deserted.

After he locked the doors, Simon put on his Heatwave CD and mixed himself a stiff Barcardi rum and Coke. While he listened to the smooth melody of "Star of a Story" he leaned back in a chair and propped his feet up onto the bar. "Ah, that's more like it," he said as he took a long sip.

Just as he was getting his relaxation on, there was a loud knock at the door. "Now what?" he said in disgust. As he went to answer the door, he was hoping it was Ariel. Although he wanted to be alone, he could finally finish giving her lessons on how to step, Chicago style. But when he peeked out the side window he didn't see Ariel's car. Instead there was a black Range Rover parked out front. It was Cynthia's.

He pulled the shades back on the doors and there she was, in a pair of dingy blue jeans, a T-shirt, and a Atlanta Falcons cap. She looked pitiful. Her eyes were red and puffy. He could tell that she'd been crying. She also seemed to have put on a little weight, especially in the face and arms. Simon thought about going to get his pistol just in case she turned fatal, but he decided not to. Cynthia was a no-good cheater but Simon doubted that she had turned murderous, too. As he unlocked the door to let her in, he could already feel the tension in the air.

"What do you want?" Simon asked before she could get into the door good.

"Don't worry, I'm not going to stay long. I just wanted

to tell you to your face how sorry I am for what happened."

"Apology accepted. Now, good-bye!" Simon said, sounding cold.

"How can you talk to me like that, Simon, after all we've been through?"

"It's easy, all I have to do is think about you screwing that phony preacher. By the way, where is your spiritual maintenance man?"

"For your information, I haven't seen him since that Sunday."

"Now, why does that not surprise me?" Simon said sarcastically. "I thought you two would be living in a big house in the suburbs with a white picket fence living happily ever after."

"Fuck you, Simon!"

"No, fuck you!" Simon yelled. "I trusted you and you went behind my back and laid down with another man. Not once, not twice, but several times. And you expect me to be sympathetic. Hell no!"

"What about you, Mr. Big-Shot Club Owner. When did you ever pay any attention to me?" she yelled back. "You've been cheating on me for three years with your damned business. Everything revolved around work. And when you finally came home, you were tired. I needed someone who was there for me, Simon. To hold me, tell me I was beautiful, and make passionate love to me," she said as tears rolled down her cheeks. "I'm not superwoman, goddammit. I need attention!"

Simon wanted to run over to her and hold her in his arms. He was in just as much pain as she was but his pride wouldn't allow him to show it.

"Is that all you have to say?" he asked callously. "I've got work to do."

"Fine, Simon. If that's the way you want it. Here, take it!"

She pulled the engagement ring off her finger and threw

it at him. "But before I go, I want you to know that I never loved James. He was just a substitute for the man that I love."

Cynthia wiped the tears from her eyes with her hand then turned toward the door. But before she walked out, Simon yelled, "So, when is the baby due?"

Cynthia stopped dead in her tracks.

"How did you know?" she asked while still facing the door.

"I have two sistahs who were teenaged mothers. And ten waitresses as employees. Didn't you think I would recognize when you had morning sickness?"

"The baby is due in April," she said softly.

"Do you know whose it is?"

Cynthia took a deep breath as she turned to face him.

"To be honest with you, Simon, I don't know. But it doesn't matter. I'm putting it up for adoption after it's born. I'm not going to shame myself or my family any further by trying to raise a child without a father. Now if you're through breaking me down, I'm going to leave. Good-bye!" she said, crying.

"Wait, Cynthia!"

Before she could get inside her car, Simon chased her down and brought her back inside the club. Without saying a word, he cleared the chairs off the dance floor and turned up the volume on his Heatwave CD. He forwarded it to the song "Always and Forever" and lead Cynthia out onto the floor.

"Simon, what are you doing?"

"What I should've done a long time ago," he whispered in her ear. "Giving you the love and attention that you need."

Chapter 38

It was just after 10:00 A.M. when Ms. Ruby rushed into my bedroom nearly hysterical.

"Malcolm, wake up!" she yelled as she shook me violently.

"What's wrong?"

"It's Melvin. He had a heart attack!"

I sprang up out of my bed in one motion and began searching through my closet for something quick to slip into. I pulled out a wrinkled pair of blue jeans and a Malcolm X T-shirt.

"When did this happen?"

"About eight this morning. Scottie found him lying on the bathroom floor at his home. The ambulance had just arrived when he called."

"Why didn't you wake me sooner?" I asked angrily.

"I turned off the ringer when I came in this morning," she said as tears began to pour down her brown cheeks. "I was only trying to make sure you weren't disturbed."

I felt like a heel for yelling at her. She was just as concerned as I was. She knew how much Melvin meant to me. I took a deep breath to calm myself down, then I walked over and put my arms around her.

"I'm sorry for snapping at you, Ms. Ruby," I told her. "Did Scottie mention which hospital they were taking him to?"

"King Drew Medical Center in Compton."

"Was Melvin still breathing?"

"He didn't say."

"I want you to try to calm down," I said as I gave her a kiss on the forehead. "I'll call you from the hospital as soon as I know something."

I grabbed my car keys and cell phone off the kitchen counter and hurried out of the door. My heart was racing one hundred miles per hour as I rode the elevator down to the lobby. The thought of losing what had become the most important man in my life again was unbearable. I frantically dialed Scottie's number trying to get through but there was no answer. "Pick up, goddammit!" I yelled. The people riding with me on the elevator were staring at me like I was going crazy. But I didn't give a damn. I needed to know if Melvin were still alive.

• • •

The emergency room at King Drew was a madhouse. Doctors and nurses scrambled to stabilize four gunshot victims. All young children no older then ten years old.

"Another drive by," I heard one nurse say. "And it's not even sundown yet. It's going to be a busy weekend."

"They don't call this place Killer King for nothing," another replied.

The sweltering Los Angeles heat had a way of increasing the body count in the black community. Although it was mid-September it was more than ninety degrees. After the commotion died down, I approached the nurse at the receptionist's desk. She was a crabby old white woman wearing wire-framed glasses.

"Excuse me, nurse. I'm looking for a patient who was brought in earlier this morning. His name is Melvin Butler."

She held up her index finger, indicating that she wanted me to wait until she finished gossiping on the phone. I stood there for another minute or so trying to be courteous, but when she continued to ignore me, I snapped.

"Excuse me!" I said much louder. "Would you please get your ass off the phone and give me some assistance."

I must have scared her to death because she slammed the phone down and gave me her undivided attention.

"When was he admitted?" she asked, looking up at me timidly through her wire-framed glasses.

"This morning about nine o'clock."

"Here he is," she pointed out to me on the computer screen. "He's in intensive care."

"Which way is it?"

"Just go down that corridor and turn left."

When I made it to the intensive care area Scottie was standing in the waiting room talking with the doctor. When I approached him, he turned and gave me a hug.

"How is he?" I asked the doctor.

"Not good. He had a hemorrhagic stroke, which means he has internal bleeding in the heart," he explained. "I'm sorry, there's nothing we can do."

"I need to see him," I said.

"No one is allowed to see him except his immediate family."

"I am the immediately family, goddammit! Now take me to him!"

Scottie waited in the hall while the doctor escorted me to Melvin's room. It was hard for me to see him lying there so helpless with all those tubes and electrodes attached to his body.

"Can you please give me a moment alone?"

"No problem, I'll be right outside," the doctor said.

I stood over the bed and held Melvin's clammy hands. His face was pale and his breathing was weak. I fought back the tears hoping he would open his wrinkled old eyes and tell me one of his dirty jokes. He had been the closest thing I had to a father in twelve years and I was losing him. I felt so helpless.

Suddenly his grip tightened around my hand. He cleared his throat and tried to speak.

"Did you open the present I gave you?" he whispered.

"Not yet, old man, but I will as soon as I get you back home." I was trying to be cheerful. "Did you get my message about my deal with Columbia Records."

"Yeah, I got it. Congratulations. I knew you would be a big star someday."

"Hey, slow down with all the hype. I haven't signed the contract yet."

"It's going to happen for you, Cool Breeze, because it's time. Just like it was time for you to meet that young lady," he said, sounding sure of himself. "I could tell by the way you talked about her that she was the one. You do love her, don't you?"

"Yes, I do," I told him. "She's everything I've ever wanted."

"I'm just glad I lived long enough to see you happy," he said as the tears welled up in his eyes. "Make sure you take good care of her. I don't want you to end up old and alone like me."

"You're not alone, I'm right here," I said as I watched him fading away. "Don't leave me, old man. I still need you!"

"Just remember, I'm proud of you, Malcolm. I've always loved you like my own son."

"And I loved you as a father," I said, crying.

I held him in my arms as his eyes slowly shut. He took one last breath, then he was gone.

Chapter 39

The day of the funeral was dark and dreary, much like the day my father died. A light drizzle fell as the mile-long procession slowly made its way down Crenshaw Boulevard to the Inglewood Park Cemetery. The mayor himself would've been envious of the multitude of people who came out to pay their respects. Melvin was practically an institution in the black community and he was going to be dearly missed.

The reading of the eulogy took place underneath a small canvas tent. Only fifty or so people were able to stand out of the rain while the minister spoke words over Melvin's casket. I held hands with Scottie and the staff from the club, and we tried to comfort one another. Aside from a distant cousin, we were the only family Melvin had.

After the eulogy, we joined hands and sang "Amazing Grace." That was the toughest part of the service to get through. Everyone broke down crying including the minister. But I held my tears for later, just like I did with my father. There were thoughts I wanted to share with Melvin that had to be shared alone.

As Melvin's casket was being lowered into the ground, we threw flowers on top of his ivory and gold-plated casket. It was our way of saying good-bye to a man who had been a father and a mentor to all of us. Once it was rested against the cold, dark ground, I threw in the first symbolic shovel of dirt. With every shovelful of dirt that fell, a part of my soul was being buried, too. "Rest in peace, old man," I said.

When the service was over, those who were outside of the tent lined up to pay their last respects. There were at least two hundred people standing in the pouring rain waiting to lay down their floral wreaths and to bid Melvin a final good-bye. I had never seen such a show of devotion.

As the procession came to its end, I saw a familiar face. At first I thought my eyes were playing tricks on me. But after he laid down the bouquet of roses that were obscuring his face, I realized it was Simon. I had successfully held back my tears up until that point. But the moment we embraced, I let it all out.

"Déjà vu, huh, partner?" Simon said as we hugged.

"Yeah, déjà vu," I said. "How did you know I was here?"

"Ms. Ruby called me yesterday. I flew out of Atlanta this morning on the first available flight."

"I know I should've called you myself. But I didn't want to burden you. I know you have enough drama to deal with."

"If we weren't in a cemetery I would slap the hell out of you. I thought we were boys."

"You're right, Simon. I don't know why I'm trippin'," I told him. "My head hasn't been right for a while."

Simon waited outside while I received the last of the guests. Once they were all gone, I grabbed my umbrella and we took a short walk together. In a strange way it was the perfect reunion. Simon had been by my side to bury both my fathers. Having him there helped to alleviate some of the pain, just as it did twelve years before.

"So, how are you holding up?" Simon asked.

"I'm hanging," I told him. "Although I've been through this before, it doesn't get any easier. Pain always feels brand new no matter how much experience you've had with it."

"Amen to that!" Simon said. "I've had all the pain I can handle for the next twenty years."

"Speaking of pain, you mind if I ask you a personal question?"

"Shoot!"

"Whatever happened to Cynthia?"

"I was hoping you wouldn't go there."

"Look, partner, we don't have to talk about it. I was just wondering how things worked out."

"I may as well tell you and get it over with. Cynthia's pregnant and we're getting married in Vegas next month," he said. "Now before you say anything . . ."

"Congratulations," I said, cutting him off.

"Excuse me?"

"I said congratulations. I wish you both all the best."

"I'm surprised you didn't try to talk me out of it, or ask who's baby it is."

"Who am I to criticize you or anybody else? My personal life is a disaster. I can't even go out on an appointment to get paid without my conscience kicking my ass," I said. "Would you believe I've been celibate for more than four weeks? That's the longest I've gone without sex since high school."

"Did Toni get that close to you?"

"Toni who? What are you talking about?"

"Don't try to run your game on me, Malcolm. I know you too well," he said. "And any blind man can see that you miss that woman. I'm sure Melvin saw it, too."

"Yeah, I miss her. But that page in my life has been turned."

"Listen to you trying to sound all hard. You ain't foolin' nobody but yourself. Why don't you stop playing the role of big-time ladies' man and go after that woman. She loves you, you arrogant fool!"

I dropped the umbrella I was holding and grabbed Simon by the collar of his trench coat.

"Shut the fuck up! Shut up!" I yelled. "You have no idea what I'm feeling inside! There isn't an hour that goes by that I don't think about her. I can't even lie down with another woman without seeing her face. So don't you assume to know shit about me. I've got a heart, too, goddammit!"

"Well, stop being so afraid and use it!" Simon said, pushing my hands away. "A good woman like Toni is not going to respond to your manipulating games. You have to be willing to be vulnerable and submit yourself to her the same way you want to be submitted to. Until you learn how to do that, you will always be alone. Alone or dead!"

Simon pulled a laminated piece of paper out of his coat pocket and handed to me. It was an article from the *Atlanta Journal Constitution.* The headline read: LOCAL STRIPPER SHOT AND KILLED BY JEALOUS HUSBAND. I only had to read the first few lines to get the point. The man killed was Theodore Simmons. He was the stripper who worked at Club Obsession. He was shot in the head when a husband came home early and caught him in bed with his wife. Ironically, it was the same story of what happened to my father.

"There are no coincidences in life, Malcolm. Everything happens for a reason," Simon said. "You have to take advantage of all the hurt and pain in life and grow from it. I learned that lesson the hard way. And if your father or Melvin were alive they would tell you the exact same thing."

Simon had hit me over the head with a five-hundred-pound dose of reality. I walked down to the bench that was a few yards away and sat down. I didn't care that my umbrella had blown across the cemetery and I was getting soaked.

"I'll be damned!" I said, laughing nervously.

"What's so funny?" Simon asked as he came and sat down beside me.

"The student has finally become the teacher," I said. "I was trying to teach you the game and here I am breaking the cardinal rule in the *Player's Handbook.*"

"What's that?"

"Never fall in love."

We hugged in that brotherly way that men do to say they're sorry. I had learned more about myself that day than any other, and I had Simon to thank. Shortly after our talk, Simon left to catch his flight back to Atlanta. I stayed at the cemetery for another hour to say my good-byes to Melvin. I wanted to tell him that I was going to be okay. And that I would do everything in my power to get Toni back.

• • •

That night, I took a long walk near the ocean to reflect on the meaning of life, the universe, and all that other philosophical shit you think about when you're trying to get your head together. I was in a creative mood so I brought along a spiral notebook and my John Coltrane "Ballads" CD. I found a secluded spot away from the crowds and laid my blanket down along the shoreline. As I watched the full moon gleaming off the still ocean, I thought about the night Toni and I spent on the lakefront in Chicago. We stayed up all night holding each other and talking about our hopes and dreams.

That romantic evening seemed like such a distant memory. Since the incident in New York with Eric, I hadn't heard from her. When I tried calling to apologize, her home number had been changed. And so had the number to her pager. The thought crossed my mind to show up on her doorstep unannounced but I quickly dismissed that idea. Not only was it inappropriate but it was the fastest way to get my feelings hurt.

My only chance at getting Toni back was to write her a letter from the heart. God had blessed me with the gift of writing music. All I had to do was transfer that same passion into words.

Dear Toni,

It's hard to know where to begin when you've lost a woman's trust. The words I'm sorry *seem so inadequate, so empty. I would've preferred to express my love for you in song on the piano. But I doubt even a melody could express the degree of pain I feel for letting you down. Lately, I've been praying at night to rid myself of the guilt from that moment. You know how religious black folks can get when things get tough. I got on my knees and prayed for another chance to hold you again, and to show you that I am the man you need me to be: caring, affectionate, and most of all, honest. Toni, I am all those things, and much more. It just took someone like you to come along to bring out that part of me. That part that wants to love and be loved uncon-ditionally.*

I know starting over would be hard. It always is when trust is involved. But I'm willing to do whatever it takes to rebuild that trust and make you happy. I miss holding you, and talking on the phone all night. And I miss watching you dance. I'll never forget the first time I saw you. You looked just like an angel. In a very short period of time you have become a neccesary part in my life, and without you nothing feels real.

Love always,
Malcolm

P.S. Whatever happens, please don't ever stop believing in me. That means more to me than anything else in the world, even more than your love.

EPILOGUE

When Players Pray

(2000)

It was a typical Thursday night. Melvin's Jazz Club was standing room only. Hundreds of people turned out for the special memorial party I was throwing for Melvin. My mother even flew in from Chicago, and she hated airplanes. Simon and Cynthia were there, too. They had just returned from Vegas and were sporting their diamond wedding bands. They never looked happier.

But behind all the champagne and celebration was a real concern that the club would be closing. Melvin didn't leave a will, which left his cousin as executor of his estate. He was a greedy old bastard who couldn't wait to sell the club to a condo developer. My lawyer had done everything in his power to block the judgment but we were running out of arguments.

I tried to put those thoughts aside as I relaxed in Melvin's office. It was a quarter to nine, fifteen minutes before show time. I wanted to stay focused on my music. To take my mind off the situation, I pulled out Melvin's old photo albums. As I turned the dingy pages, I was in awe of the artists who had performed at the club over the years. Ray Charles, Thelonious Monk, and Sarah Vaughn, just to name a few. Melvin was his usual flamboyant self, all decked out in his pinstriped suits with his hair slicked back. And of course, he was chewing on his trademark Cuban cigar I smiled just thinking about how smooth he must have been back in the day. "Knock'em dead in heaven, you old playa," I said.

The sudden roar of the crowd broke my concentration. The band had taken the stage to warm up. That was my cue. But I had promised myself the day before, and the day before that, to open the birthday present Melvin had given me. It was still wrapped tightly with the red bow on top, the same as it was back in June. I don't know why I waited so long to open it. Maybe I was afraid of the responsibility attached to whatever was inside.

As I tore away the colorful wrappings, my hands began to shake. It was as if I were opening some sacred artifact like Harrison Ford in *Raiders of the Lost Ark*. Once I got the paper off, I searched for something sharp to remove the thick tape. But before I could find a pair of scissors, someone pounded on the door. I knew it had to be Scottie.

"Malcolm, let's go! It's show time!"

"Give me a couple of minutes," I said while trying to bite the tape off the box.

"You don't have a couple of minutes. Everybody is waiting."

"You're not getting away today," I said to the box. "I'll be back!"

As I made my way toward the stage, it finally hit me that it could be the last time I walked down these historic halls.

Forty years of blood, sweat, and tears, down the drain. All for the love of money. Just as I was being introduced, I bowed my head in silent prayer. If this was to be my last performance at Melvin's, I wanted it to be my best ever. "Don't forsake me, Lord," I prayed. "Not tonight!"

When I walked onto the stage I was greeted with cheers and thunderous applause. My legal battle to keep the club open was well advertised in the local media. *The Los Angeles Times* dedicated an entire page to the story. "Thank you very much," I said as I took a bow.

When I sat down at the piano, I noticed something was different. The house piano had been switched. In its place was my Steinway, the one my father had given me on my eighteenth birthday. I ran my fingers across the engraved initials M.T. to make sure I wasn't dreaming. As I scanned the room through the bright stage lamps, I saw Simon sitting on the front row with a shit-eating grin on his face. I was so overwhelmed with gratitude that I walked over and gave him a hug.

The audience applauded us as we embraced, no doubt celebrating that two black men could openly show affection for each other. In a town like Los Angeles where brothers shoot one another over gym shoes, it was a welcomed sight.

"I love you, man," I said to him.

"I love you, too, partner," he replied. "Now, do me a favor and turn this place out."

"You got it!"

I walked back toward my piano fired up and inspired. I had intended on playing a song by Cole Porter, or perhaps Thelonious Monk. But my spirit compelled me to play what was in my heart. As I pressed down on the keys, a hush came across the crowded smoke-filled room.

"This song is dedicated to the two men who taught me everything I know about music and life. My father, Joseph Tremell, and Melvin. And also, to the woman who without knowing it, taught me the meaning of love. The name of the song is 'When Players Pray.' "

It was the song I had written for my father before he died twelve years ago. Ironically, I wrote the lyrics on the same night I wrote Toni the letter. I wasn't much of a singer, but I was going to give it my best shot. The melody of the song was similar to "Fortunate" by Maxwell.

I played the game for selfish reasons
The love you gave so freely was for but one season
My heart was so very cold and locked away,
Never to feel the warmth of a holy wedding day

After that first verse, the audience was swaying back and forth to the rhythm and holding up their cigarette lighters. It was a very spiritual and emotional experience.

Never love more then she, that's the rule
A man who masters his sensitivities will seldom play the fool
But the game is not eternal, there is always a spiritual price to pay
Heavenly father is it too late to repent? Is it too late for a player to pray?

After that second verse, there wasn't a dry eye in the house. I continued to play even though I was overwhelmed with grief. All the repressed feelings I had toward my father, Melvin, and Toni came pouring out onto the keys. It was my most intense performance ever. At the end of the song I was given a standing ovation. "Encore! Encore!" the crowd screamed. I inconspicuously wiped the tears from my eyes and stood up to take a bow. My mother, who was sitting at the table with Simon, was wiping the tears from her eyes, too. More than anyone else, she understood how significant that moment was for me.

As I exited the stage, one of the waitresses approached me carrying a bouquet of red roses, eleven to be exact. Attached to the bouquet was a small card that read: I STILL BELIEVE IN YOU!

"Where did you get these?" I asked anxiously.

"The woman over there." She pointed in the direction of the bar, but no one was there. "At least that's where she was standing a minute ago," she said.

"What did she look like?"

"She was a very classy-looking lady about five-eight, medium-length hair, and brown skinned," she said.

I knew it had to be Toni. The card could have come from anyone, but the eleven roses were a dead giveaway. I gave her eleven roses when I met her at the Fox Theater in Atlanta for the first time. I rushed through the thick crowd after her. The audience was still applauding as I made my way toward the front door. Judging by the sly expression on Simon's face as I passed by him, he knew what was going on. I suspected he was responsible for her being there.

Once I made it outside, I saw a woman in a long sheer black dress stepping inside a taxi. She was across the street so it was hard to make her out. But just as her head disappeared inside, our eyes briefly met and I knew it was her. "Toni, wait!" I yelled. I ran across the busy intersection almost getting myself run over. But I was able to catch her before her taxi drove off. Or maybe she was simply waiting. I didn't know for sure and I didn't care.

When I bent down to peek inside the taxi she was staring at me with those beautiful brown eyes.

"Hello, stranger," she smiled nervously.

"Hello to you," I replied. "Leaving so soon?"

"I—I have another stop to make," she stuttered.

"I guess you were just in the neighborhood, huh?"

"Actually, I wanted to stop by and pay my respects to Melvin. I know how much he meant to you."

"How did you find out what happened?"

"I went by Club Obsession to say hello to Simon and he told me what happened."

"Look, I don't mean to break up this romantic reunion

but I've got a job to do," the taxi driver asked. "Are you going or not, Ms.?"

"Yes," Toni said.

"No!" I quickly replied.

"Which one is it going to be?" the driver asked, sounding frustrated.

"Toni, don't go like this," I begged. "I know you didn't come all the way to Los Angeles just to give me flowers. Can I talk to you for just a minute, please!"

Toni sat there for a moment to contemplate. Then she gave the driver five dollars for his inconvenience and stepped out of the taxi.

"Malcolm, before you get started, I want you to know that I can't stay long. Eric is waiting for me at the hotel. We're engaged again."

"Eric?" I said in disgust.

That was the last name in the world I wanted to hear. Anybody but him, I was thinking. My heart all of a sudden became heavy.

"I guess there isn't much for me to say after all," I said. "I'll call you another taxi."

I escorted her back toward the club. I couldn't even look at her pretty face knowing she was back with him. It was too painful an image. Just as we were about to cross the street, Toni grabbed me by the hand and pulled me back.

"Malcolm, why won't you look at me?"

"How could you go back to him?" I asked, trying my best to hide my pain.

"Because I can trust him, that's why!"

"Is that all you need to be happy?"

"No, but it's the most important thing in a relationship," she lashed out. "But I guess you wouldn't know anything about trust and honesty, now would you?"

"Why are you saying these things to me when you know how sorry I am. Didn't you get my letter?"

"They're just words!"

"Words are all I have since you won't let me close enough to look you in the eyes and tell you how I feel!" I said as I grabbed her by the shoulders and looked her dead in the eyes.

"Well, here I am!"

Toni was trembling as she stared back into my eyes. Her strong and agile dancer's legs felt like spaghetti as she tried to take a stance. I was tense, too. This was my final chance at redemption. I set aside my male insecurities and spoke from the heart.

"You are the most important person in my world. I didn't know how incomplete I was until you came along and filled that void. You taught me to believe in myself and to never give up on my dreams," I professed. "What I'm trying to say is, I love you, baby. And I need you in my life."

"I'm scared, Malcolm," she said, crying. "I don't want to end up hurt and alone."

"I'm scared, too. I've never been in love before. But I'm ready to take that chance in order to be happy. What about you?"

Tears rolled down her cheeks as she looked deep into my eyes. I held my breath and prayed she would give me another chance to be the man I knew I could be.

"I'm ready, baby," she said.

We embraced each other and kissed on the corner of that busy intersection. People were driving by blowing horns and whistling. But I didn't care. It had taken me thirty-seven years to find my soul mate. I wanted the whole world to know she was mine.

"Wait a minute," I said after we came up for air. "What about Eric?"

"Eric who?" she said bluntly.

I didn't touch that. Hell, that was his issue, not mine. Toni and I ran across the street hand in hand back to the club.

"Wait right here," I told her. "I'll be right back."

"Where are you going?"

"I'm going to get something out of the office, then we're outta here!"

"Malcolm, this is an important night, you can't just leave."

"Watch me!"

I ran back inside the club to get my birthday present out of Melvin's office. On the way out, I congratulated Simon and Cynthia on their marriage. It was the first time I ever kissed Cynthia. And it felt good to finally put my issues with her to rest. Then I gave my mother a kiss on the cheek and told her I loved her. She just looked at me and smiled. I had never seen her so happy. She knew Toni was good for me. Mothers always know what's good for their sons.

It felt strange walking out of those historic old doors knowing it was possibly for the last time. Melvin's Jazz Club had been my home for nine years. That was hard to handle. But I had to get on with my new life as a recording artist and as a husband. And I couldn't think of a better start than to drive down to the ocean and watch the sunrise, just like we did on our first date in Chicago.

It was another full moon that night and the breeze off the ocean was brisk, perfect for snuggling. With Toni by my side I finally worked up the courage to open my birthday present. The box contained a Bible and a white envelope. On the envelope were the words *To My Son* in cursive writing on the back. Inside was a copy of Melvin's Last Will and Testament. I couldn't make out the fine print but one thing was definitely clear, I was the beneficiary of Melvin's Jazz Club.

Maybe I should've been elated by my newfound wealth but I wasn't. I celebrated within by holding Toni tight and giving thanks to God. I had been blessed so much that night and I wanted to remain humble.

Finally, I pulled out the old King James Bible. It was the same one Melvin's father had given him before he died.

There was a marker inside the book of Proverbs with the inscription, 18:22. I turned to the chapter and read the verse out loud.

"He who finds a wife finds a good thing, and obtains favor from the Lord."

"What a coincidence," Toni said.

But I knew better. Simon told me that there were no such things as coincidences. "Everything happens for a reason," he said. I had finally come to understand what that meant. In life, and especially in love, everything happens in God's time.

ABOUT THE AUTHOR

Success did not come easy for this Chicago native, who was born in 1963. In 1994 he was driving trains for the Chicago Transit Authority and struggling to keep a small business from going under. In 1995 he released his first book, *Never Satisfied: How & Why Men Cheat*, a controversial book of short stories about unfaithful men and the women who support their irresponsible behavior. The large New York publishing companies rejected his work, saying it wasn't marketable—which basically meant, it wasn't good enough. Not willing to concede defeat, Michael decided to self-publish. He borrowed money from friends and family, charged his credit cards to the limit, and sold his automobile.

Within eight months, he sold more than 50,000 books and was on *Essence* and *Emerge* magazines best-sellers lists. He toured with black expos, sorority conventions, and book fairs. He even signed books at local nightclubs and hair salons. "I was determined to make it!" he says. "I would sell books at a funeral if they let me." Eventually, his popularity grew and so did the demand for his next book. This time, instead of writing another book on relationships, Michael took a gamble on a novel. "There was a void in African-American novels written by men," he explained. "I wanted to destroy the myth that men don't read."

In July 1997 he released his second book, *Men Cry In The Dark*. Once again, the book was a big success, selling 30,000 hardcover editions during the first six months. This time the national media paid attention. Michael has been a guest on several local and national radio programs, including the syndicated *Tom Joyner Morning Show*. His electrifying personality has earned repeated appearances on talk shows such as *Ricki Lake, Sally Jessy Raphael, Maury Povich, Queen Latifah,* and *The View*. He has also been a guest host for Tavis Smiley on *BET Tonight*.

Michael is happily single and is currently living in Atlanta, Georgia, where he is working on another controversial book.

For more information about when the *Love, Lust, & Lies* seminar is coming to a city near you, log on to Legacy Publishing's Web site at
www.michaelbaisden.com
Or you may send a brief letter to request information on how to schedule a seminar for your organization, convention, or exposition to:
Legacy Publishing
P.O. Box 49644
Atlanta, GA 30359
Or send e-mail to **mb@michaelbaisden.com**

All book clubs: Please e-mail your web address *or* write to the above address.

Never Satisfied
"HOW & WHY MEN CHEAT"
by Michael Baisden

What methods will a man utilize to conceal his affair? And how many lies will he tell to maintain these sordid relationships? These tricks, or games as women refer to them, have been the reasons behind many break-ups and divorces. It seems technology has made the game of cheating much simpler to play with the innovation of pagers, car phones etc. But regardless of scientific advances, one simple fact remains, a man must forever keep his lies straight, because with one slip of the tongue, his world could come tumbling down around him.

Chapter 1. Pg. 1 - The Hunt
Any successful hunt must begin with the selection of the ideal geographic location to find a particular animal. The cheating man understands this fact and has carefully considered where he will lay his insidious traps. The most commonly preferred places are the bars, night clubs, and lounges. These modern day meat markets provide the perfect stalking grounds for any man with the desire to "temporarily resign" from his existing relationship. Nowhere else can such an alluring combination of women, alcohol, and immorality be found under one roof. He feels right at home in this perverse jungle where cordial admiration is but visual assault, and the art of good conversation has been degenerated to nothing more than a prerequisite to sex.

Chapter 3. Pg. 159 - Vamp, Tramp, Traitor
If it is true that men who cheat are dogs, then the other women must be the dog catcher. Because without her full and unconditional the husbands and boyfriends of the world would have only one place to go, *home*. Single handedly she can turn a happy home into a house of horror. With little or no shame she will aggressively pursue, wrongfully date, and shamelessly screw any man who tickles her fancy. And she doesn't give a damn if he just happens to be married, engaged, shacking, or seriously involved.

For more information about book signing dates and to subscribe to our newsletter, log on to our Web site at
www.michaelbaisden.com
You can also purchase books and tapes for 20% to 30% off retail.
To order by phone, call **1-800-772-0524**.

Men Cry In The Dark

Another best-seller by Michael Baisden

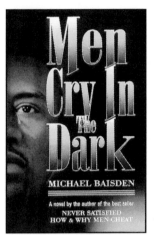

The bad boy of literature is back! Michael is taking the book world by storm once again with a provocative book that is sure to stir controversy. *Men Cry In The Dark* is an entertaining and realistic novel about relationships, fatherhood, and interracial dating from the man's perspective. And in an industry dominated by female writers, it's long overdue!

Men Cry In The Dark has been called the male's version of *Waiting to Exhale*. The story centers around four men and how they deal with their relationships, but that's where the similarities end. Michael's characters are strong successful men who live in two worlds, the world of big business and the streets. Like many men who have made it out of the inner-city ghettos, his characters, Derrick, Tony, Ben, and Mark, represent the thousands of men who struggle with the challenges of their professional lives while trying not to forget where they come from. Never before has a book tackled so many controversial social and relationship issues: fatherhood, golddiggers, and interracial dating. It has all the makings of another best-seller, and hopefully a major motion picture. Michael says, "It's *Boomerang, Love Jones,* and *Boyz N the Hood,* all rolled into one."